Computers into Cla

Computers into Classrooms
More Questions than Answers

Edited by

John Beynon and Hughie Mackay

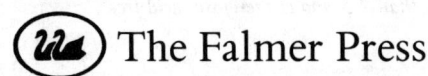 The Falmer Press

(A member of the Taylor & Francis Group)
London • Washington, D.C.

UK   The Falmer Press, 4 John St., London WC1N 2ET
USA   The Falmer Press, Taylor & Francis Inc., 1900 Frost Road, Suite 101,
Bristol, PA 19007

First published 1993

Library of Congress Cataloging-in-Publication data are
available on request

**A catalogue record for this book is available from the British
Library**

ISBN 1 85000 644 x cased
ISBN 1 85000 645 8 paper

Cover design by Caroline Archer

Set in 9.5/11pt. Bembo by
Graphicraft Typesetters Ltd., Hong Kong

*Printed in Great Britain by Burgess Science Press, Basingstoke on
paper which has a specified pH value on final paper manufacture of
not less than 7.5 and is therefore 'acid free'.*

Contents

Contents

Preface and Acknowledgments

This is one in a series of three books published by Falmer Press, one edited by Mackay, Young and Beynon, and the other two by Beynon and Mackay. Each addresses the question: 'Of what should technological literacy consist?' Our view of technological literacy is very different from a narrow, skills-based, technical perspective. We see the cultural and social as central to the technology curriculum, not marginal. This book and its companions, taken together, push forward and explore the possibilities of a new, expanded, cultural definition of technological literacy, one that can inform National Curriculum Technology and IT across the curriculum.

In this enterprise our greatest debt is to Michael Young of the London University Institute of Education, our co-editor in the opening volume, *Understanding Technology in Education.*

The advent of the National Curriculum allows for the first time the opportunity for a systematic understanding of technology's significance in our lives. The danger is that, separated from the social sciences and humanities, technology is reduced to no more than a combination of artefacts and specialized knowledge. As Young argues

> What will be needed will be knowledge about how technological choices are enmeshed in organizational, economic and political choices . . . what is needed is a concept of technology as a social phenomenon . . . we have to find ways of making explicit how different purposes are involved in its design, its implementation and its use, and how at each stage there are potential choices and decisions to be made. This means a technologically literate population and an increasingly wide debate about the content and meaning of technological literacy. [Young, 1991]

It is our hope that this book and its companion volumes will contribute towards these debates.

We also extend our debt to Malcolm Clarkson (Managing Director) and Carol Saumarez (Editor) of Falmer Press for their patience and unfailing courtesy; to all of our contributors who stuck with us through what turned out to be a protracted project; to Peter Bartlett, Phillip Bassett and Patricia Lovering of the Cardiff Institute of Higher Education for permission to use extracts in the Teacher

Case Studies from work originally presented as coursework for their Diploma in Educational Computing; and to Joyce Fox, whose word-processing skills and good humour even when under pressure ensured that the final stages of manuscript preparation were relatively trouble-free.

John Beynon and Hughie Mackay
The University of Glamorgan
(formerly The Polytechnic of Wales)
August 1992

More Questions than Answers

John Beynon and Hughie Mackay

This edited volume is the final one in a series of three, published by Falmer Press, in which we have brought together a range of writers, each of whom has attempted to understand or 'read' technology. Brief details of the other two (*Understanding Technology in Education*, edited by Mackay, Young and Beynon; and *Technological Literacy and the Curriculum*, edited by Beynon and Mackay) are provided below. This volume focuses more specifically on classrooms and classroom processes involving computers: it deals directly with pupil and teacher usage of microcomputers in teaching and learning. Moreover, whereas the previous volumes had as their common theme *learning about* technology (in terms of technological literacy), this volume changes the emphasis to *learning through* technology. What this volume reveals (as the subtitle clearly states) is that there are more questions than answers concerning computers in classrooms. This is partly due, of course, to the regrettable paucity of high quality research data: the fact is that (ethnographic) evidence of what *actually* happens when computers are introduced into classrooms (as opposed to what it is *assumed* happens) is rather thin on the ground.

Our introductory paper is in three parts. In the opening section we detail the origins of this book and our hope that it might act as a catalyst for a more educationalist, classroom-sensitive, qualitative research-based approach to pupil, teacher and computer interactions (see Kemmis, 1988, discussed below).

In the second section we review two views of computers into classrooms, namely from the standpoint of those who have sought to 'advise' teachers as to good practices through what we term (and we do not intend to be derogatory, just descriptive) 'cook-books'; and from those who have attempted in the UK over the past decade or so to evaluate outcomes.

Finally, we outline the major concerns of our contributors, showing how their work provides valuable evidence and insights into areas in which comparatively little research has yet been done.

Origins

The origins of this book reveal much about the way in which technology in education is generally viewed. We both teach Communication Studies at the Polytechnic of Wales, a degree programme which has pioneered the study of the social shaping and historical development of a wide range of technologies (notably television — see O'Sullivan, 1991; Hartley *et al.*, 1985; radio — see Moores, 1989; computers — see Mackay and Gillespie, 1989). Moreover, we both shared an interest in classroom processes (Beynon, 1985) and structures of schooling (Hall, Mackay and Morgan, 1986), and we were concerned, throughout the 1980s (but especially during Kenneth Baker's period as Education Secretary) at the unseemly speed at which microcomputers were being placed in classrooms. There was, we felt, little informed analysis, research or critical reflection, either from technologists who were developing and promoting IT in education, or from sociologists of education, who did not seem to have identified IT (or, later, technology) as a key area of contemporary educational policy and practice. We expressed our misgivings in a paper published in the *Journal of Education Policy* in 1989. We were especially concerned by the dominance in the UK of a narrowly technology-inspired discourse in discussions of computers into classrooms, and — conversely — the absence of a sociologically informed one. Meanwhile one of us acted as consultant to the exciting research into teacher and pupil deployment of micros in Ontario schools based at Altmaster College, the University of Western Ontario (Beynon, 1989b; also Blomeyer, in this volume). The absence of a major project based on qualitative research of this kind in the UK has been rectified, in part, by the Impact Project based at King's College, London (see Moore, in this volume).

At the Annual Conference of the British Educational Research Association (BERA) in Manchester in 1987 Hughie Mackay outlined this and our concern that an unfortunate dichotomy was developing between sociologically-inclined 'voices' (for example, Michael Apple, 1986) and essentially technological ones, with little opportunity for a dialogue between them. We followed this up by organising a day conference at the same event a year later in Norwich. At Norwich we attempted to set up a bridgehead between the technologists and educational technologists on the one hand, and the sociologists and cultural theorists on the other (for example, versions of Newton's, Culley's and Beynon's papers included in this volume on the gender differentiation associated with computers in classrooms were presented on that day).

In the spring of 1989 we organized a day conference on New Technology at the Polytechnic of Wales in which the lead lecture ('What is *new* about New Technology?') was given by David Albury of the North East London Polytechnic and whose co-authored book (*Partial Progress*, 1982) we still regard as a key text in grasping the essentially *social* nature of technology. At the end of 1989 one of us was asked to comment on plans for a television documentary on the theme of the influence of the microcomputer on young people. At the end of the day most of the advice proffered was jettisoned and the final product sensationalized the issues, focusing on the dangers of addiction to home-based hobbyism and game-playing. All attempts at a discussion of the benefits as well as the shortcomings of micros and their place in young people's lives was lost. The formula was repeated: technology as addressed by the media has to be either 'glitzy and exciting' or 'threatening and potentially evil'. Rare is the media treatment which steers a middle course.

The outcome of this activity has been three edited volumes for Falmer. The first, *Understanding Technology in Education* (edited by Mackay, Young and Beynon, 1991) brought together between two covers writers whose disparate concerns nevertheless constituted a powerful political, social and cultural account of technology. The second, *Technological Literacy and the Curriculum* (edited by Beynon and Mackay, 1991) continued the endeavour by suggesting how teachers (and, of course, through them their pupils) might start to understand (or 'read') technology as a text embodying ideological subtexts and meanings. Such a 'reading' was presented as being at the heart of technological (as opposed to computer) literacy. The argument was advanced that technologists had much to learn from Cultural and Media Studies. Moreover, the claim was forcefully put that technologists are not the only people entitled to talk about technology and that technology in education demands a new set of 'non-technological discourses'; and that these must now inform both National Curriculum technology, and Information Technology as it operates across the curriculum. To be technologically literate demands more than the hands-on capability of being able to use a piece of technology: it also demands the ability to be able to 'read' it.

From that second volume we were left feeling that, whilst we had provided something of a cognitive framework for teachers to make sense of technology, we had not dealt with what this might mean in practice. Meanwhile, of course, the National Curriculum was being developed, and we felt the need to inform that development. Teachers and researchers, though, have generally not yet applied to their teaching the social and cultural approaches to technology which we have proposed. Some teachers, however, are beginning to raise questions which seem on the right lines. The present volume is a collection of work in this vein; our aim is to provide ideas towards the possible direction of techology teaching.

We see this as a crucial area because of the limitations of so much of the existing literature. We now review the literature on computers into classrooms — which can be divided into two broad categories; that associated with advisors, and evaluators. The selective examples detailed below should give readers a flavour of the characteristic strengths and shortcomings of each of these.

The Advisors and the Evaluators

The Advisors

'Cook-books' about educational computing fall into two general categories:

- those which provide ideas for teachers of 'things to do' and catalogue and comment upon available resources;
- those which raise wider issues and are primarily academic in their intent rather than pragmatic and written for educationalists rather than teachers.

The earliest 'cook-books' took a behaviourist stance, an example being De Cecco (1964), with its strongly Skinnerian overtones and its intention to 'bring together research reports and theoretical discussions of both psychology and education which have so far contributed to knowledge about educational technology, programmed learning and the psychology of learning'.

A similar stance is taken by Rushby (1979), an early book which basically asks 'What is computer assisted learning and how might teachers best employ it?'

Payne *et al.* (1980), similarly, show teachers what computers can do, indicate available materials, and suggest how they might best be used. *Perspectives* 7 (1982), meanwhile, encourages teachers to become confident users. Another advice book is that by Wayth (1983) who puts both the case for, and the possibilities of, computing to teachers, and a strong advocacy of LOGO as 'an introduction both to computing and to thinking' is that by Gascoigne (1984). Meanwhile, Steinberg (1984) is a book about how to maximize the computer's capacity as a teacher. Terry (1984), too, constitutes a beginner's guide, with particular attention being paid to micro usage in teaching creative writing, whereas Wellington (1985) lays emphasis upon teachers finding their way around the types of micros available and their suitability for different subject teaching. Meanwhile, Martin (1986) explores the possibilities of LOGO use; and the tradition of advice for teachers of 'good practices' continues with, for example, Straker's (1989) volume, with its chapters on computers and language and the arts, mathematics, science, social and environmental studies, problem solving and information handling. More recent additions to the 'cook-book' (suitable ingredients and how they might best be prepared) category relate computer resources and uses to changes in the curriculum leading up to the National Curriculum (for example, Jones and Scrimshaw, 1988).

One of the most comprehensive and valuable recent texts on how children might best use computers (primarily 'as fun') is by Straker (1989). She comments that technology 'should find a place in all subjects which are able to take advantage of the facility to store and process information and to generate further information'. She sees technology as having an important place to play in at least six areas of the curriculum (in addition to the technology area), namely: science; moral education; mathematics; literary and linguistic studies; the human and social; and the aesthetic and creative.

By far the largest and most interesting category is the second — those texts that, whilst still being books of advice and good practices, succeed in articulating more philosophical questions concerning technology in education. For example, Stonier and Conlin (1981) are hugely enthusiastic in their advocacy of computers into classrooms but temper this with a warning:

> I am sure we do not know enough yet about how to take full advantage of technology or about how to avoid some of its dangers, but experience is beginning to accumulate. We are seeing the emergence of synergy as different choices and systems are brought together, combining powerfully their effects, and synergistic systems may soon become multipurpose systems, serving learners in many ways.

Maddison (1983) writes from a lifetime of experience as a teacher and from the background of someone who introduced Media and Film Studies into his schools. Teachers, he argues, must control and guide technology when it penetrates into education; foreshadowing Michael Apple's (1986) argument, he argues that democratic values and freedoms are best safeguarded through education. Therefore, education must both address and use technology and, ultimately, be transformed by it. He calls for a multi-media approach to curriculum that results in 'a genuine symbiosis of the whole innovative panoply of methods, materials and techniques through which science (in the guise of technology) can open up the prospect of a new and enriched concept of education'. Maddison's may not be a detailed discussion of a media literacy which encompasses computers, but he does make a number of interesting connections in this respect. The theme of futurism is picked up and extended in the Stonier and Conlin (1985) volume, which prophesies a switch from school to home-based learning:

> This book is about computer-based education (CBE) and that means we are considering the computer not merely as another piece of educational technology, not merely as just another tool. What we are saying is that the entire education system will begin to revolve increasingly around the computer as such a tool. Combined with teachers and parents, books and classrooms, the system over the next few decades will change. At the core of it will be the computer.

They go on to offer advice for teachers and parents concerning the computer's role in the teaching of literacy and life skills. However, a far more challenging discussion of technology and its impact on schooling is that edited by Schostok (1988). Education must respond to technology and that response must not simply be to teach how to program and develop keyboard skills and electronic circuitry. Rather, the response must involve an attempt to 'identify the philosophy, styles of teaching and educational organization which will best serve to liberate humanity from its own illusions and self-made traps'. It discusses the options for changing the role of teachers, pupils, organization and the secondary curriculum. Technology must not be allowed to change education: rather, the change it occasions must be controlled by teachers and their pupils, not by machines:

> What use is made of the machine will depend entirely upon what ends are chosen. The choice open to teachers in terms of curriculum and role has not changed significantly with the advent of the computer age. However, the choice has, perhaps, become more critical.

Computers put to educational use and in the hands of well-informed teachers offer pupils an expansion of information and cultural experiences. A similar case for teachers controlling technology rather than becoming appendages of it is made in Garland (1982). Contributors to that volume examine how micros might best serve the curriculum, and the role of computer simulation is especially noted. The attitudes, values and priorities of teachers must be taken into account when choosing, implementing and using both hardware and software, and the danger of mundane and irrelevant computer-based activities is stressed. Although Pogrow's (1983) book is primarily a how-to-do-it manual for teachers, it advocates a transformation by computer of the education system. Schools must teach both about and through micros which should not, therefore, be mere incremental additions, but means of transforming current practices. Another practical guide that nevertheless raises wider ethical, philosophical and political matters emerging from the 'technologizing' of education is that by Coburn *et al.* (1982).

The Evaluators

The emphasis here is upon documenting the kind and extent of microcomputer deployment in schools and making policy-related recommendations. The data-collection methods employed are often eclectic and the model stays close to the practicalities of implementing technology in education, seldom raising broader questions about technology. Much of it is given to evaluating technology in education policy formulation and implementation, and the identification of instances of 'good' and 'bad' microcomputer practices across the curriculum. Studies tend to be relatively small-scale, autonomous, and not accumulative or generalizable in terms of either findings or theory. Below we briefly detail a small sample of evaluation projects in recent years, namely:

- work carried out at the CARE Unit of the University of East Anglia;
- that based at the Educational Computing Unit, King's College, London;
- a few individual studies which are best considered under the general rubric of the evaluative.

The Centre for Applied Research in Education at the University of East Anglia, Norwich, has been linked to IT in Education evaluation for over a decade, notably through the evaluation of the National Development Project into Computer Assisted Learning in the late 1970s, and in the 1980s for the evaluation of the Department of Trade and Industry's Micros Into Schools initiative. The former (termed the UNCAL Project) is best remembered for its attempt to obtain critical purchase on the computer's contribution to the curriculum at different levels of demand; and then to draw up a typology of student-computer inter-actions. What can happen when students use micros is mapped in terms of four curricular models:

- instrumental CAL, involving drill, practice and tutorial activities;
- revelatory CAL, utilizing simulations and 'trial-and-error' exercises;
- conjectural CAL, relating to the creation by the pupil user of 'new' knowledge;
- emancipatory CAL, encompassing activities that free teachers and pupils from routine, time-consuming tasks.

Further, a five-fold typology of student-computer interactions was developed, as follows:

- recognition tasks, involving 'yes-or-no' types of response;
- recall tasks, typically requiring 'fill-in-the-blank' kinds of responses;
- reconstructive understanding tasks, usually of the 'multiple-choice' variety;
- global reconstructive tasks, calling for open-ended responses and analytic, synthetic and creative solutions;
- constructive understanding tasks, demanding even more open-ended and original responses.

Whilst these types may be too narrowly task-oriented to describe the range of individual and group responses and spin-off activities occasioned by the best practices in current uses of technology in education, they still constitute a good research starting-point in spite of describing interactions rather more from the nature of the demands circumscribed by the particular technology as opposed to pupils' actual sense-making and behaviour when using micros.

Another CARE-based project was the evaluation of the Micros Into Schools Support Scheme, 1981–1984, along with recommendations for future action. The general conclusion is that the DTI intervention had been decisive in promoting computer awareness but that judged in purely educational terms some policy decisions had been ill-advised, with little time for teachers to prepare given the inadequacy of in-service training (see Beynon and Mackay, 1989). Moreover, for the most part, software was 'educationally retrogressive' and few teachers were aware of the full capabilities of the hardware: as a result ineffective use was often made of micros. The scheme had been too rushed and would clearly have been strengthened if it had been based upon prior research. Furthermore, although the literature has consistently advocated exciting uses of open-ended enquiry learning, in practice usage has been generally pedestrian and dominated by drill and practice. However, the evaluation reported different overall pictures in primary and secondary schools. The former are presented as generally engaging in more fruitful micro usage, although there is a continuing need for more resources. The primary school environment, being more flexible, has made it easier for teachers to experiment and fit the computer into the curriculum, unhindered by rigid timetables and subject boundaries. Conversely, the tighter organization and management of secondary schools has obstructed the use of micros for cross-curricular work. As a result computers in secondary schools have been used primarily in examinable subjects (Computer Studies and Business Studies, for instance) so that only some pupils (and some teachers) have had ready access to them. Whereas, in general, children are well disposed towards computers, teachers in UK schools are not that favourably inclined, either because they feel incompetent, or because the available facilities are inadequate, or because they have yet to be convinced of their educational potential. Nevertheless, the evaluation stresses that the long-term implications of IT in Education on curriculum, pedagogy and school organization and management are likely to be considerable.

In 1985 Hall and Rhodes, based at King's College, London, undertook case studies in six Inner London Education Authority (ILEA) primary schools to identify factors that may promote or inhibit the uptake of Information Technology and, also, to examine classroom attitudes arising from uptake. Amongst the most useful practical points that emerge are that:

- whilst children were observed capably organizing themselves when working with the micro it was noted that a small number of children were gaining superior knowledge in comparison to their peers;
- children working in pairs were more successful then in groups or individually, but the pairing of children of disparate abilities required a high degree of teacher supervision to be beneficial;
- children were observed to maintain concentration over longer periods than might have been expected when working on the same topic with different media;

- valuable task-oriented social activity frequently occurs when children engage in micro activity;
- word-processing programs are particularly beneficial to the advancement of literacy skills because the editing and printing facilities are highly motivating and aid the production of texts which can be put to a variety of uses;
- strong teacher direction of the micro activities of primary-age children is necessary to ensure they employ to the full software potential;
- few teachers considered that the use of a micro had significantly influenced their curriculum, teaching style, or relationships with children;
- several factors were identified that inhibited micro usage, amongst these being lack of appropriate training, access problems, dissatisfaction with software, and lack of convincing evidence that there are, in fact, educational benefits;
- affording only some children the opportunity to use a micro should be avoided and the overall responsibility for computers should be entrusted to a single member of staff;
- it is important that both the technical and wider educational aspects of microcomputers in primary schools be addressed in pre-service and in-service courses. Moreover, there is an urgent need for quality research into the educational benefits of microcomputers and the best ways for teachers to use them.

Surprisingly there have been few detailed studies to date evaluating the implementation of micros in schools. An exception is that by Bliss, Chandra and Cox (1986), who examined the introduction of computers into Barnaby Comprehensive at the levels of teachers, departments and school. They conclude that although the overall attitude of staff was positive, most had serious misgivings. They felt that their traditional role as 'imparters of knowledge' was being threatened. However, amongst the advantages mentioned are that micros were:

- motivational tools promoting individual learning;
- statistical tools offering dynamic visual displays;
- an opportunity to reform learning through the visual medium.

Amongst the reservations itemized were:

- the poor educational quality of much software and the danger of encouraging solely game-playing;
- difficulties associated with access and infrequency of use;
- the problem of brighter pupils monopolizing micro usage and the less able thereby losing out.

The obstacles specifically encountered by girls and women teachers are referred to in two of the projects detailed above. In their Microcomputers into Primary Schools Project, Hall and Rhodes (1988) record that:

- teachers must avoid prioritizing male pupils by involving all pupils in using micros;
- whilst more male teachers must attend courses and make use of micro-computers, female teachers must be given far more opportunity to become involved and so redress what is an unbalanced role model currently being presented to children;
- there is a need to monitor constantly whether girls are receiving the same opportunities to use the micro as boys.

Similarly, the CARE-based study reports that

> There is clearly still a need to ensure that girls are encouraged to use micros and shown positive models of women teachers using them effectively. There is no evidence that girls are hesitant in using micros in the early years of the Primary School, but they often begin to be hesitant towards the end of Junior School.

In the same vein Lorraine Culley's (1986; 1988) research (reported in this volume) is highly significant in that she shows computing in secondary schools to be essentially a masculine domain, one that re-creates existing social and gender relations, attitudes and assumptions. It is massively associated with male staff, and with mathematical concepts and departments; it fits in neatly with the gender differentiation of subject/option choices; and, as a result, it plays relatively little part in girls' hopes for the future, whereas it is central to those of many boys. Since home computing is dominated by fathers and sons, girls are less familiar and confident with computers and boys assume this lack of interest and incompetence is part and parcel of 'being a girl'.

Further examples of the evaluative studies in the UK are: Jackson (1987) on English teaching and technology; Wright (1987) on teachers' views on technology in two primary schools; Medway (1988) on the Technical and Vocational Education Initiative (TVEI) and its implications for English teaching (and further reports referring to the same project by Barnes, 1987; Medway and Yeoman, 1988) and Hughes *et al.* (1987) on pupils' perceptions of computers; the small-scale case studies undertaken by teachers and reported in the UK/USA Final Report of the Micro-Electronic Project (1987); Jackson, Fletcher and Messer (1988) on primary school micro usage; and Crook (1989) on evaluating open-plan computing in a primary school.

A Canadian example of technology in education evaluation is the Ontario-based Schools, Computers and Learning Project (Miller *et al.*, 1988) which, from the mid-1980s on, examined the use of computers in an elementary school. The conclusion was that as children worked through programs they appeared to be 'floating' several hypotheses simultaneously concerning both the activity and the operation of software. Moreover, these hypotheses were often formed on the basis of 'fuzzy' or partial knowledge. Overall, the establishment of a computer-rich classroom environment occasioned considerable modifications to curriculum content and pedagogy, and the project concluded that 'although ample examples of computers becoming a natural aspect of teaching and learning could be found, an equal number of counter examples were observed as well'.

Although the evaluative approach has provided a number of useful individual studies whose classroom-related findings are clearly helpful to practitioners, it hardly constitutes a coherent and coordinated research tradition. This book attempts to point the way towards a more educationalist, classroom-sensitive view of computers in teaching and learning. Before looking in some detail at the approaches adopted we refer to two 'windows' onto technology which, we believe, further the way in which it might be viewed and studied in a way beneficial to teachers. The first is the research position adopted by Kemmis (with whose emphasis upon the ethnographic study of 'real life' processes we are in agreement); and the second, perhaps surprisingly, is taken from literature, namely Thomas Hardy's novel *Tess of the D'Urbervilles* first published in 1891, but depicting life in the Wessex countryside in the 1850s. Hardy, indeed, makes vivid the far from neutral nature of technology in a vivid manner.

Stephen Kemmis, a former CARE evaluator, now Professor of Curriculum Studies at Deakin University, has written most interestingly (Kemmis, 1988) on what should *not* occur when evaluating IT in Education and calls for a more comprehensive and theoretically vigorous approach, namely:

- research which depends upon pseudo-objective tests and on too-narrow focus on aims-achievement;
- research which ignores the concerns and perspectives of the participants (teachers) and the formation of these;
- research which serves decision-makers outside the setting as opposed to serving those within through rational and collaborative decision-making within these settings;
- research which disturbs the on-going reflection and action necessary for the development of education in the setting;
- research which ignores the ways in which processes of formation are conditioned by social constraints beyond participants' control.

He rejects positivist approaches to IT in Education research as partial and misleading because they invariably adopt an instrumental view of classroom computing, construing it as only a technical means to educational ends. Kemmis argues that there are two general functions of education: an individual function (the development of knowledge) and a social function (the development of the culture of a society through processes of reproduction and transformation). The problem, as he sees it, is that the evaluation of IT in education focuses too narrowly on student learning outcomes and ignores technology in education's functions in social and cultural reproduction. He employs, for example, Habermas' (1987) distinction between system and lifeworld, between the societal structure and division of labour and the social construction of group identity and cultural presuppositions within a site (whether family, neighbourhood or school). To interrelate these individual and social functions in the context of IT in Education requires, argues Kemmis, new educational theories. We would want to argue that Kemmis' point concerning technology and social and cultural reproduction bears directly upon the discussion later in this paper of a fuller and revitalized definition of technological literacy for the 1990s.

From Kemmis we turn to Thomas Hardy and this extract from *Tess of the D'Urbervilles*:

The long chimney running up beside an ash tree, and the warmth which radiated from the spot, explained without the necessity of much daylight that here was the engine which was to act as the 'primum mobile' of this little world. . . .

They were soon in full progress, after a preparatory hitch or two, which rejoiced the hearts of those who hated machinery. The work sped on till breakfast time, when the thresher was stopped for half an hour; and on starting again after the meal the whole supplementary strength of the farm was thrown into the labour of constructing the straw-rick, which began to grow behind the stack of corn. A hasty lunch was eaten as they stood, without leaving their positions, and then another couple of hours brought them near to dinner time; the inexorable wheels continuing to spin, and the penetrating hum of the thresher to thrill to the very marrow all who were near the revolving wire cage.

The old men on the rising straw-rick talked of the past days when they had been accustomed to thresh with flails on the oaken barn floor; when everything, even to winnowing, was effected by hand-labour, which, to their thinking, though slow, produced better results. Those, too, on the corn-rick talked a little; but the perspiring ones at the machine, including Tess, could not lighten their duties by the exchange of many words. It was the ceaselessness of the work which tried her so severely, and began to make her wish that she had never come to Flintcomb Ash. . . . The hum of the thresher, which prevented speech, increased to a raving whenever the supply of corn fell short of the regular quantity. . . . In the afternoon the farmer made it known that the rick was to be finished that night, since there was a moon by which they could see to work, and the man with the engine was engaged for another farm on the morrow. Thence the twanging and humming and rustling proceeded with even less intermission than usual. . . .

Hardy is alluding to the mechanization of farming through the mid-nineteenth-century technology of the steam-driven belt and cylinder thresher. Tess, of course, is trapped by more than a machine, but it is emblematical of her tragic predicament. Hardy shows how the steam thresher, even more than the steam train, changed the lives of farm labourers and their relationship to the land. It was not just a machine, but a transformer of labour relations and skills in the face of the thrust of capital (here embodied by the avaricious owner of Flintcomb Ash) to rationalize threshing and, thereby, cut costs, increase profits, and strictly regulate labour.

Technology, whatever its form (whether stocking and lace frames, steam threshers or telegraph lines), is not, and can never be, neutral and apolitical. Neither does it necessarily contribute to universal progress: that rather depends where you stand in relation to it. Two points emerge:

1 Perhaps we ought to be more alert to the 'use-values' and practices encoded in so-called 'neutral' and 'naturally evolving' technologies and ask whether they really are the products of a benevolent and disinterested science.

2 Separate technologies (whether steam thresher or silicon chip computer) have their own design histories and purposes, but should not be

decontextualized from the broader context of technology at work at a particular period in history.

We want to argue that in the research and evaluation of Information Technology and its application to education there is an urgent need for a new way of making sense of and theorizing it. There is, moreover, a need for a 'paradigmatic shift' (Kuhn, 1970) from a perspective which reifies the technical and cognitive aspects to one which includes the social, interactionist and cultural. To date, research into IT in Education in the UK has been dominated by what might be called the Cognitive Psychology/Artificial Intelligence (CP/AI) paradigm. Conversely, there has been comparatively little input into the debate from the sociology of education which, in the recent past, has been swift to address issues of great actual or potential social significance. Given the potentially transforming role of technology in Western society in general, and education in particular, the absence of a well-developed sociology of technology in education is surprising and, indeed, given the extent and rapidity of technological advance and its significance, worrying.

This Book

The work summarized above, whether prescriptive 'cook-book' or cautious evaluation, reminds us of how little we really know, as yet, about the impact and influence of computers on classrooms, pupils and teachers. Rist, in his introduction to an American collection of papers on IT in Education (Blomeyer and Martin, 1991) shows how the same situation exists in the USA. In 'technologizing' schools the research community has been marginalized (or, it can be said with some justification, has marginalized itself) and some basic questions remain unanswered, for example:

- the cognitive impacts that computers have on students;
- the ways computers have changed the style and content of teaching;
- the impact on children from different class, gender, racial, regional and linguistic backgrounds.

Rist points to the fact that we know little about how technological change is introduced, modified and reacted to by schools.

The papers that follow attempt, in small measure at least, to start to fill in some of the gaps; to stimulate new research ideas; and to inform practice at a time of crucial educational change with the advent of the National Curriculum and its across-the-curriculum Information Technology.

Richard Ennals' central thesis is that 'the means are now available to offer considerable freedom and power to ordinary people, and to free their information from the constraints of conventional applications. The remaining restrictions are not primarily technical, but derive from human attitudes to knowledge and property, oriented towards the individual rather than society'. He explores the concept of 'Mindtools', tools for active learning, which he asserts can provide authentic, rich environments in which that learning can take place. He illustrates by reference to the use of databases in historical simulations, and to the Kingston

College Development Unit for knowledge-based tools; and he refers in passing to organizations as diverse as the Artificial Intelligence For Society Club and the World Press Centre and Third World Educational Clearing House. He acknowledges that any attempt to replace teachers is doomed to fail and that what is really needed is a broader view of both people and technology in their institutional and cultural contexts. But, he warns, 'acceptance that models and systems can only ever be partial, and that cultural and environmental factors will affect the applicability of software tools, limits our expectations of the power of technology'.

Alec Moore's study is an important contribution towards understanding, through careful ethnographic observation and interviewing, what *actually* occurred when a pupil used a particular Mathematics program. Siuli, a 12-year-old Bangladeshi girl, arrived at a correct answer by means of an incorrect and incomprehensible (for her) process. Moore argues that such computer-pupil 'interactions' often characterized as progressive, exploratory and child-centred are, paradoxically, instances of the most rigid transmission style of operating, one which isolates the pupil. Learning is not a private, but a social, business and to narrowly circumvent and control learners in this manner is a denigration of both pedagogy and curriculum. Teachers must view such programs as bearers of ideologies since all technologies are invested with the ideologies of their creators. The activity Siuli undertook was more about the production of an obedient, passive and uncomprehending workforce and not the progressive, exploratory mode it was presented and accepted as by designer and teacher respectively. Moore's message is that to study bad practices is to better understand and advance the good, given the potential of computers to enhance learning in mathematics. The paper raises important issues concerning how programs should be employed; how outcomes might be evaluated; the technical skills required by teachers and pupils; and the social and cultural knowledge required by both to become both computer competent and computer literate. Moreover, it alerts teachers to the fact that it is necessary to adopt a more evaluative stance towards apparent surface benefits and outcomes, given that Siuli's attaining of the 'right answer' was more the product of trial and error guesswork than planning and comprehension.

Robert Blomeyer's study (in the style of American descriptive classroom anthropology) refers to the exciting research currently under way in Ontario, where teachers have long been encouraged to become software designers and developers. He makes it clear that the cultural and political contexts of implementation are the most significant influences in the success or failure of a technology. This expanded perspective on IT in Education is expressed thus: 'Student and teacher activity accounting, construction of both oral and institutional histories of site development, and personal histories of key participants are all strategies that may be used to create an accurate and verifiable account of CAL or other interactive technologies' impact on instructional settings'. Blomeyer tells the story of computer use in two high schools, one in commercial art and the other in fine art. In assessing the value of CAL as an alternative delivery system he argues that computers encourage new forms of circulating and facilitating behaviour between teachers and their pupils. The tools he saw in operation were, in CARE terms, emancipatory as opposed to instructional, revelatory or conjectural, allowing the student both to save time and create sophisticated and complex visual imagery.

Les Watson colourfully illustrates, by means of an analogy of a camping stove and cooking utensils, how the introduction of computers into UK schools throughout the 1980s was uncoordinated, haphazard and wasteful in resource terms. As a consequence there is still an urgent need for teacher training in computer usage; for time for practice, assimilation and planning; and for access to more appropriate, pupil-sensitive equipment, as well as for a freer sharing of curriculum ideas. Watson puts the case that the use of 'micro-worlds' can revolutionize teaching and learning, but first teachers must be released from their enforced dependence on frequently unsuitable, commercially produced programs. He describes some of the products of the teacher-led group PEG, which is 'an enabling force to enhance teaching and learning through the impact of IT' and aid technologically naive teachers. At the heart of PEG's activities is the philosophy that hardware and software must start with what teachers and pupils need to be able to do, not *with* technology per se but *through* it. A second strand is a rebuttal of the view that IT in the secondary school requires more sophisticated equipment than in the primary school. The overall picture that emerges is a most exciting one: that teachers and their pupils 'educationalize' (and, in the process, 'decommercialize') technology in the primary classroom.

Graham Peacock's paper, a study of word-processing in the primary school, questions its widely accepted 'benefits'. It indicates how little we yet know about the influence of word-processing on children's linguistic and cognitive development and on the writing process itself.

Christopher Pole writes about the role of especially designed programs on records of pupil achievement at Benton, a Midlands secondary school. He stresses that the software was sensitive to individual needs and flexible enough to accommodate a wide range of pupil abilities and achievements. The Benton study showed that specifically targeted software enhanced dialogue between teachers and pupils. Although some teachers expressed disquiet, the overwhelming feeling was that computer-aided Records of Achievement had improved teacher-pupil rapport and the overall institutional ethos. In the process they pointed the way to a new and additional role for IT in schools. Pole comments that rigid perceptions of computers as cold, super-efficient machines without soul or conscience would certainly not encompass such a deployment of the computer as go-between, arbiter and facilitator of an enriched interaction between teachers and pupils. However, he warns that such systems should never result in pupils being left alone to talk to a floppy disk! Rather, in order to ensure that they serve and support the Record of Achievement process and do not lead or direct it, 'primacy must remain with dialogue'.

The papers by Nicholas Peacey and Oleg Liber are best treated together as each details interesting applications of IT to expand participation and access to resources and facilities for teachers. Peacey's account of the Training Materials Network details the exchange of learning materials between a group of IT centres in order to cut down on the duplication of effort. He characterizes it as 'a democratic and decentralized model for generating and distributing a wider range of learning materials than would otherwise be possible, by enabling teachers to write and publish materials'. He explores both the social and technological contexts within which the project operated and provides guidelines for any attempt at institutional and teacher collaboration in the centring and disseminating of resources. The author warns that teachers must only use a technology

over which they have a strong sense of control. They must participate, if possible, early in the design process. Meanwhile, Oleg Liber tells of the role of technology to coordinate and rationalize a special needs project. He and his colleagues,
acknowledging that communication both within and between educational
institutions in the UK is poor, constructed a database of all available special needs
courses and conferences and, thereby, highlighted the huge potential for online
communication in in-service training. Liber concludes that 'online communication is not effectively used in educational administration ... communications systems could offer a way of assisting the proper identification of needs and
thus help to avoid taking people away from their classes to courses they see as
valueless'.

Peggy Newton and Eevi Beck point out that for many reasons computing
appears an ideal occupation for women, yet the proportion studying and entering it is dropping. Women are not, on the other hand, if measured by university entry figures, turning away from science and technical subjects. They show
that the manner in which computers were introduced into UK schools in the
1980s resulted in them being overwhelmingly associated with secondary school
mathematics and male staff. They argue that if women and girls are to take computing more seriously then computing must first take them more seriously and
the cultural connotations associated with technology as a male domain must
be attacked and eroded. But the difficulty of changing things must not be
underestimated. Single-sex schools appear to be more supportive and successful
in attracting girls into computing, whereas girls in mixed schools are likely to
need an extra measure of determination to put up with the overt and covert
discrimination they frequently experience. Many girls form a negative perception
of computing early in their school careers, but — the authors claim — such negative connotations are not as widespread in schools in the USA, France or the Far
East. In this country the high technological imagery of male power and dominance persists even though 'much of computing is about communication, about
the interface between people and computers, about organizing information, and
about devising new ways to work'. A new definition of computer literacy must
take this fact into account.

Lorraine Culley's work clearly shows how the use of computers in UK
education is following (and, thereby, reinforcing) the traditional lines of gender
bias and demarcation: put bluntly, boys use them more, dominate resources, and
ensure that computing is overwhelmingly a masculine arena. She comments upon
some of the impediments to computing equity (whether schools' administrative
structures or pedagogical practices) and outlines a set of interventionist strategies
which would undoubtedly raise the level of girls' (and women's) participation
in computing activities. This, however, is not going to be an easy matter:
deep-rooted, interrelated and often invisible sets of factors are involved in the
different levels of male and female participation and the construction (largely
unintentionally) of computing as a highly gendered activity in schools. The
identification of the structures and processes which constrain girls' participation
and shape their adverse perceptions is a pressing task at hand. One immediate
step that might be taken (as part of a new computer literacy) is to use the computing curriculum as a place where 'gender divisions in school and in employment
could be made visible and discussed'. Such a project would demand that teachers
appreciate more the ways in which boys come to dominate computing and

computers, and get pupils themselves to discuss the gendered nature of much of their classroom interaction.

Continuing this topic, John Beynon's ethnographic case study illustrates the means by which boys achieved dominance over girls during computer-based activities in a primary school classroom. He shows, moreover, how the introduction of computers into the school was very much in the hands of a male teacher and was shaped by his responses to a series of pressures and contradictions in the wider culture of the school at that point in its history and development.

It is important that teachers' voices should feature in a book such as this in that it is directed — in part at least — at teachers and intended to influence both the deployment of computers in their classrooms and their thinking about Technology in the National Curriculum. The final contribution is made up of three mini case studies which were produced as part of the coursework demands of a Diploma in Educational Computing. They show practitioners closely observing their pupils using computers and asking questions about what appears to work and what does not, as well as formulating future lines of enquiry. Over and above any substantive 'findings' (which must, given the small-scale nature of the work, be regarded with extreme caution), these mini case studies highlight the value of teachers actively 'researching' within their own classrooms and, thereby, clarifying their thinking and formulating future developments concerning computer usage.

Finally, in the Epilogue Beynon attempts to pinpoint and summarize some of the most important educational issues and debates to emerge from the book, issues and debates which we hope teachers implementing National Curriculum Technology will now take further.

References

ALBURY, D. and SCHWARTZ, J. (1982) *Partial Progress: The Politics of Science and Technology*, Pluto Press.

APPLE, M. (1986) *Teachers and Texts*, Routledge and Kegan Paul.

BARKER, P. and YEATES, H. (1985) *Introducing Computer Assisted Learning*, Prentice Hall.

BEYNON, J. (1985) *Initial Encounters in a Secondary School*, Falmer.

BEYNON, J. (1989a) 'Technology as Text', Opening Paper to IT in Education Colloquium at BERA Conference, UEA, Norwich.

BEYNON, J. (1989b) Consultant's Report on RUCCUS Project. London, University of Western Ontario.

BEYNON, J. (1990) 'Researching technology: the need for an educationalist paradigm', c/o Computers and Classrooms Project, Altmaster College, University of Western Ontario.

BEYNON, J. (1991) 'Just a few machines bleeping away in a corner', in BLOMEYER, R.L. and MARTIN, C.D. (Eds) *Case Studies in Computer Aided Learning*, Falmer.

BEYNON, J. and MACKAY, H. (1989) 'IT/Education: towards a critical perspective', *Journal of Education Policy*, 4, 3, pp. 245–257.

BLISS, J., CHANDRA, P. and COX, M. (1986) 'The introduction of computers into a school', Computer Education, 10:1.

BLOMEYER, R.L. and MARTIN, C.D. (1991) *Case Studies in Computer Aided Learning*, Falmer Press.

BROUGHTON, J.M. (1988) 'The surrender of control: computer literacy as political socialisation of the child', in BROUGHTON, J.M. (Ed.) *The Computer in Education*, Teachers' College Press.

CAPEL, R. and YOUNG, M.F.D. (1988) *Critical Perspectives on IT Across the Curriculum*, Post-16 Centre, London University Institute.

CROOK, C. (1987) 'Computers in the Classroom: defining a social context', in RUTHOWSKA, J. and CROOK, C. (Eds) *Computers Cognition and Development*. London, Wiley.

De CECCO, J.P. (1964) *Educational Technology: Readings in Programmed Instruction*, Holt, Rinehart and Winston.

CHANDLER, D. (1984) *Young Learners and the Microcomputer*, Open University Press.

CHANDLER, D. and MARCUS, S. (Eds) (1985) *Computers and Literacy*, Open University Press.

COBURN, P., KELMAN, P., ROBERTS, N., SNYDER, T.F.F., WATT, D. and WEINER, C. (1982) *Practical Guide to Computers in Education*, Addison Wesley.

DUNN, S. and MORGAN, V. (1987) *The Impact of the Computer on Education*, Prentice Hall.

GARLAND, R. (Ed.) (1982) *Microcomputers and Children in the Primary School*, Falmer Press.

GASCOIGNE, S. (1984) *Microchild: Learning through LOGO*, Macmillan.

GIANNELLI, G. (1985) 'Promoting computer use in the classroom', *Educational Technology*, April.

GOLBY, M. (1982) 'Microcomputers and the primary curriculum', in GARLAND, R. (Ed.) *Microcomputers and children in the Primary School*, Falmer.

HABERMAS, J. (1987) *The Theory of Communicative Action*, Beacon Press.

HALL, J. and RHODES, V. (1988) 'Microcomputers in primary schools', The Educational Computing Unit, King's College, London.

HALL, V., MACKAY, H. and MORGAN, C. (1986) *Headteachers at Work*, Open University Press.

HARTLEY, J., GOULDEN, H. and O'SULLIVAN, T. (1985) *Making Sense: A Course in Media Studies*, London, Comedia.

HAWKRIDGE, D. (1983) *New Information Technology in Education*, Croom Helm.

HEAFORD, J.M. (1983) *The Myth of the Learning Machine*, Sigma Technical Press.

HEBENSTEET, J. (1986) 'Children and computers', in BLAGOVEST, S. *et al.* (Eds) *Studies in Educational Technology*, New York, Holt Rinehart and Winston.

HOWE, J. (1983) 'Towards a pupil-centred classroom', in MEGARRY, J. (Ed.) *Computers and Education*, Kogan Page.

HOYLES, C. (Ed.) (1988) *Girls and Computers*, Bedford Way Papers 34, Institute of Education, University of London.

HUGHES, M., BRACKENRIDGE, A. and MACLEOD, H. (1987) 'Children's Ideas about Computers', in RUTKOWSKA, J.C. and CROOK, C. (Eds) *Computers Cognition and Development*, London, Wiley.

JACKSON, A.C., FLETCHER, B.C. and MESSER, D. (1988) 'Effects of experience on microcomputer use in Primary Schools', *Journal of C.A.L.*, 4, 214–26.

JACKSON, V. (1987) 'English teaching and the new technology', *Educational Review*, 39:2, Abingdon Press.

JONES, A. and SCRIMSHAW, P. (Ed.) (1988) *Computers in Education 5–13*, Open University Press.

JONES, R. (Ed.) (1984) *Micros in the Primary Classroom*, Edward Arnold.

KEMMIS, S. (1988) 'Educational computing: how do we know what we are getting?', Paper to Educational Computing Conference, Melbourne, July.

KUHN, T.S. (1970) *The Structure of Scientific Revolutions*, University of Chicago Press.

MACDONALD, B. (1977a) 'The educational evaluation of N.D.P.C.A.L.', *British Journal of Educational Technology*, 8:3.

MACDONALD, B. (1977b) *The Programme at Two*, Norwich, UEA, CARE.

MacDonald, B. (1988) *D.T.I. Micros In Schools Support, 1981–1984*, Norwich, UEA, CARE.

Mackay, H. (1988) 'Computer literacy: issues and debate', paper presented to IT in Education Colloquium at BERA Conference, UEA, Norwich.

Mackay, H. and Gillespie, G. (1989) 'Ideology in the social shaping of technology', Unpublished paper, Polytechnic of Wales.

Maddison, J. (1983) *Education in the Microelectronics Era*, Open University Press.

Martin, A. (1986) *Teaching and Learning with LOGO*, Croom Helm.

Medway, P., Yeomans, D. and Layton, D. (1989) 'Technology in TVEI 14–18: the range of practice', Sheffield, Training Agency.

Miller, L. *et al.* (1988) *Schools, Computers and Learning*, Ontario, Ministry of Education.

Moores, S. (1989) 'The box on the dresser', *Media, Culture and Society*, Vol. 10, pp. 23–40.

Obrist, A.J. (1983) *The Microcomputer and the Primary School*, Hodder and Stoughton.

O'Shea, T. and Self, J. (1983) *Learning and Teaching with Computers: AI in Education*, Harvester Press.

O'Sullivan, T. (1991) 'Television memories and the culture of viewing, 1950–1965', in Corner, J. (Ed.) *The Homely Image: Essays in Television History*, British Film Institute.

Payne, A., Hutchings, B. and Ayre, P. (1980) *Computer Software for Schools*, Pitman.

Perspectives 7 (1982) Exeter University School of Education.

Pogrow, S. (1983) *Education in the Computer Age*, Sage.

Robinson, B. (1985) *Microcomputers and the Language Arts*, Open University Press.

Rist, R. (1991) 'Computers, clay pots and case studies', in Blomeyer, R.L. and Martin, C.D. (Eds) *Case Studies in Computer Aided Learning*, Falmer Press.

Rushby N.J. (1979) *An Introduction to Educational Computing*, Croom Helm.

Schostok J. (Ed.) (1988) *Breaking into Curriculum: The Impact of IT on School*, Methuen.

Shepherd, I.D.H., Cooper, Z.A. and Walker, D.R.F. (1980) *Computer Assisted Learning in Geography*, Council for Educational Technology and Geographical Association.

Straker, A. (1989) *Children Using Computers*, Blackwell.

Steinberg, E.R. (1984) *Teaching Computers to Teach*, Lawrence Erlbaum Associates.

Stonier, T. and Conlin, C. (1985) *Children, Computers and Communication*, Wiley.

Terry, C. (Ed.) (1984) *Using Microcomputers in School*, Croom Helm.

Van Weert, T. (1987) 'A model syllabus for literacy in IT', in Rahtz S. (Ed.) *IT in the Humanities*, Ellis Harwood Press.

Walton, D. (1982) 'Shall we have a microcomputer in our primary school?', in Garland, R. (Ed.) *Microcomputers and Children in the Primary School*, Falmer.

Wayth P.J. (1983) *Using Microcomputers in the Primary School*, Gower.

Wellington, J.J. (1985) *Children, Computers and the Curriculum*, Harper and Row.

White M.A. (Ed.) (1983) *The Future of Electronic Learning*, Lawrence Erlbaum Associates.

Wright, A. (1987) 'The process of micro technological innovation', *Educational Review*, 39:2, Abingdon Press.

Young, M. (1991) 'Technology as an Educational Issue: Why it is so Difficult and Why it is so important'. In Mackay, H., Young, M. and Beynon, J. *Understanding Technology in Education*, London, Falmer Press.

Chapter 1

Computers and Exploratory Learning in the Classroom

Richard Ennals

Introduction

Powerful low-cost computer systems are now available to educational and community users, providing potential access to the products of research in the field of cognitive tools for learning. Groups such as the PROLOG Education Group (PEG) and the Artificial Intelligence For Society Club (AIFS) have been developing new tools through collaborative projects, and the Information Technology Development Unit at Kingston College of Further Education has provided an institutional framework to facilitate open and exploratory learning. This chapter describes experience of the introduction of a new generation of integrated low-cost software for exploratory use in the classroom and in the community. The central objectives of liberating people and information are pursued using expert systems, hypertext and information albums, raising broader implications for education and society.

Mindtools

Crucial to computer-aided exploratory learning in the classroom is the concept of Mindtools. Mindtools are partial models, generalizable knowledge structures within which exploratory learning can be facilitated and generated, and have enjoyed increasing popularity following the work of Papert with Turtle Graphics (Papert, 1980) and the development of powerful computer learning environments. For a Mindtool to be effective it needs to mediate between the cultural and institutional context and the technology with which it is constructed, providing a natural entry point for the user. The elements and objects within the Mindtool must be both authentic in themselves and conducive to constructive thought in a larger practical context. Mindtools are tools for active learning, which presupposes a commitment from a motivated learner, and an acceptance, at least at an instrumental level, of the representation and knowledge structures offered by the Mindtool. This does not suggest easy widespread use in practical education, where the habit of 'playing with' computers has often authenticated an undemanding superficial approach.

Richard Ennals

Designing and Implementing Educational Mindtools

My own research in this field began with the development of experience-centred role-based simulations to assist in the teaching of history and social studies in secondary schools, deriving from experience in writing and directing plays and musicals, normally workshop-style with students. The production of a series of historical simulations required the formulation of a common methodology and approach to structuring knowledge. At this stage, in the 1970s, the physical technologies used were paper, card, paper-clips, light, paint, sound and musical instruments, which can serve as 'Mindtools' but lack the potential power of the computer.

Escalating information requirements of participants in classroom historical and political simulations forced a number of theoretical and practical developments. Models had to be idealized from reality to the status of stimulating Mindtools, freed from the detail of the original situation. If the quality of thinking and decision-making within the simulation was to match the normal performance of the learner, appropriate information needed to be readily available in the form required, which became impractical beyond a certain level of complexity, for example in a simulation of the European Parliament in 1979. Accordingly we began to make use of computer database facilities. Conventional educational software, and languages such as BASIC, did not offer the means of combining rich knowledge representation with the modes of reasoning appropriate to the domain and user interaction appropriate to classroom simulation use. A knowledge-based approach to computing was needed.

From 1980 the 'Logic as a Computer Language for Children' Project, directed by Robert Kowalski in the Logic Programming Group at Imperial College, London, developed software tools, methods and teaching materials for the use of logic in the classroom. Different representations were used in classroom teaching, exploiting the equivalence of semantic networks and predicate logic. Initial work focused on the teaching of logic, using the 'SIMPLE' front end to Micro-PROLOG (Ennals, 1983), but from 1981 attention was also given to the different requirements of particular curriculum areas, the knowledge structures involved, and the software tools which might provide support in the development and use of Mindtools (Ennals, 1985). From 1982 educational work was increasingly focused on the PROLOG Education Group at the School of Education, Exeter University. The initial concentration was on the teaching and learning of history, but affiliated projects internationally in subsequent years have addressed a vast range of curriculum areas, including English, ecology, electronics, geography, physics, chemistry, mathematics and biology (Yazdani, 1984; Ennals, Gwyn and Zdravchev, 1986; Nichol, Briggs and Dean, 1988). In 1990 the PROLOG Education Group led a theme of the World Conference on Computers in Education. PEG have developed a range of classroom tools for teachers and students, supporting a variety of modes of exploratory learning, and driven from extensible but self-contained examples. They have been translated into many natural languages at the interface level, and modified to suit local cultural and institutional requirements, facilitated by their implementation in compiled PROLOG for personal computers.

Exploring Real-World Problems in the Classroom

By 1984 there was considerable experience with the use of knowledge-based tools in secondary and middle schools, and growing commercial awareness of the potential of expert systems technology. Interest was expressed from Further Education in bringing these two elements together: offering support for learning in areas of vocational and commercial interest. Further Education Colleges have a crucial role in technology transfer, educating skilled manpower for industry in light of the latest technical advances, and it was suggested that Expert Systems tools on personal computers could provide a valuable stimulus.

Following a report for the Further Education Unit (Ennals and Cotterell, 1985), the Information Tecnology Development Unit was established at Kingston College of Further Education in January 1985. The intention was to provide an appropriate institutional setting for the development and use of knowledge-based tools in education, acting first as a catalyst for innovative work in established departments, then assisting in embedding good practice and support materials into the College Culture.

A succession of linked research and development projects, involving KCFE and partners, have explored the use of different metaphors for individual and collaborative computer use.

One early approach involved the development of a family of 'front ends' to PROLOG. Having first simplified the surface syntax of PROLOG in work at Imperial College, using SIMPLE and MITSI (Man In The Street Interface) (Briggs, 1985a), the next steps in the provision of user environments constitute Mindtools. Jonathan Briggs' PLAN (Briggs, 1985b) system enables children to develop and play their own adventure games, deriving the metaphor from the popular commercial systems which permit play only. Similarly the LINX system (Briggs, 1988a) enables children to develop and play their own simulations, providing a new interactive narrative medium, particularly useful in history and English curriculum contexts, and finding a valuable role in work with students with special educational needs.

Each of these systems proved useful in classroom situations but required the motivation of initial appealing examples to establish the dominant metaphor for the Mindtool. If we regard the 'system' in the classroom as comprising the teacher, students and the computer in a curriculum context, then in many cases the context defines the framework of the Mindtool, but this requires sensitivity and confidence from the teacher, including competence in newly emerging teaching methods. A 'freestanding' package for wider distribution would require considerable development and testing effort, refining the model of the teacher and student embodied in the software. More realistic has been the evolution of a collaborative network, offering support to new practitioners in this educational medium, and facilitating the sharing of knowledge and experience. In building this human network we have sought to separate the transfer of knowledge from the transfer of money: teachers and students contribute 'sweat equity', and should not be obliged to pay to think.

Crucial to the development of the 'Learning with Expert Systems' Starter Pack at KCFE (Briggs, 1988b; Cotterell, Ennals and Briggs, 1988) was the involvement of subject specialist lecturers in the implementation and application of a family of expert system shells. Exposition and practical use was driven first by demonstrators then by well formed and motivated examples, the best of which could be ascribed the status of Mindtools in themselves, while also paving the way for the patterns of reasoning and interaction to be applied to new domains of the user's choice. (This had become apparent during the early days of Micro-PROLOG, when the murder mystery example 'Who killed Susie?' (Ennals, 1983) captured the imagination of international audiences, even being taken up in the slightly adapted form of 'Sherlock Holmes' in the documentation for the Danish/American Turbo-PROLOG).

The ADEX Advisor could offer advice on clothes, AIDS, good practice in equal opportunities, and the prior learning and achievement of electrical and motor vehicle engineers (Mansell, 1990), working from a knowledge base of rules in ASCII format input using either the shell or a standard word-processor. Where the examples fell neatly into place it was because the knowledge was naturally represented in the form handled by the shell, and the shell did not impose distortions on normal practice. Teachers and students could build their own examples within minutes.

The EGSPERT Browser, working from the same form of rules, supported explanation of potential culinary disasters, the possible replacement of the Prime Minister, racism in science teaching, and self-profiling for staff development. The appropriately chosen example would provoke the class to extend, edit and improve it interactively, thus making the transition from passive users to active system builders. The EGSPERT Browser could also been seen as a form of simple hypertext, supporting links up, down and across the tree structure of the knowledge base, driven by menus and 'hot spots', and also offering a trace of the journey.

The Q-VIT database provided a user-friendly front end which assisted queries and explanations concerning the vitamin content of foods and related health implications. The knowledge was probably not unfamiliar to teachers, and the structure was uncontroversial, but the volume of detail was hard to recall, and the system could handle a large set of facts and rules, providing explanations of its conclusions. As a bonus Q-VIT offers an introduction to the working of PROLOG facts and rules, and to the construction of queries to the database, formulated incrementally with the assistance of menus.

In each case a rich, well-structured, commonly-understood domain and representation helped the Mindtool to provide a credible bridge between micro world and real world. The task of the researcher undertaking technology transfer, and then of the teachcer, was to gauge the interests, language use and sense of humour of the 'target group', and to introduce examples to catch their imagination, empowering them to pursue their pre-existing interests to greater effect.

A more recent development derives from the world of AIDS. In the spring of 1987 Kingston College held a seminar series for staff on key medical aspects of AIDS providing a basis for discussion. It was clear, however, that more than mere medical facts were involved, for the question of AIDS touches on deep-seated attitudes and prejudices. A project initiated at Kingston Polytechnic in association with the ACET AIDS charity and Brunel University, then continued at Kingston College, has sought to support the work of AIDS educators equipped wth personal computers (Smee, 1990). In a manner reminiscent of my history simulations a decade earlier, a scenario is presented to which the individual or group must respond. The YOSSARIAN system explores the implications of different decisions, and draws inferences about the attitudes to the respondents, provoking further discussion.

The same YOSSARIAN shell has been applied to the world of drugs education, and experimental work has begun investigating applications in equal opportunities and industrial relations. The AIDS and drugs applications were developed by Pete Smee, acting as both software engineer and knowledge engineer, and drawing on his experience as an AIDS worker, working with acknowledged experts. It is likely that the success of subsequent YOSSARIAN applications will depend on a number of factors, including the extent to which users find the subject matter immediate, the effectiveness of the presentation of the early frames of material, and the extent to which the belief system and commitment of the designer is shared by users. It appears that YOSSARIAN can serve as a tool to animate discourse in well-understood but loosely structured areas, perhaps working from a basis of existing interview schedules or questionnaires. Pilot work with senior college managers, college governors, and the Business and Technician Education Council is producing encouraging results.

Experience in this field over the past decade leaves some issues apparently resolved, while a new agenda is opened up by technical advances in related fields. We should not expect to develop many Mindtools whose applicability is global, as the Mindtool provides a common representation with which issues of cultural relevance can be addressed. The development of a set of tools enables us to provide a flexible range of learning experiences in the real world. Those tools are often by-products of collaborative research in Artificial Intelligence (Ennals, 1987), whose ideas can be applied in affordable software of personal computers. Their use will be more effective if users have been involved in design and development from the earliest stages, and their dissemination will be eased if the Mindtools are expressed in familiar language and representations. It turns out that to produce Swedish or Danish versions of our KCFE shells involves more than simple verbal translation: different user interfaces are also needed. Work with French researchers in France and La Réunion suggests that knowledge may be viewed in very different ways in different cultures, and exposes dangers of computational cultural imperialism.

Importantly, the new agenda is partly motivated by the proliferation of personal computers among educational and voluntary groups. Where there are common objectives and commitments, common beliefs and assumptions, the provision of a rich software environment may open up new possibilities for learning. We are currently investigating extending the approaches above with the use of interactive hypertext, information-handling tools and improved interfaces for communications. The same 'flat' ASCII text describing a domain of knowledge can be animated by a variety of software environments, with few additional keystrokes. We can carry a range of powerful tools in our knowledge tool-boxes, without being obliged, given that we have hammers, to treat every problem as if it were a nail. Similarly we may come to appreciate the broad range of skills possessed by our colleagues and students, brought out and often enhanced by the use of different stimulus devices.

Information Studio and the Kingston Data Library

David Hopson of UNET and KCFE comes to Further Education from many years of working with unemployed and community groups, seeking to empower them by increasing their access to and control over information. In asssociation with the Artificial Intelligence For Society Club, and with technical assistance from computer professionals in both the public and private sectors, he has developed a system, Information Studio, which is easy to use, self-copying, and requires only a standard personal computer. Users of a range of standard applications can save their files onto Information Albums, making them available for printing, searching and distribution. As voluntary and educational bodies see the advantages of sharing information, and financial mechanisms are evolved to reward the originators of particular materials, we can expect to see the world of information opening up. Already the Kingston Data Library offers a vast range of materials, for distribution by disk or by electronic mail. The new World Press Centre and Third World Educational Clearing House (Thompson, 1989) offers the prospect of a worldwide information service on Third World issues, again assuming access to a personal computer.

Experimental Results

The work I have described has not been conducted by psychologists in laboratory conditions, but by collaborating practitioners in the real world conditions of education, and, more recently, community work. Our emphasis has been on practice, though our work and tools have been open to evaluation by others. The extensive literature describes the context of use, the real world situations in which the Mindtools have been established, suggesting that the results of Mindtools are more than merely technical, involving new ways of learning and working.

Much can be learned from the emerging limitations of Mindtools. Once we accept that experts could never give a full rule-based description of their expertise, as there is always a residue of tacit knowledge, we learn to appreciate the instrumental value of partial models used appropriately. Similarly, skills could never be fully captured by progressive fragmentation into conclusions and conditions, but apply within a culture, involving participation in a form of life. Paradoxically, the limitations can be turned into strengths as Mindtools need not aspire to completeness, but can provide rich culturally authentic environments for learning.

Implications for Education and Society

Work in exploratory and open learning using Mindtools gives increased emphasis to the essentially human-centred nature of useful systems (Ennals, 1986; Goranzon and Josefson, 1988; Goranzon and Florin, 1990; Ennals and Gardin, 1990). Acceptance that models and systems can only ever be partial, and that cultural and environmental factors will affect the applicability of software tools, limits our expectations of the power of technology. Attempts to replace teachers by technology will necessarily fail: what is needed is a broader view of people and technology in their institutional and cultural context. This in turn suggests that the narrow technical training of many computing specialists, and the separation of technology from humanities studies, are counter-productive and dangerous. The means are now available to offer considerable freedom and power to ordinary people, and to free their information from the constraints of conventional applications. The remaining restrictions are not primarily technical, but derive from human attitudes to knowledge and property, oriented towards the individual rather than society.

References

BRIGGS, J.H. (1985a) *MITSI*, Kingston College of Further Education.

BRIGGS, J.H. (1985b) *The PLAN*, Kingston College of Further Education.

BRIGGS, J.H. (1988a) *LINX*, PROLOG Education Group, Exeter University School of Education.

BRIGGS, J.H. (1988b) *Learning with Expert Systems*, London, FEU.

COTTERELL, A., ENNALS, J.R. and BRIGGS, J. (1988) *Advanced Information Technology in Education and Training*, London, Edward Arnold.

ENNALS, J.R. (1983) *Beginning Micro-PROLOG*, Chichester, Ellis Horwood.

ENNALS, J.R. (1985) *Artificial Intelligence: Applications to Logical Reasoning and Historical Research*, Chichester, Ellis Horwood.

ENNALS, J.R. (1986) *Star Wars: A Question of Initiative*, Chichester, John Wiley.

ENNALS, J.R. (Ed.) (1987) *Artificial Intelligence State of the Art Report*, Oxford, Pergamon Infotech.

ENNALS, J.R. (1990) *Artificial Intelligence and Human Institutions*, London, Springer.

ENNALS, J.R. and COTTERELL, A. (1985) *Fifth Generation Computers: Implications for Further Education*, London, FEU.

ENNALS, J.R. and GARDIN, J.-C. (Eds) (1990) *Interpretation in the Humanities: Perspectives from Artificial Intelligence*, London, British Library.

ENNALS, J.R., GWYN, R. and ZDRAVCHEV, L. (Eds) (1986) *Information Technology and Education: The Changing School*, Chichester, Ellis Horwood.

GORANZON, B. and FLORIN, M. (Eds) (1990) *Artificial Intelligence, Culture and Language*, London, Springer.

GORANZON, B. and JOSEFSON, I. (Eds) (1988) *Knowledge, Skill and Artificial Intelligence*, London, Springer.

HOPSON, D. (1990) *Information Studio*, London, UNET.

MANSELL, J. (1990) *The Assessment of Prior Learning and Achievement: The Role of Expert Systems*, London, FEU.

NICHOL, J., BRIGGS, J.H. and DEAN, J. (Eds) (1988) *PROLOG, Children and Students*, London, Kogan Page.

PAPERT, S. (1980) *Mindstorms*, New York, Basic Books.

SMEE, P. (1990) *YOSSARIAN*, Kingston College of Further Education.

THOMPSON, P. (1989) *The World Press Centre and Third World Educational Clearing House*, London, WPC.

YAZDANI, M. (Ed.) (1984) *New Horizons in Educational Computing*, Chichester, Ellis Horwood.

Chapter 2

Siuli's Maths Lesson:
Autonomy or Control?

Alec Moore

Introduction: Divided Opinion

Some extravagant claims have been made recently relating to IT use in schools. In the area of social development, Burke *et al.* (1988, pp. 16–17) maintain, for example, that the introduction of the computer into the classroom can have a positive anti-sexist effect, while in the area of cognitive development Papert (1980, p. 995), supported by Noss (1988, p. 75), has claimed that if properly introduced to LOGO at an early enough stage children can develop computational concepts 'even earlier than the numerical', thereby 'reversing what has appeared to be a universal of cognitive development'. Clark, meanwhile, (1985, p. 19), taking a stage further Papert's view that the regular availability of computers at home could result in children learning to write almost as soon as they learn to talk, suggests the exciting possibility of some kind of computer-inspired socio-literacy revolution, in which children become 'no longer passive consumers of the written word' but — along with their teachers — 'producers' who 'make books'. For each of these observers, there seems to be no questioning the need to get microcomputers into schools urgently and in large numbers, and no doubting their beneficial impact on all sorts of social, cognitive and academic achievement.

Theirs is not the only view, however, and, as one would expect with the advent of anything perceived as 'new', the introduction of IT into the world of education has been characterized by a wide range of responses on the part of both educators and researchers. Beynon (1989) has defined the major of these responses in terms of five IT-related research paradigms. These paradigms are:

- the Cognitive Psychology/Artificial Intelligence (to date, the dominant one), which focuses on 'the relationship between AI and developmental issues and how these might be used to generate theories of cognitive development';
- the Accolatory, which comprises 'uncritical advocacy' and is 'often based on general, unresearched presuppositions and prejudices';
- the Dismissive, which objects to CAL in ways that are 'sweeping, general and extravagant';
- the Social Literacy, which focuses on the role of the teacher as ensurer that new technology exists in classrooms for (Apple, 1986) 'politically,

economically and educationally wise reasons, not because powerful groups may be redefining our educational goals in their own image';

- the Evaluative paradigm, which places the emphasis on 'documenting the kind and degree of microcomputer deployment in schools and making policy-related recommendations'.

Not all commentators, of course, can be fitted neatly into one particular paradigm; however, there are tendencies among researchers to pursue certain lines and interests, and clearly the views referred to in the first paragraph of this chapter are those of people whose work generally falls within the Accolatory paradigm (a paradigm, it could be added, particularly highly populated with researchers who have specialized in working with LOGO). *Why* teachers and researchers pursue different lines and form different conclusions is an interesting question that is partly to do with personal histories and cannot be pursued in any real depth here. There is one aspect of such disagreement that I do want to highlight, however, and that is concerned with each observer's *own initiation* into the use of microcomputers in school classrooms. This initiation seems, as I hope will become clear, crucial in determining whether microprocessors are used to good effect and for admirable purposes or to bad effect and for purposes that do not challenge existing pedagogies and power-bases but tacitly support and prolong them.

Teacher Initiation into IT Use

The picture painted by IT enthusiasts is rosy partly because it is painted *by* enthusiasts. These are people who have enjoyed or witnessed the successful use of microcomputers in the classroom and who quite properly want to share their positive feelings with colleagues and other interested parties. Significantly, they are themselves often the initiators of computer use in the classrooms they write about. They may, as in Papert's case, be programmers who have brought educational software into a large number of schools, or, as in the case of Burke *et al.* practising teachers who have developed computer use in the particular school or schools in which they teach. Either way, they have seen a clear educational value in one or more items of software, that has sat comfortably with an existing philosophy and pedagogical style. They have, in short, brought computing into the classroom to produce particular social/cognitive/academic effects; and with it they have brought very clear ideas about how the software should be used, including how it should be used to challenge the existing pedagogical styles of other teachers.

The scenarios described by such enthusiasts are often idyllic: scenarios in which, for example, 'the computer is integrated with other resources, and a corner will probably have been set aside for its use, with the screen positioned so that pupils can choose when to share their work with others and when not' (Hoyles, 1988, p. 14); scenarios in which, at other times, teachers and pupils sit crouched together over a microprocessor, intimately absorbed in some joint learning enterprise, or in which pupils working concurrently in more traditional ways leave their seats of their own accord to use the class computer in the same way that they would, to use Papert's analogy, use a pencil. In such scenarios, independent as well as collaborative learning is nurtured and encouraged, both by the nature of the program used (typically, LOGO in mathematics, word-processing packages in English) and by the teaching style of its adult mediator.

There is no doubt that such scenarios do exist, and that the 'right' program in the hands of the 'right' teacher is likely to have the kinds of beneficial effects the enthusiasts describe. It is equally true, however, that for many teachers and pupils a very different reality applies, and that at least one of the sources of that difference lies in the history of computer use both in the institutions in which they work and in their own individual lives generally.

The fact is that when it comes to IT there are far more users than there are developers. That is to say, most practising teachers have seen computers brought into their schools in ways that make them at worst reluctant and fearful, at best incompetent and uncertain how best to use them. They have not developed programs, nor, prior to the machines' arrival on site, have they developed notions of how computers might be used to improve teaching and learning in their subject area. Computers arrive and are often left largely neglected. (Dillon, 1985, p. 99, quotes the statistics that '75 per cent of US schools that own micro-computers leave them idle over half the day' and '25 per cent of schools use their computers for only one hour per day'. It would be surprising indeed if a significantly different set of figures resulted from a similar survey in the UK.) When told they have a shared responsibility to initiate their pupils into IT skills and uses, it becomes, not surprisingly, a question for most teachers of *incorporating* available facilities into existing practices. That is to say, most teachers' deployment of microcomputers in educational settings becomes a largely *ad hoc* affair and consequently, as we shall see, a potentially damaging one.

Several commentators (see, for instance, Dillon, 1985, and Smith, 1981) have gone to some lengths to point out the actual and potential dangers of the *ad hoc* use of computers in schools, and it is within that tradition of criticism that this essay belongs. It is not my intention, however, that it should also fall within Beynon's Dismissive paradigm: rather, by offering evidence of certain kinds of computer use in the form of brief case studies, it is intended that it should fall into the Educationalist paradigm whose necessity he argues as an alternative to the other five. That paradigm is based upon qualitative, ethnographic-style research and upon the 'feeding-in of critical, analytical insights . . . which address Technology in non-technological but nevertheless highly rigorous and challenging ways'. It is a paradigm within which researchers must examine closely, by reference to specific examples, the nature of programs in use, in the context of teacher-pupil and teacher-pupil-computer relationships and in the light of the stated and unstated pedagogies and educational philosophies that underpin such use. The following study, of a secondary school pupil using a SMILE program in mathematics, is presented in order to illuminate the ways in which the new technology, rather than revolutionizing learning, can all too easily be slotted into and reinforce existing practices in ways that should concern us: it is offered in the belief that by looking at the bad we may be better equipped to address the rather more difficult question: What is 'good'?

'SMILE' Maths and Autonomous Learning

A 12-year-old Bangladeshi girl, Siuli, has come into her school library to work on a SMILE program, there being two computers here but none currently available in her classroom. The previous day, she has come in with a Bangladeshi classmate whose English and maths are regarded by the maths teacher as 'more advanced' than Siuli's. Together, with the librarian assisting, the girls have worked through the program several times until Siuli appears to have got the hang of it. Today, Siuli comes in to try the program on her own.

The program — presented as a game — runs as follows. The computer displays a random set of fourteen low numbers, e.g. (to use those thrown up on the occasion of this observation):

3	9	11	14	15	18	19
22	23	26	27	29	31	34

One of these numbers has been 'selected' by the computer as the object-number. By identifying and eliminating groups of numbers/characteristics of the object-number, the pupil has to work out what the object-number is: i.e. (in the librarian's words to the researcher) 'what number the computer is "thinking of"'.

The pupil can ask any of four basic questions to arrive at the solution:

Prime number?

Square number?

Factor of . . .?

Multiple of . . .?

If she types in 'Prime number?', for instance, and the computer has 'chosen' 9 as the object-number, the display will read NO and at the same time eliminate from the screen all the prime numbers. If the pupil types in 'Square number?' the display will read YES and simultaneously eliminate all the numbers that are *not* square numbers, leaving only the square numbers showing: in this case, 9, which is the answer. The trick is to guess the 'chosen' number in as few attempts as possible.

The final display for Siuli's first finished game looks like this:

3	9	11	14	15	18	19
22	23	26	27	29	31	34

Prime number?		9		14	15	18
NO	22		26	27		

Multiple of 3?	9	15
YES		27

Multiple of 5?	9
NO	27

Square number?	9
YES	

On the face of it, Siuli seems to have grasped the game very well. Certainly, she is very pleased to have finished it in five goes. But as Hoyles says: 'correct answers may well hide incorrect processes' (Hoyles, 1985, p. 10) — and perhaps it is pertinent to ask: What exactly *has* Siuli done, and what does she *think* she has done?

The librarian's concept of the game is stated very clearly in conversation with the researcher:

> The computer selects a number and you have to work it out by asking questions: a sort of problem-solving exercise involving a process of elimination and selection. Also, it reinforces the ideas of square numbers, factors and so on.

The game, then, as far as she is concerned, has two distinct objectives:

1 to develop and reinforce certain key concepts to do with numbers;
2 to encourage problem-solving through a process of elimination and selection: a key mathematical concept in itself.

(These objectives are subsequently confirmed by Siuli's maths teacher.)

Is this, however, Siuli's perception of the game? A brief discussion with the researcher reveals that it is not:

Researcher: Siuli, what's the point of this game?
Siuli: To get all these numbers out and leave only one.
Researcher: I see. Does it matter what number it is?
Siuli: No . . . You have to ask questions.
Researcher: I see . . . And what do all these Yes and Nos mean?
Siuli: These? . . . I don't know . . . Miss! . . . Sir wants to know what Yes and No are for.

As far as Siuli is concerned, the idea of there being a pre-selected number simply does not apply. She is not 'discovering' a 'chosen' number at all: she is merely reducing a large number of numbers to a single one — and though she will eventually arrive at the 'right' answer by asking appropriate questions (appropriate, that is, to the problem she believes she has been set), her misconception clearly affects the efficiency with which she arrives at that answer and alters the kind of questions she asks. The words YES and NO remain utterly meaningless to her in the context of the game; however, since she is still able to achieve some measure of success (as evidenced by ending up with a single number) this is of no consequence to her.

How Siuli has arrived at her misunderstanding has something to do with adult mediation, and something to do with the program itself. In fairness, it has to be said that the librarian, though an excellent librarian, is not a trained maths teacher (and should probably not have been put in the position of having to act as one): a fact brought into sharp focus when, in quickly reminding Siuli of the program again on her arrival, she attempts to explain to the pupil factors and multiples (Siuli's apparent lack of knowledge of these concepts may lead us to enquire why she has been sent off to use this particular program in the first place):

Librarian: How many threes in four?
Siuli: Eight.
Librarian: Eight? Eight threes in four?
Siuli: Oh . . . twelve.
Librarian: Twelve? Twelve threes in four? Are there? If you had four, how many threes could you get out of that? *Could* you get twelve?
Siuli: No.
Librarian: No . . . So . . . How many threes in three? If you had three (holding up three fingers) . . . How many threes is that? . . . It's one three, isn't it? One lot of three.
Siuli: Yes.
Librarian: So if I had four . . . Is that enough to get any more threes? (Shaking head.)
Siuli: No.
Librarian: So . . . How many threes in four? (Holding up one finger.) One.
Siuli: One.
Librarian: Right.

As Lorenz (1980, p. 18) says: 'There is no other subject in which the teacher is tempted to misinterpret a (numerically) correct student response as an insight into the underlying problem structure; and nowhere is the student more willing to accept overt or covert prompts in order to conceal problems of understanding'. It is not surprising that Siuli never once uses the question: 'Factor of . . .?' in her several playings of this game, since the expression has no meaning for her; while her regular use of the question 'Multiple of . . .?', always suffixed by the figure 3 or the figure 5, represents no more to her than another meaningless question which, however, has the wonderful effect of clearing away a few more numbers from the screen.

The librarian, however, is only one of two adult mediators: we could say, the less significant of the two. Back in the classroom is the second mediator, Siuli's maths teacher. He it is who has selected this particular program as suitable material, directed Siuli towards it, and taken the very important decision that she will work at the program 'on her own' (he has no inkling that the librarian's role will be anything more than that of technician, and is surprised subsequently to learn of the extent of her pedagogical involvement). He has apparently made these decisions for two possibly contradictory reasons:

1 'Siuli has been working on these things in class.'
2 'She's been having some difficulty with number.'
3 'She really likes to work on the computer.'

Siuli may well have been working on these things in class and may well enjoy working at the computer; however, her difficulty with number has clearly not been eased by exposure to the program and there is at least the possibility that existing misconceptions have been reinforced. The problems with the program itself, meanwhile, are twofold.

First, there is a problem with its presentation in that it obscures the true nature of the task it purports to set. Had the pupil using it been asked the question '*Is it* (a prime number, a square number, etc.)?' those two words 'Is it' would almost certainly have clarified the true nature of the task, or at the very least have prompted the student to ask (herself or the librarian) 'Is *what*?' As it is, 'computer-talk' ('Prime number?'; 'Square number?') merely serves to reinforce Siuli's perception that she is not after a pre-selected number at all, that she has merely to clear a number of numbers from the screen until only a single number remains. This is, of course, crucial to how she sets about the task and to her subsequent opportunities for concept development: if she knows she is after a particular number, the terms 'prime number', 'multiple', etc. will prove useful to her; if she thinks she only has to reduce the number of numbers to one, their importance is reduced drastically (especially when she discovers that virtually any question will assist this process).

The second problem is to do with the *kind* of program that this is. Kemmis (1977) proposed four paradigms relating to educational software: the instructional; the revelatory; the conjectural; and the emancipatory. The program we have looked at may have pretensions to being a simulation (and therefore located within the 'revelatory paradigm') but effectively it is instructional. That is to say, it presents the child with a set of related problems to each of which there is a right answer. That answer is get-at-able by the child by taking 'independent' decisions (i.e. on which of certain pre-set questions to ask), feeding those decisions in, and having the possibility of learning from those decisions in the process. It is the kind of program that has proved highly popular with some teachers, partly because, once the child knows how to feed her decisions into the machine (i.e. which buttons to press), it obviates the need of a teacher at the child's side. With programs such as this, hard pressed teachers need not contribute more than the most minimal input, nor, significantly, do they have to put their own 'computer literacy' on the line as they might have to do with word-processing programs or with LOGO. They can send pupils off to work quietly and (they can reassure themselves) productively on the computer from time to time on a topic or project related to what they are doing in the classroom, and in her absence from the room the pupil can be handily perceived as developing in this way an autonomous learning style that is part of a wider, publicly stated pedagogical and philosophical aim of 'putting the child in control of her own learning.'

This all sounds very wonderful, both from the teacher's and from the pupil's point of view. However, it ignores some very important things about learning and teaching.

First, it ignores the fact that learning is essentially not a private but a *social* business — that cognitive development, as Vygotsky (1962) points out, has to take place through dialogue both with one's teachers and with one's peers. If we accept such a view of learning, we must be suspicious of any programme of study that has the effect (intended or unintended) of physically and socially 'isolating' individuals, however progressive or child-centred its underlying philosophy may purport to be. Sending Siuli off to the library may, in her maths teacher's words, be 'only one of many different learning situations to which she is exposed during the course of her mathematics lessons', and it is true that on this occasion her learning has involved some dialogue (however unhelpful) with another human being: it is equally true, however, that the kind of software she has been sent off to use lends itself very readily to the kind of isolated, individual work that many other teachers have come to associate with control rather than learning and, in the wider context, with the creation of a future corpus of obedient, unquestioning, unorganized workers.

Second, it ignores the 'hidden agenda' of the program itself. Programmers are very keen these days on talking about software that is 'teacher-proof'. To say that a program is 'teacher-proof' is to say that teachers won't get in the way of it, won't muck it up through their own ideas or ignorance. But it is also to suggest that the program itself is some sort of ideal 'disinterested logician', whose sole function is to serve the learner. The program is, of course, no such thing: it was designed by a human being with a particular idea of how children learn and what they need to learn (possibly not a trained educationalist at all), and it must be made available to the pupil by a teacher who, for all the program's 'teacher-proofness', obviously thinks the program worthwhile. The notion that children like Siuli are learning 'autonomously' at such programs is, consequently, a sham: it is every bit as false and misleading as Siuli's sense of academic achievement each time the program is brought to a successful end. She has not been free to choose this particular piece of work to do, nor, once she is in front of the machine, is she free to take part in any discourse other than that set for her by the program's designer. As Dillon (1985, p. 92) says of such software,

It is the student who must fit in with the program's structure, to respond to the machine's initiative, to be evaluated by the machine.

In short, the illusion of autonomy created by the sight of pupil working at machine minus teacher merely masks a more worrying reality in which teacher 'conspires' with programmer to reinforce a certain kind of learning that is actually the very opposite of autonomous, a kind in which 'knowledge and expertise' (to adapt Hoyles, 1985, p. 25) is assumed to reside not 'solely with the teacher' but with the teacher's trusty representative: the computer.

It is a conspiracy which is not to be underestimated. As Dillon (1985) goes on to say,

In effect, much of the interaction with the machine is just like the 'teacher initiates — pupil responds — teacher evaluates' pattern of inter-action that has been discovered in so many classrooms before the advent of computers.

In other words, not only do programs such as this encourage a physical and social isolation of the user that reflects notions of how children learn (and remind us of the 'silent, sitting-in-rows' teaching of the old grammar schools): they also, however innocent, friendly or neutral they may appear to the user, promote and support a certain style of teaching which very strictly controls *what* they learn.

Computers and Ideologies

'Can a computer,' asks McCormick (1983, p. 33), 'in its role as "surrogate" teacher, embody an ideology?' — while Beynon (1989) argues: 'Technology . . . is not, and never can be, neutral and apolitical.'

Computers, clearly, have not just 'turned up' in schools, any more than their programs have just 'appeared': both have been developed and promulgated by individuals and groups of individuals with distinct, if often disparate, motives. Ideologies can be transmitted overtly or covertly; they can have high or low visibility, and they can be accepted or questioned. One of the problems with computers is that they are machines; and machines, having the capacity neither for independent thought nor for generating and using their own language, often have their ideological content overlooked. There may be social, political and economic reasons behind the invention of a machine like the computer, for the forms in which it exists and for the ways and areas in which it is deployed, but these reasons tend to have relatively low visibility: the existence of the computer often gets taken for granted as yet another aspect of some sort of 'natural' technological progression — a socially, politically and economically neutral development that, to quote one teacher in a high-IT-using school, 'does not take sides' for the very simple reason that it is 'not human'.

'Not human' may be a perfectly reasonable description of a computer itself — that is to say, of the microchips and wires and various other components out of which it is made: however, a computer is nothing without its programs, and these in a very real sense *are* human: that is, they are clearly invested with the ideologies of their human creators. In the field of educational software, it is the programmers who most often decide what problems to set, what questions to ask and how to ask them, what forms of answer are acceptable, and so on. It is their biased, human voices that 'talk to' computer operators, not the unbiased, in-human voices of neutral machines with no axes to grind.

Common sense suggests that the ideological content of a computer program ought to be more obvious — that is to say, of higher visibility — than that of the existence of a computer viewed apart from its programs. Certainly, when discussing computer hardware, teachers appear generally most concerned with matters of mechanical reliabilty, ease of use and compatability with other machines, whereas their discussion of software is far more likely to involve issues related to curriculum and pedagogy. Children, too, usually find little difficulty in distinguishing in conversation between the computer as an artefact and the programs it is constructed to operate, generally attributing to the latter a rather higher status than to the former. (One child at Siuli's school interestingly talks of the 'dead' computer 'coming to life' on the insertion of a disk, while another describes the computer itself as 'like a human body' and the various items of software 'like its brain'.)

Interestingly, despite this widespread theoretical differentiation of program from machine, a difficulty appears to remain for many computer users *in practice*, in separating out the 'unbiased', 'non-human' machine from the biased, human voice of the program: that is to say, perceiving the program *in use* as 'neutral' because the machine itself appears, to common sense, to be neutral. (When the teacher quoted above — whose view is echoed by several teachers at Siuli's school — states that 'the computer does not take sides', he is, of course not referring to the computer as a *potential* resource but to its actual deployment in his lessons and therefore to its programs.) In computer-use in schools, this has particularly interesting implications, since it could reasonably be argued that the ideology embodied in a computer program perceived as 'unbiased' and 'non-human' is even less likely to be questioned by pupils (and teachers themselves) than if it were being conveyed by a teacher. Whereas teacher authority occasionally gets questioned by pupils (sometimes to the extent of pupils claiming their teachers to be mistaken, unreasonable or incapable) the authority of 'the computer' has a tendency to remain intact. The observation 'This computer is stupid' or even 'This program is stupid' is not, certainly, an uncommon one in school class-rooms, and is regularly heard at Siuli's school; however, the complaint is in-variably directed at a program's ease of operation rather than at any ideological content or at the 'rightness' or 'wrongness' of its answers or its approach.

The problem of ideology has been raised by several commentators, includ-ing Chandler (1985) and McCormick (1983), who answers her own question: 'Designers and programmers, like teachers and school architects, may transmit ideologies consciously or unconsciously.'

McCormick, initially concerned with the possibilities of the deliberate mani-pulation of educational software on the part of government or government agencies, concludes that the nature of future software is 'far more likely to be determined by individual choice, market forces, and the ability of learners (or their parents) to pay for what they want to learn.' To those familiar with the current commonsense majority view of what is and is not worth learning and of the character of 'market forces', this will come as small comfort: indeed, there may be little difference in the end between the 'government manipulation' and the 'individual choice' that McCormick talks of.

Chandler takes McCormick's concerns a stage further, focusing not so much on the overt content and style of programs as on the pedagogical assumptions that underpin their creation and the kinds of pedagogy invited at the 'receiving end'. Thus, for Chandler (1985, p. 10):

> The current reification of technique reflects a belief that the only import-
> ant learning is that which can be precisely described in quantifiable terms
> ('the Basics'): it is a value system which champions instrumental reason
> at the expense of human values. And the computer is a powerful tool for
> technocrats who think like this; it takes no imagination and little effort to
> make the computer function as a monitor of mechanical operations.

The ideologies that lie within the SMILE program used by Siuli have already been described. But consideration of ideologies embodied in software prompts a further question related to ideologies embodied in pedagogy generally, and in particular to the relation between teachers' existing classroom practices and the kinds of educational software they place before their pupils.

It might be assumed that for a teacher to make use of an item of software, some element of ideological *accord* must exist (or failing that, must be believed to exist) between the teacher's and the programmer's educational philosophies: that if there is an ideological *mismatch* the particular item of software will simply not be deployed in that classroom. In the case of Siuli's program, this certainly seems the case: whether we look at the program from the teacher's viewpoint or from a more critical one, a clear commonality of approach appears to exist. (This is hardly surprising, since the program has been designed specifically for use by teachers already committed to SMILE maths generally). Thus, Siuli's maths teacher's perception of his own pedagogy is that he pursues a teaching style that is 'child-centred and progressive', in which, in a mixed ability classroom, each child has the opportunity to 'proceed at her own pace' without missing out any 'key concepts' or 'being made to feel in any way inferior or superior by being segregated'. For this teacher, the computer program tackled by Siuli is appropri-ate since 'it gives this pupil the chance to work at a particular thing that has given her difficulty but that she's begun to make some progress in, in an environment that promotes concentration, that is interesting for her, and that is not at all threatening: she can make as many mistakes as she likes, and she's far more likely to learn from those mistakes'. To take a more critical view, it could be said that in Siuli's normal maths lessons she finds herself working in unhelpful isolation through a fairly rigid programme of work at a pace dictated by the programme, and that to be sat in front of a small screen, on her own, engaged in silent, 'in-head' reasoning sits equally comfortably with an isolationist, 'transmission' model of teaching and learning. These are differences of opinion that are interpersonal but not intrapersonal: basically, if you like SMILE maths you are likely to like SMILE computer software; if you do *not* like SMILE Maths you are unlikely to like SMILE software. It may safely be assumed that Siuli's maths teacher and the designer of the program she is using have a shared belief in the value of SMILE and in the strategies and philosophies it entails. What is equally likely is that neither teacher nor designer has seriously assessed the *problematics*, either of the scheme of working or of the particular program in question.

Conclusions: Autonomy and Control

Siuli's maths teacher certainly sees nothing but value in the task he has sent Siuli to complete: nor, indeed, does the librarian, who has unwittingly been called in to help and who is particularly impressed that here is a girl (not only a girl, but a bilingual girl to boot) not previously noted for her confidence 'actually using — and enjoying using — a computer with the utmost confidence'. What is interesting, however, is that Siuli herself has been drawn into this unquestioning praise of the program. When asked how she likes working at the computer generally, she says:

> I like it a lot. It helps you to concentrate better, and you get on much better than when you're in the classroom 'cos you don't get distracted so easily. Also it's more interesting, it makes you want to do the work more.

When asked about the particular program she is working with, she is equally enthusiastic but less specific:

> It's fun. It teaches you about numbers. I like it.

On the face of it, it would seem churlish to be critical of what must seem to many to be a small triumph for the introduction into school and into one girl's life of the new technology. We should not forget, however, either what took place while Siuli was working at the computer or the context in which it occurred. It may have pleased Siuli's maths teacher to believe that what Siuli was doing in her absence from the classroom was beneficial to her, and there is no doubt that Siuli was delighted every time she 'got' the right answer: to any uncommitted observer who was there, however, it would be very hard to acknowledge that anything of any real educational value to Siuli was taking place.

As for the librarian, her perception is, perhaps, the most interesting. She sees the computer as something that has given Siuli not only a measure of self-confidence but a measure too of 'independence': a belief that she transmits to Siuli through her every smile of congratulation and reassurance. That independence, like the 'autonomy' referred to by Siuli's maths teacher, is, I suggest, no more than a dangerous illusion. What exposure to the computer has done for Siuli is not to make her less dependent but, by creating an illusion that she is working alone and at her own pace, to make her dependence less visible and therefore less likely to be challenged. As Foucault (1977) has pointed out, the most successful kind of political and social control is that which is carried out in the very minds of those being controlled: one person's autonomy is thus another person's thraldom.

All of this is not to say: Let us not use computers in our schools. Chandler (1985), having himself raised serious doubts about current uses of computers in school classrooms, concludes:

> This is no justification for rejecting the tool: rather, it demands the raising of our consciousness of the bases of all technologies, and a positive discrimination in favour of using them, where appropriate, to meet genuine needs.

This essay intends to support such a view. Not only do we as educators and educationalists have a duty tirelessly to examine educational computer programs, to exhibit them not as neutral items but as the bearers of ideologies that we may — as teachers and pupils — wish to question; we must also examine, critically, the ways in which those programs are presented to the people they are meant to help. Through that examination we should seek to promote examples of 'good practice' as well as of good software, while at the same time exposing computer uses which support discredited transmission models of teaching and learning and attempt to 'privatize' learning through the effective denial of its social character.

References

APPLE, M. (1986) Teachers and Texts. A Political Economy of Class and Gender Relations in Education, London, Routledge & Kegan Paul.

BEYNON, J. (1989) 'Researching Technology: the need for an Educational Paradigm', Polytechnic of Wales.

BURKE, J. *et al.* (1988) 'My mum uses a computer, too', in HOYLES, C. (Ed.) *Girls and Computers: General Issues and Case Studies of LOGO in the Mathematics Classroom*, Bedford Way Papers 34, Institute of Education, University of London.

CHANDLER, D. (1985) 'Computers and literacy', in CHANDLER, D. and MARCUS, S. (Eds) *Computers and Literacy*, Milton Keynes, Open University Press.

CHANDLER, D. and MARCUS, S. (Eds) (1985) *Computers and Literacy*, Milton Keynes, Open University Press.

CLARK, M. (1985) 'Young writers and the computer', in CHANDLER, D. and MARCUS, S. (Eds) *Computers and Literacy*, Milton Keynes, Open University Press.

DILLON, D. (1985) 'The dangers of computers in literacy education: who's in charge here?', in CHANDLER, D. and MARCUS, S. (Eds) *Computers and Literacy*, Milton Keynes, Open University Press.

FOUCAULT, M. (1977) *Discipline and Punish*, Harmondsworth, Penguin.

HOYLES, C. (1985) *Culture and Computers in the Mathematics Classroom: An Inaugural Lecture*, University of London, Institute of Education.

HOYLES, C. (Ed.) (1988) *Girls and Computers: General Issues and Case Studies of LOGO in the Mathematics Classroom*, Bedford Way Papers 34, Institute of Education, University of London.

KEMMIS, S. (1977) *How Do Students Learn?*, Working Papers on CAL, Occasional Paper No. 5, University of East Anglia, Centre for Applied Research in Education.

LORENZ, J.H. (1980) 'Teacher-student interactions in the mathematics classroom: a review', *For the Learning of Mathematics*, Vol. 1, No. 2.

McCORMICK, S. (1983) *Computers and Learning*, Open University Educational Studies: A Second Level Course. Purpose and Planning in the Curriculum. Block 3, Unit 23. Milton Keynes, The Open University.

NOSS, R. (1988) 'Geometrical thinking and LOGO: do girls have more to gain?', in HOYLES, C. (Ed.) *Girls and Computers: General Issues and Case Studies of LOGO in the Mathematics Classroom*, Bedford Way Papers 34, Institute of Education, University of London.

PAPERT, S. (1980) *Mindstorms — Children, Computers and Powerful Ideas*, Brighton, Harvester Press.

SMITH, F. (1981) 'Demonstrations, engagement and sensitivity: the choice between people and programs', *Language Arts*, 58, 6, Sept, pp. 634–42.

VYGOTSKY, L. (1962) *Thought and Language*, MIT Press.

Chapter 3

A Case Study of Microcomputers in Art Education

Robert Blomeyer

Introduction

The concept for this formative study evolved as a result of conversations and correspondence between Professor Ivor F. Goodson and the author. The CAL intervention project now referred to as 'Curriculum and Context in the Use of Computers for Classroom Learning' is being conducted by the Research Unit for Computers and Curriculum Studies (RUCCUS) at the University of Western Ontario in London, Ontario. There, Professor Goodson and his staff were to initiate a major study examining the use of Computer Aided Learning (CAL) in schools located in the vicinity of London, Ontario. The study was funded by the Ontario Ministry of Education as a part of their on-going efforts to evaluate the impact of CAL on curriculum in the Ontario school boards.

During the 1980s the Ontario Ministry of Education developed a consistent educational philosophy and generalized policy statement to guide the acquisition and implementation of new instructional technologies in the Ontario school boards (Nielsen, 1989). During that same period the Ministry sponsored the development of the ICON 1 and ICON 2 microcomputer systems. Their approach to materials development and curricular integration has encouraged creative and experienced classroom teachers from Ontario school boards to become software designers and developers.

The result of Ontario's efforts to develop appropriate instructional technology systems and policies to guide their implementation is the evolution of a microcomputer hardware and software system that is unique to the educational philosophy and curricular content of the Ontario schools. The Ministry's purpose in commissioning the study 'Computers in Context in the Use of Computers for Classroom Learning' was

> ... to assess and examine the use of computers in classroom learning at the secondary level; to further assess how computer practice might be adapted to maximize learning opportunities; and to provide a series of case studies of how innovative activities in the school can be initiated, implemented, and sustained. (Goodson *et al.*, 1989, p. ii)

During an initial visit to London, Ontario as a consultant in the autumn of 1988, we discussed the feasibility of a 'condensed fieldwork' case study to be conducted soon after implementation of the CAL intervention in the selected school or schools. We also discussed the possibility of creating two field sites so that contrasts and comparisons could be made between particular logistic and administrative protocols that would probably evolve in the cooperating schools.

The author agreed to and subsequently wrote a paper on methodology which outlined my ideas about using qualitative methods to document initial implementation of new instructional technologies. That paper (Blomeyer, 1989a) provided the concept that was negotiated into a field study during subsequent interactions with Professor Goodson. I lobbied for an ethnographically-oriented descriptive study to be initiated at the outset of initial classroom use of the new ICON microcomputers. Because of the scope and scale of the intervention it seemed obvious that the project would be difficult to study initially as a whole. I proposed to conduct a formative case study of one curricular area within the total project to make an initial inquiry more manageable.

This choice of timing was based on the author's assumption that the effects of CAL on classroom learning are strongly context-dependent and that the technological, cultural, and political contexts of implementation efforts may be the most significant influences driving the success or failure of technological innovations. My background as an arts and humanities teacher and training in the evaluation of art education programs made selection of the art education curriculum area a logical choice.

My prior experience working with computer graphics applications in instructional settings suggested to me that the art teachers would probably be among the first to discover hardware and software problems that might lurk behind any CAL system. Graphics applications are generally memory-intensive and often interact in unpredictable ways with operating systems, file servers, and other system software. My hunch was later supported by observations of classroom events, but that's getting a bit ahead of the story.

The formative study was agreed upon in concept by November 1988 and a tentative date for April was set in January 1989. Arrangements were finalized with Professor Goodson by March 1989. We agreed that the field study would be conducted in two schools located in London, Ontario between 10 April and 22 April 1989. One school was to be a comprehensive high school with studio-based art classes taught in a traditional manner and the other school was a vocational high school having a highly specialized graphic arts curriculum. The comprehensive high school was configured with four distributively networked ICON microcomputers in each cooperating classroom and one printer per classroom. The vocational high school was configured with a centrally located ICON laboratory installation having twenty-five networked work stations and two shared printers.

During the two weeks that I was was resident in London, the art classes in both schools were observed over a nine-day period for a total of seventeen hours and five minutes. I also observed two board of education ICON teacher training classes for a total time of two hours and fifty-five minutes. During nine days of observational fieldwork, the fine arts classes in the comprehensive high school were observed for a total of eight hours and twelve minutes and the vocational art classes for a total of eight hours and fifty-three minutes.

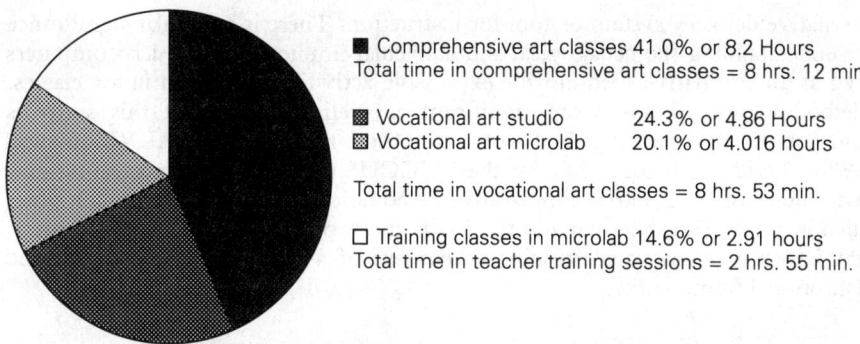

Comprehensive art classes 41.0% or 8.2 Hours
Total time in comprehensive art classes = 8 hrs. 12 min.

Vocational art studio   24.3% or 4.86 Hours
Vocational art microlab   20.1% or 4.016 hours

Total time in vocational art classes = 8 hrs. 53 min.

☐ Training classes in microlab 14.6% or 2.91 hours
Total time in teacher training sessions = 2 hrs. 55 min.

Figure 3.1:   Observational time in field sites

In the fine arts classes, there was only one forty-minute class where the ICONs were not being used by the students present. Otherwise, students from all the traditional art classes were systematically rotated on and off the computers at intervals that coincided with assignment of new studio projects.[1] In the commercial art classes, four hours and fifty-two minutes were spent observing in a studio (where only one Macintosh and a laser printer were a part of the regularly shared art equipment) and four hours and one minute were spent observing the graphic arts students working in the centralized ICON laboratory (see figure 3.1).

During the first five days of the study, the researcher's verbal interactions with the students and teachers were limited to avoid unnecessary intrusion on the classroom settings. On the sixth day of the field study, interviews were begun with the teachers and with a self-selected sampling of their students. All interviews were tape-recorded and tape recordings were taken in the classroom settings when ambient noise levels were low and classroom activities offered suitable subject matter (i.e. a class critique or initial group-mode instruction on a technique).

Foreshadowed Problems

One of the conventions usually followed in planning and conducting naturalistic studies is formalization of a tentative research agenda framed as a list of 'foreshadowed problems', questions, or issues like those deliberated by Malinowski in *Argonauts of the Western Pacific* (1922). As shown by Lou Smith and Paul Pohland in their seminal study 'Education, Technology, and the Rural Highlands', problems and issues evolve from observational fieldwork as events in the real world play themselves out (1974, p. 40). This new case study will attempt to *tell the story* (Stake, 1988) of computer aided learning in two teachers' art classes within contrasting secondary school settings. In telling the story, the problems and issues that become evident from examination of the new findings should contribute to a clearer focus on the details relevant to understanding the curricular integration of computer aided learning.

The story told here has potential for understanding the value of CAL as an alternative delivery system or tool for instruction. There is particular significance for understanding the pedagogical and curricular implications of microcomputers used as an alternative medium for expressive activities conducted in art classes. Methodological questions are significant as well. Much about this study is common to the growing body of naturalistic research on CAL (Blomeyer, 1989b). Perhaps a broader role for the RUCCUS project will be integrating new case studies of CAL into a comparative or ethnological perspective on computer aided learning. But, like many of the issues and problems relevant to this project, that is being renegotiated within the context of a changing technological and institutional framework.

Questions on CAL

The questions that I brought into the study of CAL in secondary art education were in themselves a third generation of questions that I have been working with since 1983–1984. In my research on CAL in secondary foreign language classes (Blomeyer, 1985) I borrowed heavily from a set of questions addressed by the Congressional Office of Technology Assessment in their report of 1982 entitled *Informational Technology and its Impact on American Education* (see Blomeyer, 1985, p. 4). In response to the OTA's questions and the particulars of my inquiry about the use of microcomputers in foreign language teaching, I proposed to address seven issues that were obviously relevant to looking at CAL in foreign language instruction. They were:

1. What were the similarities and differences of successful implementation strategies?
2. How do the teachers integrate instructional computing into the foreign language curriculum?
3. What are the optimal levels of functional computer literacy for foreign language teachers?
4. What are the state, district, and individual school policies that are affecting the classroom use of computer-assisted language teaching?
5. What are instructional and administrative practices with possible long-range influences on commitment to instructional computing?
6. What is the impact of instructional computing on the 'dominant core' of teaching practices?
7. What are the effects of instructional computer use on the equity, efficiency and quality of an instructional program?

Conclusions from my dissertation, further study on the mechanics of curricular integration (Blomeyer, 1986), new research on microcomputer use in elementary curriculum (Blomeyer and Bright, 1987), and four years of work with K-12 teachers from all area specializations and discipline bases have provided new perspectives on my old questions. Most recently, my review and synthesis of the growing corpus of naturalistic studies on CAL (Blomeyer, 1989b) provided the resources for reorganizing a list of questions or issues to guide new research to monitor the implementation of new interactive technologies:

A   the design characteristics of instructional technology applications (with particular attention to the interactive characteristics of CAL);

B   curricular and disciplinary sources of lesson materials;

C   pedagogical characteristics attributable to the content domain or the training of teachers as content specialists;

D   hardware and site implementation (logistic and technical considerations),

E   availability or access to necessary hardware (e.g., work stations, etc.);

F   the effects of specialized technology training on the abilities of students and teachers to use new technology applications.

(Adapted from Blomeyer, 1989a)

To summarize the changes in my research questions, I have narrowed general questions from earlier research to new issues and questions having answers that may be answerable in quantitatively verifiable ways. Questions A to D above can be addressed by careful content analysis of interactive materials and by carefully documenting and analyzing logistic and instructional activities in particular school sites. Student and teacher activity accounting, construction of both oral and institutional histories of site development, and personal histories of key participants are all strategies that may be used to create an accurate and verifiable account of CAL or other interactive technologies' impact on instructional settings.

The case study presented here on initial use of ICON microcomputers and graphics software in art curriculum uses this modified typology as an initial focus to orient data gathering. Data from this new case study on CAL will contribute to the evolution of new, contextually grounded categories for describing computer aided learning. New categories will then be used to report findings and interpret events. So begins a new iterative cycle of heuristic enquiry and interpretation.

Two School Contexts

ICONs in a Comprehensive High School
(Field Notes: 10 April 1989)

Marshall and I pulled into Brock student parking lot at about the same time as Valerie. Both cars drove far back into the lot before we found free space. Although it was April, there were still small patches of ice and snow on the steps and I hurried in because I didn't have a proper coat for the Canadian 'spring'. The building was brick construction, had two floors, and looked typical of suburban high schools where classrooms with exterior windows are constructed on both sides of locker-lined hallway. As we walked down the hall I was stuck by two things.

First, the environment in the halls was clean, light and cheery. The students were smiling and talking; getting their books out of the lockers and carrying on typical friendly patter. They were cute, well scrubbed, and looked like cutouts from an Archie comic book. Was I in a time warp? This is like I remember from when *I* was in high school! Where were the skinheads and punks? Why wasn't I hearing obscenity and where were the security guards? If this school is any example, this experience is liable to be very different from that I've grown used to in suburban and inner-city America.

As we walked down the hall, I looked into the classrooms. The numbers of desks indicated class sizes no larger than the low-mid twenties. The science rooms were well equipped, there were racks and shelves of books, charts, and supplementary materials in every classroom, and although the warning bell had not yet rung, teachers and students were already in the classrooms beginning discussions as preliminaries to the day's business. The polite behaviour of the students was outstanding! Virtually every student we passed in the hall smiled and bid us a good morning. A real contrast to the boisterous and rude behaviours I'd encountered recently at home.

We stopped in at the art room where Val and Marshall introduced me to Margarete, the cooperating teacher. She was about five feet and ten inches tall, short blonde hair, glasses, a broad and infectious smile, and had the vigorous and energetic appearance of someone who works out or competes in sports. We told her we had an appointment to meet the Board Liaison Officer in the Media Center in a few minutes. She walked along with us and started a conversation by asking me what I thought about London, Ontario, so far. I replied that if everything about London is as pleasant as her school, I will like it very much.

Classes were just starting when we reached the second floor and entered the school's library or Media Center. A large part of the available space was taken up by a large group of kids that were engaged in some sort of activity that was apparently a great deal of fun. They were working in small groups on some sort of collaborative writing project. After we walked through the students, toward some ICON terminals in the back of the room, we were approached by a tall slender man sporting a white turtle-neck pullover, neat but curly black hair, a beard, and wearing glasses.

Marshall introduced me to the Board's Liaison Office for the CAL project. Peder told us that the students were here today because a nurse working for the London board was there to conduct sex education classes. He pointed out a blonde and attractive young woman who was right in the centre of the student activity. He suggested that before we went any further, we should go down to the school office so that I could have a proper introduction to the principal.

The five of us walked down to the first floor to the main school office. Out in the hall were two well-dressed men discussing a subject related to the day's activity. Both men were wearing ties and looked senior enough to be school administrators. One came forward toward us, looked at Peder and said: 'Well, this must be our visiting researcher!'

Peder introduced me to the principal and assistant principal of the school. The principal, who came forward to address me earlier, continued: 'Welcome to London, Ontario, and Brock High School. I gather that you've had a look around with Peder and Margarete. What do you think?'

I stopped for a minute to consider my response . . . and then said: 'Your school is beautiful and open, your students are polite, and your faculty is charming. In fact, would you consider letting me ship the whole operation back to Texas with me? If we can't work that out, can we schedule tours for Houston inner-city teachers so that they could see tangible proof that schools like this can still exist?'

The principal weighed my response for a second, and then broke out into a beatific smile. He took my hand, shook it, and said: 'Well! I've heard that things are a bit rougher in the States. So, you really think that we've got things well under control, eh?'

I replied, continuing to shake his hand vigorously: 'Why, it reminds me of what high schools were like when I was a student myself in the American Midwest. . . .' I seemed to have made a hit with Margarete's principal. He continued to chat with me for a few minutes about yesterday's unseasonably late snowfall and a bit about the local history of their school.

After a polite few minutes I excused myself and suggested that we were probably keeping him from his appointed rounds. I knew that Margarete had a second hour class and I wanted to get back to her room so we could discuss our first observation. I also wanted to get a look at the distributive network installation and see how the printers were hooked up in the classroom sites.

The principal said goodbye to Peder and the rest of our party, wished us a good day, and walked into his office. Peder left us to make an appointment in another school and the rest of us went back downstairs toward the art room. On the way down I asked Margarete how she felt about having so many people as observers in her classroom this morning. She indicated that three observers might be 'a bit much'. I suggested that Val and I might observe her second hour class and that Val and Marshall might switch for the third hour. . . .

ICONs in a Vocational High School
(Field Notes: 12 April 1989)

I was still without a car this morning so Valerie arranged to pick me up at about 8:10. By about 8:45 we were slowly circling a parking lot across the street from Tecumseh School. As we got out of her car, I looked across the street at Tecumseh. It was a large, grey, three-storey structure that was partially stone, partially concrete, and partially brick construction. In fact, the different materials roughly matched to different buildings or additions that had evidently been joined together during various expansion or remodelling efforts. The sides of the building were stained by weathering and it had a dingy but massive and solid appearance; like a factory or prison. In short, had great similarity to urban high schools that I was familiar with in the US.

I had already been briefed on Tecumseh's history by Ivor Goodson, the RUCCUS project director. It was a vocational high school with a very long and distinguished history. It had been founded in 1912 as one of the first fully technical schools in the province. It was at the forefront of educational reforms intended to make the Ontario schools more responsive to the industrial and commercial needs of Ontario's developing industrial economy. It was opened with an initial enrolment of 150 and its growth to the present 2700 students probably corresponds with the types of materials used in constructing various wings of the building.

As we approached the school, we could see groups of students standing around close to the building. They were sheltered from the wind, having a last smoke before going in. As we got closer, we could hear the music from jam boxes that the students had outside with them. The students were not dressed as neatly as those in yesterday's suburban school, but there was a carefully crafted element to their disarray.

Many of the students were wearing trendy faded jeans with patented holes, leather coats, shirts-tails outside oversized wool pullovers with the sleeves rolled back and cuffs stylishly unbuttoned. Many wore expensive sneakers (running shoes) but some of the girls were sporting leather lace-up boots that went part way up ankles covered by argyle socks. In short, these students spent a great deal to get this casual appearance. They seemed to be making a statement about their group identity, or status.

As Val and I came closer and moved toward the doors, the students moved aside to let us through. They were not discourteous, but they were not openly friendly. Their general language usage did not include excesses of obscenity, but there was occasional roughness and vulgarity. They were socially involved with one another to the point that I felt nearly invisible as Val and I threaded our way in through the various group boundaries.

Marshall caught up with us inside. He said that he was going to go immediately to the microcomputer lab. It was located in this older part of the building in a room that had previously been a studio for displaying student art exhibits. When we came to the door, Marshall went in and Val and I went on down the hall to stairs. The plan called for me to meet Sandi and observe in her 9:00 class. I was to go back down to the ICON lab later and observe a training session that Peder was conducting for a group of the teachers from the Board's 'back-up' group. These teachers were trained in case any of the primary project teachers were taken out of their jobs for any unforeseen reason.

Val and I climbed up to the third floor. We went down the hall toward the art room, but it was still locked. No Sandi. Val stopped off at a media centre on the third floor to see about an overhead projector for Peder's demo. She checked one out and decided to take it down to Peder in the ICON lab. I said that I would wait for her in the hall outside the media centre, just down the hall from the art room door.

Watching the students in the hall was fascinating. I'd noticed as Val and I walked back and forth by the media centre, that the groups of students clustered around the lockers were roughly grouped according to ethnicity. I recognized a variety of mother tongues including Thai, Vietnamese, Cambodian, French, Spanish, Portuguese, Russian, two different Eastern European languages I could not identify, Greek, Turkish, Arabic, and Persian. The students up here in the halls were not the group that were determined to stay outside in the drizzle for that last cigarette. They were colourfully and stylishly dressed. Some were Reebok casual, but others were European stylish.

Once again, I felt almost invisible because the students in the different language/culture groups were so involved with one another that they seemed unaware of even the members of the next nearest group. Since mother tongue use was dominant, I couldn't follow the conversations. The body language indicated that it was standard high-school talk and flirtation.

After student watching for about seven to eight minutes, a very tall and attractive woman wearing a grey, floor-length greatcoat, and long neck scarf, came flowing down the hall. She had shoulder-length blonde hair and was wearing a hat that matched her coat and scarf. She walked with her hands in her greatcoat pockets, taking long strides, threading her way through the jumble of students. She looked too old to be a student and too unconventional to be anything but an artisan. I thought . . . that is Sandi. She walked around a corner and down the hall out of my vision.

Just then, Val walked up and said: 'Well, now that I've gotten rid of that overhead projector . . . let's see if Sandi has arrived yet.' We walked over to the art studio, went in, and found Sandi taking off her grey greatcoat and scarf.

Valerie introduced us and we began a standard introductory conversation about the unseasonable weather. After the opening formula, she said: 'Well, I'm sorry to be the one to tell you this, but there has been a little change in plans since we set it up for you to observe my class today. Today is the change between the semesters and I don't have a class to observe! We start back with regular classes tomorrow and I will have most of the same students that I had last semester.'

I said that there was no problem. Peder wanted me to come downstairs and observe his training anyway, so things would work out quite nicely. I asked her to show me around in her art studio. She hung her coat in a hallway between her office and the studio and started to give me the Cook's tour. She showed me her MAC Plus and laser printer first.

She said: 'I've really been working with computer graphics for quite a while. Before I came to London to teach, I had a job as a commercial artist in Toronto and learned to do computer graphics on Intergraph work stations. In fact, I sort of became the local expert on the operations of the Intergraph. I had to field strip it and carry pieces in for repairs a couple of times. I really hated that part of my work back then. It was a high-pressure job with tight deadlines and every time the darn thing went down, we stood to loose big bucks. So, I found myself under pressure to both turn out work and maintain the machine. Now I never have to mess with hardware problems or repairs. That's someone else's job and I just turn in a work order.'

She went on to tell me all about how the MAC was in constant use by her students doing both text and graphics to be used as part of their designs and projects. She showed me the other more standard graphic arts equipment including a camera table, presses, air brushes, compressors, drawing tables, and other assorted hardware.

She said: 'All of this stuff is really old, but we're lucky to have it. Most of these drawing tables were used when they were obtained a few years ago and we could use more of them. But, we would need more floor space if we got a lot more of them. The light in here is good for art work.' (There was a sixteen-foot ceiling with windows all the way to the top.) 'Sometimes we get pretty crowded in here but we make do.'

She went on to say a great deal about her father, who was the chair of an art department in a public school, her prior activities as a serious amateur athlete before the onset of back problems from scoliosis, her background working in the commercial graphics industry and her transition to education after more health problems due to job-related stress.

From there she went on to say more about the problems related to getting better technologies for her students to use in doing their work for her classes. In fact, considering that I had not meant or even tried to start a formal interview, she said a great deal indeed. She talked very easily and seemed willing to tell me her whole life's story right then and there.

Toward the end of the conversation, Val asked her to tell me about an 'event' that had happened in her class a couple of weeks ago, involving a generalized crash of the network. Sandi said: 'We were using SPECTRICON for the first time with the class and some of the students had been working on initial efforts to do colour graphics on the ICONs. They were used to doing computer graphics in black and white on the MACs, so some of them were doing pretty complicated compositions. Something happened and first one terminal went down, then another, and another . . . until finally all but two of the ICONs had crashed or frozen up and lost their graphics that they were building. I think some of them had saved or were trying to save at the time that the melt down occurred. We never figured out what caused it, but it makes all of the students really careful about saving their work.'

Val caught my attention by looking obviously at her watch and saying: 'Well Sandi, we know that you want to get some work done. So why don't we reschedule Bob's observation for the next available day (Thursday) and go ahead on down to observe Peder's training class in the lab downstairs.' We arranged with Sandi for me to observe her next ICON class on Thursday afternoon. We said goodbye and went downstairs.

ICONS in Fine Arts Education
(Field Notes: 11 April 1989)
Note: YL = Young Lady and YM = Young Man

Margarete is talking to in-coming and out-going students and putting a colour wheel up in front of the room that I assume she will be using on the next lesson. She's telling the students in the in-coming class that today is 'absolutely the last day' for the current assignments to be finished and she wants the work turned in by period's end so they can go on to the next project.

Margarete: '—, . . . what about your art history project?' Student: 'Well, uh . . . I'll have it tomorrow.' The interaction pattern repeats with four or five more students. A female student (YL1) stops to show her some sketches and discuss her work. She also discusses a college that she's visited and seems to be suggesting that the student check it out.

The team has changed. Marshall is in and Val is out. Students are still coming in and handing in due or overdue work. At 11:42 there are about thirteen students present. About six are started doing some sort of art project. They appear to be working on hieroglyphics and other stuff that is thematically related to some Egyptian relics that are being built for the school 'show'.

YL1 is going to paint on a large pharaonic wall painting that is near my temporary table site. We had to move some stuff around so she can work. No problem.

The teacher said that two students were to be working on the computers today. The two designated went back into the ICON booth. The regular class are all started on their respective projects (11:47). I'm floating back into the booth.

I've moved the work station to the back so I don't disturb YL1. The teacher is talking with the class about pyramids and scrounging jewellery for the show . . . Egyptian jewellery is hard to find. . . .

The boy (YM1) working on the ICON was adding to a surrealistic pyramid motif piece he had saved . . . but he didn't like his modification and ditched it. The girl (YL2) is having a hard time starting a graphic drawing. She said '. . . yours is really nice. I'm having a hard time. I don't have much experience with this.' She's *fooling around* learning to use the features.

Margarete chased out a third student (YL3) who was talking to both students on ICON. YL2 mentions that she had an elaborate drawing on the library computer and the thing crashed on her. (A discussion ensued between researchers and teacher about other bugs and crashes that have occurred with the graphics program.)

YM1 has started a new drawing. YL2 is still building up the upper left-hand corner of her screen. Marshall, Margarete and I were all in the back room. Margarete left saying 'Well . . . these guys don't need three adults watching them.'

In the studio two students are painting on a giant poster of hieroglyphics, etc. Two boys are collaborating on another similar poster near the back. YL3 is still off task and there is generally an informal atmosphere in the studio overall. YL3 wandered out of the room. The teacher is helping YL1 mix tempera. A late student (YL4) just arrived and was asked by Margarete to go 'sign in' and come back. YL3 floated back into the booth. Margarete said to YL3: '—, time line!!'

YL3: 'I'm getting there! It's stupid! I don't know what I'm doin'!' (i.e., commenting that she did not understand the time line assignment).

YM1 is apparently doing a street layout in perspective. He's outlining the scene with white lines on a black background. He's apparently figuring out his idea on the fly.

YL2 is still playing with features on the ICON. She doesn't yet have anything resembling a composition . . . but more like a pad full of doodles.

The teacher went out of the class momentarily and came back with a roll of brown paper. She announces to the class that people that need the paper should get pieces the right length and cut them off the roll.

Students who have been working on the big black-on-white posters are now trying to put their work up on a wall. YL4 came back into the class.

The teacher is trying to keep a student from falling over backwards while she is stapling up a poster. She's also trying to help the two boys who were collaborating on a poster to find a wall space for theirs.

Margarete floats back into the booth and asks 'How are you guys doing??' YM1 is starting to use colour fills on some parts of his drawing. The teacher checked on YL2's progress and intervened. YL2 was having trouble erasing and Margarete showed her an area erase procedure. YL2 then used the procedure after Margarete left to clear some more doodles off the screen. YM1 *seems* more self-directed and sure of what he is doing. The girl *seems* more tentative and still doesn't have anything clearly resembling a composition.

The teacher is now helping the two boys tack up their poster. Lots of 'ladder work' going on. YL3 is looking at a source book containing drawings of the Egyptian gods. She asks Margarete to comment on what she's doing and Margarete refers her to another source book.

Three boys putting a poster up. YL1 is still painting. One cutting cardboard. Two working on gold wrapping paper. Three painting a prop. YL3 is doing research and YL2 and YM1 in the booth. The teacher asks this class if they can put up posters for the production around town: 'Can your mums and dads put them up in the workplace??'

YL1 is cleaning up.

YM1 is still working to fill in more of the areas that he has blocked. YL2's doodles are accumulating into a kind of eclectic composition. Themes are the word ART and a kite. She shows good functional knowledge of using the various colour palettes. Some features she seems to know a lot about. Some she is apparently unaware of.

The teacher in back room: 'Anybody need help?' No response. She then goes outside into the studio and says: 'Be sure and watch the time. Don't anyone leave dirty paint brushes lying around.' The students are already cleaning up. The studio is winding down. The computer art students are still working intently.

'Is it time to go??' 'Yeah. It's time to go. Everybody put everything away!' The students in the booth are asking Marshall some questions about the graphics program. He's helping out as needed. He answers questions but doesn't offer much more than direct answers. At 12:42 YL2 leaves. She talked to the teacher on the way out and Margarete asked her if she was sure that she exited so that the work was saved. At 12:43 YM1 left and Margarete also asked him if he exited and saved.

(Contextual background from field notes: After completing the first observation in the fine arts education classes, the RUCCUS project's art education specialist Roger Clark came through the school and took the art teacher to lunch. From my own discussions with Roger, I knew he was providing the art teacher with planning support and that he was pursuing his own data-gathering activities concerned with the ICONs and art education.)

Distributive Computer Aided Learning

It has become relatively commonplace to discuss the technical and logistic significance of local area networks for supporting the instructional use of microcomputers. A local area network (LAN) simply connects all the work stations in an installation to a shared data path through some sort of coaxial cable, twisted wire pair, or modular telephone wire (Bright, 1988).

The installation of a LAN enables the shared use of network printers and file servers. File servers permit data files and multiple-user software programs to be loaded into individual work stations through the network. In effect, a file server functions as a shared, high-capacity disk-drive, attached to every microcomputer in the network installation. This means that one printer or one installed copy of a legal, multiple-user application can service multiple microcomputer work stations on a LAN. This eliminates the cost of multiple printers from the lab installation and improves the speed and efficiency of software distribution to the end users.

For several years, a shared assumption common to many school microcomputer installations has been that individual work stations should be housed in secure, centralized lab sites. *The Electronic Schoolhouse* (Cline *et al.*, 1986) was one of the earliest serious works to discuss policy and practice concerning the curricular integration of microcomputers. Referring to the initial IBM/ETS dissemination project undertaken in 1983–1984, we find the following:

> The program plan specified that all donated PCs be kept together in the high schools in centralized labs. (p. 28)

> . . . suggestions were made to the high schools concerning security. This advice included: (a) having all the equipment gathered in one room on the second floor, (b) securing all windows and doors against unauthorized entry, (c) restricting all off-hour access through building coordinators, and (d) using other security precautions such as bolt-down systems, burglar alarms, or additional security personnel. (p. 31)

Attention to administrative details like security, air-conditioning (to avoid heat build-up in sensitive equipment), providing lab aides or site managers to assist with the mechanics of a new technology, and scheduling shared access to a limited amount of hardware has meant that microcomputer laboratories are the dominant hardware configuration in US secondary schools (Becker, 1986).

The art education class described above details a significant departure from the typical centralized lab site. The individual work stations were installed in mini-sites within the classrooms of the cooperating art teacher. Individual students were rotated on and off the ICON work stations. The ICONs were used as graphics production tools for specifically devised art studio assignments. The particular computer-based art projects were thematically and contextually similar to the projects undertaken by the majority of the students working with traditional art media and materials.

The behaviour of the classroom art teacher did not differ significantly in the way she addressed and related to the students engaged in traditional art or computer-based art projects. She rotated or circulated throughout the classroom, answering questions, demonstrating techniques, and offering encouragement and direction to all the students. While the particulars of her interaction with the computer artists was occasionally technical in nature, her role in the whole class was clearly that of a facilitator and mentor for all of the student artists.

In summary, the art education described above is distributive in two distinct ways. The microcomputer installation in the fine arts programme utilized a distributive network with shared microcomputer resources and the teacher equally shared her attention among the students working on both traditional and computer-based art projects. Both of these distributive attributes have a significant impact on the pedagogy and instructional outcomes.[2]

Microcomputers in Commercial Art Education
(Field Notes: 13 April 1989)

I'm at Tecumseh and entered Sandi's class (meeting in the ICON laboratory) a few minutes after the period started. Sandi is floating around the room helping various students play with features. Just a second ago a student was overheard to say 'I am playing! I want to play with animation!'

One student is at the centre table cutting out from magazines. Everyone else is on ICONS. . . .

It looks like Sandi has shown them where the clip art is and quite a few of them are using it to experiment with. Three or four I'd say. . . . Two of the girls have found the crosswords program. . . . One is doing a cursive name (YL2). . . .

The young lady doing the name (YL2) is erasing a circle she got accidentally. Sandi working with the girl sitting at the terminal next to her. She is apparently having a hard time getting used to the tool. She's doing a lot of one-on-one support with her.

Sandi has taken over the screens using ROBOTEL. It routes the video output from a selected work station into all the ICON monitors so they see her screen. (When she kicks in the ROBOTEL, there is almost an audible *snap* and the students look like they've been hit. They don't like to have control over their work stations taken away from them.)

She has designated control over ROBOTEL to YM1, who is taking them through a demo of IPAINT II. Sandi is explaining the limits of the program (ten frames) and letting the student (YM1) do the demo. (Marshall has set up their fancy tape recorder. The external mike makes it really obtrusive but I'll bet it cuts a good tape.)

Sandi has moved the control of ROBOTEL back to her own terminal. Now she's doing the demo. She has drawn a box (2D) and is doing a series of frames simulating the rotation of the 2D figure. The lines in the shape always have to be drawn in the same order. (The students can't wait to get control of the program themselves. Overheard: 'This is some kind of wonderful machine!')

She's getting closure on the demo. She tells them that they can also create a background scene for the animation to overlay on.

One boy is still into the crossword. Two of the girls are still using SPECTRICON. Everyone else is getting into IPAINT II.

I wandered over to ask Sandi if IPAINT could fake a 3D figure. She said yes and explained to me how it could be tricked to rotate a 3D figure or blow a figure apart for a dramatic effect.

She explained that she's intentionally letting them play around including looking at the other stuff on the server. She says that because they've used Cricket Draw etc. on the MAC, she gets them right into IPAINT because it lets them do some different stuff. Six students are using IPAINT.

The person in the middle that was cutting pictures is leaving. (Maybe a non-student?)

Sandi is talking two more into IPAINT (including YL1) through AMBI-ENCE (the ICON operating system; a bright blue background).

The majority of the students leave with Sandi to go and sing happy birthday to another of the art teachers . . . taking a cake along. Two students stay behind and continue working.

Sandi and company have come back in and the students are 'playing' with IPAINT and a few other assorted programs. (Some of the students have tried the drill and practice software that is available through the network and AMBI-ENCE. They never seem to stay with the drill and practice programs or more traditional instructional software for very long.)

YL1 finally got her simple animation to work. She was really pleased with it and did it over three or four times. She said: 'Wow! Where was this when we were doing film last year!?! I had to do 130 drawings for how long?? A minute and a half??'

Two of the boys go out. One comes back and asks if the room upstairs is open. Sandi says yes . . . that one of the girls is working up there on the MAC. Another girl (YL3) comes in to ask Sandi a question about what she is working on. Sandi works with her one-on-one at the centre table.

(Sandi explained to me that YL3 is a student who is very talented and has a spelling and writing disability. She told me that she really can't spell and doesn't get the sort of help she needs to remediate the disability so she can work up to her level. Sandi has made herself available to YL3 whenever she needs any help working out art or any other assignments.)

Five students are using IPAINT . . . one is doing a drill . . . and one is using a program to build up a seashore with shore birds and plant life.

YL2 (did the cursive name) has animated a simple wing flapping. She says: 'Sandi . . . am I through with the assignment?' Sandi answers: 'No . . . you have to find a commercial application for it. You have to explain its use to us.'

YL1 is still working with her animated wing and talking. . . . 'We have to find some commercial use for *this*? I wonder what we can use it for?'

Sandi's students are starting to save and clear out. Only three students are still on. YL4 asked Sandi's help to figure out how to save her figures. She asked: 'Is today a play day? Do we get serious tomorrow?' Sandi: 'You were supposed to fool around with it today and discover its capacity. Tomorrow you can work with it.'

Sandi is helping YL4 log off after an extended one-on-one. Help. She's chasing students out. She says that she has to get outside for the track practice. The art teacher leaves to go and coach track.

A Commercial Art Studio
(Field Notes: 14 April 1989)

I am in Sandi's classroom/studio. There are six students in the room. Five are at drawing boards working on individual projects and one young man is working on the MAC. Their cassette player is playing heavy metal music. Sandi is looking for something in her office. She just entered the classroom.

One of the students immediately asked her a question about the animation program they used yesterday. YL1: 'Do I have to change my drawings to accommodate the program?' Sandi: 'No, but you have to work it out on paper and acetate before you put it into the animation program. I don't want you to change your idea to fit the computer program, but I want you to work it out first. You have to be all prepared when we have time on the computers so you can make maximum use of your time.'

YL1 goes on to explain her idea about a truck ad. Sandi: 'Today is the day I'm going to explain your new project to you. Where is — . . . Where is — . . . (She's taking attendance.) OK . . . — is the other one that is doing that. . . .'

YM1: 'So . . . are you going to explain this thing to us before 10:00??' Sandi: 'Yeah, I'm just trying to wait for everyone to get here first.' The students are continuing to work. The students are anglo except for one black student. Three males and three females are present.

Sandi: 'You can turn the music off now. I just want to go over what we've got going now. We've got the illustration and the animation piece.'

A discussion is going on about access to the computers. Sandi is explaining to them why access to computer is limited to certain class times. The students want to know why they can only have access at certain times. 'We're really taking advantage of the situation now because a lot of teachers in the computer programme haven't figured out how to use them yet in curriculum. I've used computers for graphics so I'm ahead of them in getting started. That way, we are getting more computer time in.'

'You only have ten frames to work with so you have to plan your drawing carefully. . . .' (She has drawn frame number ten and a diagram on the board showing ordering of lines in a drawing. She has accumulated three diagrams illustrating consequences of line ordering.) 'So what we have to do is start numbering out lines on the roughs so that we can always order them in the same sequence. From the drawing we will move to acetate so that we can register the lines. We all know how to register a drawing, right?'

Sandi goes on to talk about the acetate phase of the planning and doing a drawing transfer to acetate through a photocopier. 'The idea of this assignment is that you will do some commercial application of animation. I don't just want shapes moving across the page . . . I want to see that there has been a lot of thought given to manipulating the images on the screen.' (She goes on to combining figures to have more than one figure on-screen.) She explains that if you want more than one figure on-screen you have to draw combined-connected figures. You can't separate them.

YL1: 'If we move a figure in front of the background, is the background erased?' Class answer: 'No, it stays in front of the background.'

Sandi: 'At the same time we are going to be working on the illustration assignment. It is going to be done in wash. . . .' (She writes illustration and text up on the board.)

The other student, YM1, comes in. He has his portfolio. Sandi is explaining that their illustrations can be illustrations for a book – for instance – but that it has to be well researched. 'You must have a *comp* and it must be done in marker!'

Student: 'You're cruel! We can't make mistakes in marker. Can't we use pencil crayon?' Sandi: 'No, you have to use marker. That's the way they want it done in commercial work. I'll bring in some examples of marker comps tomorrow. . . . You also need to give some careful thought to how you're integrating text into the illustration. . . . You have to put your entire illustration and text onto a grid. . . .' (This entire sequence is about *planning* the illustration layout.) 'What do we do about contrast between the text and the illustration?'

YM1 is working on the MAC the entire time Sandi is explaining the assignment. Some of the other students are continuing to work too.

YM2 — the black student – asks Sandi about an idea for his illustration. Sandi is now showing some sample commercial illustrations. Sandi is showing examples of compositions and explaining the tricks to each and particularly going into details on what techniques were probably used to create the illustration.

(Sandi is holding up an NTEL ad.) 'What message do you get from this illustration? . . . Where are you going? . . . Can you wait for just two minutes?' (They give a good answer about space and friendliness and simplicity.)

The YM2 is still holding before going to make his call.

She directs them to some books as examples, including Sendak. 'I know — is anxious to go make his call, so you can take a short break early today.' The students don't change what they're doing very much.

(Class takes a ten-to-fifteen-minute break.)

Break has been dragging on. Sandi is calling the class back to order despite the fact that some of the students are still missing. Three students are present.

Sandi gave me a copy of her last class's 'magazine' to look over. A girl comes in from the hall and joins the class; wasn't with previous group.

Sandi is seated with the four students in the centre of the room. They are going to do a demonstration of using wash. YL1 speculates that they have '. . . used wash before. They don't want to be told how to do it again.'

One of the YLs from the first part of class came in . . . and another who wasn't there but was in the computer lab yesterday joins the group.

YM1 comes in too.

Sandi: 'So . . . we can control the wash just by controlling the consistency of the pigment in the water. . . . It all has to do with the consistency of the water. . . .

'You see how I can start layering? . . . It is basically like what you can do with water colour. . . .'

'But what we can also do is by controlling the consistency of the paint, we can control the spread of the wash. What I usually do if I want an opaque area is I paint the wash and let it dry. Then I put another coat over it.'

The wash demo is going on. They're watching her and she's explaining to them what she is doing and why.

YM2 comes back in '. . . they couldn't get through.' Sandi continues demo.

YL1: 'If you *do* make a mistake when you're doing this, can you paint over your mistakes?'

Class: 'No. You have to do it over again.'

Two gentleman come in. They look very official and ask to talk to Sandi asap. They go to wait in her office. She tells them that she'll be with them in just a minute. At 11:07 Sandi goes on with her wash demonstration. At 11:11 the demo is still going on.

Sandi: 'I want you guys to experiment with this and I'd like for you to do it right now. Play around with it. I want you to know what it's capable of doing.'

Sandi goes into the back room to discuss whatever. The students shuffle around through the transition and gravitate toward their work stations. YL3 is now using the MAC.

The students are starting to work again. . . . YM2 wanders out. . . . One student on MAC . . . one looking at mag illustrations . . . three looking at and commenting on the content of a drawing.

One student is experimenting with wash. YL1 leaves at 11:22. Sandi and the two gentleman come out of her office and look at a poster that YL3 has done and has in her portfolio.

Sandi gives the class a good explanation of her discussion with the *printer* in the back room. The other guy was from graphic communications. They were clarifying a misunderstanding about a rumour that her students were doing a commercial typesetting job using desk–top publishing. (Possible paranoia from local graphic arts and publishing interests that aren't up to using desk–top publishing.)

Sandi is working with the student using the MAC. Three female students are in the room with Sandi. The period ends.

Before leaving, I initiated a discussion on scheduling future visits and interviews with Sandi. Before leaving I gave her some student permission forms and explained that I'd probably observe Monday and Tuesday of next week, then try and do interviews. I asked her to basically pick the kids for me and see if they would volunteer. We scheduled an interview for her at school next Wednesday.

Integration of Technological Tools
and Commercial Graphic Arts Curriculum

The two commercial graphic arts classes described above provide a contrasting portrayal of microcomputer use in art classes. Several important differences exist between these commercial arts and fine arts classes. The students in the commercial art curriculum are more experienced as artists and generally older than many of the fine arts students seen during the earlier observation. The commercial arts students displayed a higher overall level of 'computer literacy' and more specific experience using graphics programs than their counterparts in the fine arts classes.

The curriculum objectives in the commercial arts classes are oriented toward application of techniques to simulated graphics production activities. In contrast, the curriculum objectives in the fine arts classes are oriented toward a balance between 'discipline-based' art education and development and application of studio techniques for creative self-expression. The commercial arts curriculum is oriented toward development of vocational skills while the fine arts curriculum is generally oriented toward knowledge about art history, visual aesthetics, and sampling the range of artistic styles and techniques available through the study of our heritage from the visual arts.

In addition to differences in the background of the students and the respective curricula, there are major differences in the way that the ICON LANs are set up for student usage. The ICONs in the vocational high school are set up in a centralized laboratory setting that is shared by all the teachers in the participating classes. This meant that there were sufficient ICON work stations for the entire vocational art class to work individually at learning to use the animation tool (IPAINT II). This allowed the teacher to demonstrate particular techniques to the entire class with the aid of the ROBOTEL device and exert more control over the pacing of demonstration and practice activities within the lab site.

In both settings, student activity was highly individualized and both art teachers supported this individual activity by distributing their support activity throughout the group of students under their supervision. However, in the classes described and in other observations made during the study, there were more frequent group-focused demonstrations of technique in the vocational art classes than in the fine arts classes. In addition, the vocational graphics classes made use of group presentations and critiques as part of the studio routine. This was true with both traditional graphic arts techniques and with computer graphics techniques.

Some differences between particular observed classroom behaviours of the art teachers in these cases may be attributable to curriculum objectives, student backgrounds, or to the philosophical and instructional differences between contrasting comprehensive and vocational high school settings. Despite these differences, the broad pedagogical similarities are striking.

One outstanding similarity is obvious in the two observed situations. The art teachers in both cases displayed similar *circulating behaviour* while they were monitoring student studio work. They typically moved quickly and smoothly around the studio or microcomputer lab setting, answered questions, offered assistance when requested, commented supportively about the students' efforts, and only occasionally redirected students' efforts if the observed activity of a particular individual went outside the established boundaries for proper technique and conduct.

Is this *circulating behaviour* a central attribute of art education or an attribute of an evolving pedagogy for interactive technology? Seemingly, in both cases the teacher's role is oriented toward support and facilitation of individual student activity rather than toward more traditionally teacher-centred instructional activity. Or, could this circulating behaviour be a particular attribute of local area networks?

In a classic case study of computer-aided mathematics instruction on the networked University of Illinois PLATO system, Bernadine Stake observed similar facilitating behaviours and movement patterns displayed by a fourth-grade teacher (Stake, 1990). Other naturalistic studies of computer aided learning portraying apparently successful technology interventions suggest that use of computer aided learning encourages new forms of interaction between teachers and students (Blomeyer and Martin, 1990).

What is the common denominator here? Does the technology support or encourage an interactive pedagogy or would these art teachers use the same strategies regardless of the fixtures in the setting? Or, are there other unobvious influences moulding the ways that these two art teachers integrate microcomputer technology into the art curriculum?

Supporting a Technological Innovation in Art Education
(Field Notes: 17 April 1989)

I am in the ICON booth at the back of the art studio in the comprehensive high school. One of the female students using the SPECTRICON program has *locked up* her ICON. Margarete and the girl are trying to figure out what to do. She tells me about how this has happened a few times before and makes jokes with the YL (YL1) that it never happens twice in the same period.

I settled in after meeting a student from U of Western Ontario that is on a teacher practicum assignment. At 12:02 YL1 comes back and restarts the ICON. She finds her way back in through Ambience. Her work *is* gone. SPECTRICON is version 1.01A. She's back to a clean slate.

The art studio is as predicted . . . Margarete mixing paint and listening to a student talk about his or her work . . . Margarete circulating around the studio and making a pass through the ICON booth. The students are all working steadily on their art projects; on and off the computers.

The second student (YL2) has frozen her screen; *locked up on SPECTRICON.* She has lost her cursor and called for help. Margarete came to her assistance and had to switch it on and off.

Margarete was explaining how to use the ICON features to select the colour palette. Then she went out to work with the art studio.

YL2 asks me if it is OK to restart the computer. I say yes. I talk to YL1 about saving. She says that she doesn't like what she's done anyway. She asks if I know how to save. I say no. (I suspect she's really used to Val and Marshall answering requests for technical information.) YL1 goes out to look for Margarete to ask her how to clear the screen . . . I think.

YL2 is back into SPECTRICON.

The students out in the hall are passing. It must be the break in the periods.

Margarete comes in with YL1 and shows her how to do full screen erase. Control F10. She also shows how to use black circles to overlay another circle. She also shows how to use the paintbrush as zone erase.

YL1 now has a clean slate. Margarete now goes to work with YL2 and shows her how to change her colour palette.

Margarete's pre-service student is floating around the lab pretty much as she does. YL1 is experimenting with the air brush feature.

YL2 is going back in and has a pretty well developed composition already. Rectilinear and ellipsoid shapes on a white field. She's using the magnifier to look at the pixel patterns and work on the fine grid.

Margarete wandered in and out with some paperwork. Six students are now in the centre of the studio . . . two are working and four are watching. A fair number of students are wandering around. One YL (YL3) wanders into the back and kibitzes with YL1.

A blonde YL (YL4) comes into the back and announces that YL1 and YL2 need to work with her on a ceiling mural now. Margarete tells YL4 that she should go on without them because they get their two or three days on the computer projects now.

YL3 wanders into the ICON booth again and talks with YL1 about SPECTRICON. YL3 complains that there aren't enough selections for controlling the screen.

Margarete comes back into the booth. YL2 asks her about the intensity scale. She reminds them both that it is time to save. She lets YL3 explain saving the files.

(Excerpt from Field Notes: 18 April 1989)

Margarete was explaining to me that for the last half-hour she would let the pre-service teacher take over the class. That is the way she handles it normally. She's not in the studio now, but in the ICON booth. The student teacher is in charge. At 11:03 Val has been in the room observing and wanders out.

YM1 has used the copy and inverse feature to duplicate the pattern of his figure drawing. It is evolving into a busy composition; the symmetry is interesting. At 11:05 another male student comes in to kibitz YM1 and YM2. He shows YM1 his poster and brags that he did it in only twenty minutes total before the project was due.

The studio goes on. The student teacher isn't interacting much with the kids. She tends to wander around and watch what they're doing but she doesn't talk with the students as much as Margarete does.

YM1 is putting some subtle variations on his figures. Two girls came back to kibitz. Ones said: 'That looks real good, —. When I did it, I kept breaking it . . . the computer. I didn't mean to, but I just did.'

I just noticed the student teacher (ST) talking with a student about her composition. At 11:13 YM2 wanders out and comments on YM1's composition. 'Terrific!'

I just commented on a fill that YM1 was doing. YM2 comes back in. He's returned with an art history book. He's apparently looking for an example of something. He had been trying to do some background.

Peder appeared and came back into the ICON booth. He had a look around and asked me to come up into the library and talk with him some after this period.

YM2 locked up his ICON! He was using the line drawing feature. I'm sure that is the trick!! He said that he thought it happened when he was moving the track-ball and hit the action key at the same time. He said it happened to him yesterday too. He said his picture was saved.

YM1 also saved his picture. He asked about saving and went through the drill. When he was finished, he was about to turn it off . . . I stopped him and made him back out to ambience. He left the booth.

At 11:25 YM1 is back into his picture and working again. At 11:27 he backed out and quit. The class is getting ready to change. Margarete is back. Val came through to tell me Peder is trying to solve a printer problem up in the library.

Margarete and I talked a bit about the last LOCK UP. A new class was coming in. I said that I was going to go up to the library and talk to Peder.

I left Margarete's classroom and went up to the library. He had a variety of things that he wanted to tell me ... that the facility to video-record ICON screens using the ROBOTEL was about ready. (He was afraid that I'd wanted to record some kid's sessions and been unable to. I assured him that it wasn't important to me, but that it was to the project.) He said the reason it is hard is that the RGB output isn't standard and converting it to composite is taking a special hardware device.

We also talked about the SPECTRICON bug. I relayed the information I'd observed from crashes from earlier in the a.m. and he re-created the crash. I'm pretty sure the developers can find the bug now that Peder knows how to re-create it.

Margarete came up into the library and asked Peder about a few things: 1. Question about power failures. Peder said we had discussed the issue the night before and that he was working on it. 2. Question about graphics film he had used for the training. Peder said he would help her get a copy. 3. Question about IPAINT. Peder told her it was installed and showed her IPAINT. Margarete can't wait to use it. After their brief conversation, Peder left the room.

At 12:10 Margarete and I left the library and are both back in the art room ... in the booth. Both YLs have developed nice graphics during the interim. The class is doing a normal studio. . . . The students are pretty well gone from the room now. I think less work got done with the ST in the room and Margarete gone.

Margarete is working with both students in the booth. She showed the near YL (YL1) how too use the UN-DO feature. She goes out of the booth: 'Where ARE all of our students??'

The far YL (YL2) is using the line feature. No ramping or other textured background. I'll watch to see if it crashes. . . .

Support Structures for CAL

Clearly, when any technological innovation is brought into the schools and used by teachers in authentic instructional activities, there are going to be difficulties and opportunities for the teachers to gain practice at solving a range of technical and pedagogical problems. Scenes where the SPECTRACON program crashed on multiple work stations were observed both in the distributive classroom environment and in the larger laboratory setting. After the teachers and project research staff had sufficient experience with these 'crashes' to describe and even re-create the conditions that seemed to trigger the events, institutional support structures were mobilized to minimize the negative impacts on learning.

Special expertise was available to support the project teachers both from the local school board and from the faculty and project staff at the University. The Board Liaison Officer worked very closely with the RUCCUS researchers and was constantly in and out of both schools as an on-site consultant and troubleshooter. He was also the primary trainer who conducted the pre-service and in-service education for the cooperating teachers.

During the period of my fieldwork in the local schools, I also became a de facto member of that support network. The possibility that technical difficulties might occur during my presence in the setting was discussed with Peder Nielsen, the cooperating RUCCUS researchers and Ivor Goodson, the project's director. In our discussions we considered acknowledging a distinction between interventions of a primarily technical nature and other types of interventions that might undermine the autonomy of the classroom teacher or influence them to modify their behaviour to accommodate the perceived values of the researcher.

In short, were I to be present in the setting when a technical problem occurred and if I had a technical fix that would repair or minimize an interruption in the student's instructional activity, I was authorized to communicate the information directly to the student and help solve the immediate problem. Additionally, Peder Nielsen and the project staff expected me to share information with them that could reconstruct problem scenarios and aid in their analysis and solution.

The analogy that we used to justify these technical interventions was the ethical comparison to a medical doctor who may encounter an accident victim. If the profession of the doctor is known to onlookers, then a lack of appropriate remedial action on the expert's part might put the physician's professional commitment in question. This ethical dilemma led me to initiate some technical interventions on behalf of the students. For instance, in the scene described above, I reminded a male student (YM1) to back out into AMBIENCE before saving his work. Implications of these local interventions will be discussed in the concluding section.

The Pedagogy of CAL: A Training Group in the ICON Laboratory
(Excerpts from Field Notes: 19 April 1989)

Peder is demonstrating WRITE on the ICONs. He's using the ROBOTEL to do a 'show and tell'. He's showing tricks (like hanging indent, etc.). He's just finishing his presentation of WRITE.

One of the teachers asks how she might set up files so she has room for *marks* in the margins. It apparently has lots of room alongside the columns for extending the work space. He shows how to put in an extended margin so there is room reserved for the teacher to put in marks or comments as an overlay on the student's document. When marks are put into the left margin, they have to erase the extra spaces that are inserted.

Peder: 'There is much more for me to show you but it will be best if I don't show you these advanced tricks *until the need arises.* That is my intention in being available to work with you individually in your schools. Save your questions for when I'm in your schools and ask me about your individual concerns then.'

Another teacher has asked Peder how to make different versions of similar files . . . i.e. boilerplates. Peder also says that WORDPERFECT will probably be better for that application than WRITE.

Peder is demonstrating *another* DEMOCALC feature. He's showing them a filename trick so that the program automatically saves their work file under a slightly different name.

He says that they may be at the point where in that next semester they will want to create a 'template file' for their students to use in their assignments.

He is stopped by a teacher who asks what the trick is to get out of the 'file' area in the application. The person has apparently got caught in the file option without naming the new file. This prevents exiting the program.

He's asked some graphing questions. The user has to cut out columns of data to create a graph. The column is then reinserted with an 'insert last column' feature . . . a kind of column undo.

Peder returns the ICONS to the teachers and suggests that they 'play' with DEMOCALC and try and develop some problems so they can ask questions. They start and he floats around the room attending to various teachers' individual concerns.

[Note: the emphasis that follows was also present in the field notes.]

(It strikes me that his lab-assisting behaviour is just like the art teachers' behaviours in studio and PARTICULARLY like Sandi's behaviour in the ICON lab!! He circulates in the same way that Sandi does, observes the students' work, and intervenes to remediate or demonstrate procedures as needed. This is the normal operating mode for art teachers, science teachers, industrial arts teachers, and music teachers (when they are in a highly individualized, group learning environment). Could it be that this is something fundamental to the pedagogy of technologies?)

He's still attending to the same teacher's DEMOCALC question.

He's floating to the other side of the lab. Valerie is up and floating too.

Peder fields a question about entering and centring cell data. Cells can only be right/left/centre justified one column at a time.

Most of the teachers are doing budgets. One is building a grade book for a class. He's put in all his students and is counting up grades on his fingers.

Peder is moving some things around in ICON setting up the next part of the demo. One of the teachers tries to get his attention again to address an individual concern: 'PEDER! PEDER! You're going to have another broken computer soon!' Peder goes over and answers his question. The trainee seems very literal-minded and unable to learn by TRYING. He wants to be shown explicitly how to do everything he's interested in so that he doesn't have to RISK making mistakes.

One of the trainees is doing a graph of the 'energy consumption' assignment. . . . That is what the majority of them are doing. It is possible to type text directly on the screen to label the graph. This makes the user interface very easy to use.

One of the more experienced trainees discovered that it is not possible to save a labelled graph screen. Once the graph is labelled, the user has to print it out immediately because it is totally lost once the user goes back to the rows and columns.

Peder has kicked in ROBOTEL again. He's doing a presentation on the 'replication' feature. He's showing how formulas can be replicated to do uniform calculations doing a function of either a whole row beneath data or a whole column alongside data.

Peder is giving an important message to the teachers . . . 'The reason for using these tools . . . word-processing, spreadsheets . . . is to save you a bit of work! It is to do some of the stuff that takes up your time that is difficult for you now.' He illustrates with a story about using a spreadsheet to keep track of his bank account; uses anecdotes about his experiences to make his point about using technology as a tool.

The Impacts of Modelling on Technology Application

The training anecdote given above had a profound effect on my perception and subsequent interpretation regarding the sources of *circulating behaviour* and interactive pedagogy observed to be a central part of the classroom routines of both art teachers. It became clear to me that the two art teachers were using the microcomputers in class the same ways that they had seen them used during their training sessions with Peder Nielsen. Circulating behaviours, supportive interaction, facilitating behaviours, and instructor participation in situational problem solving were all modelled in the training classes.

Peder Nielsen's training sessions were based on the teacher-trainee's participation in a variety of application task structures that were illustrated by anecdotal explanations and contextual elaborations. This information made the task structures as realistic as possible, engaged the learners in reality-based practical simulations, and encouraged all the teachers to apply the new techniques to problem solving. The problems they engaged were like those that they might reasonably encounter with their own students while using the ICON system and its graphic tools.

Student Voices[3]

Tell me about yourself. Why are you in this class? What is your art medium of choice?

Commercial Art Student 1:	I started by taking a course at another high school and going through an application procedure. I don't consider myself to be a 'fine' artist. I do studies. I prefer traditional drawing materials and wash as media.
Commercial Art Student 2:	Art is only something I've done for the last twenty-six months. This is a career change for me. My husband has opened a trucking business and I started the commercial arts course because of possible linkages to his business.
Commercial Art Student 3:	I like presenting information to people in pictorial form. I want to be a fine arts teacher. I work in a variety of media.
Comprehensive Art Student 1:	I love art. I love anything that is expressive. I have trouble writing and I love anything that will help me express myself. I love to draw and paint.
Comprehensive Art Student 2:	I like to draw. I'm a business major. Art is just a hobby for me. I like to sketch and do watercolours.

Comprehensive Art Student 3:	I'm not planning on art as a career. It is just a hobby for me. I like to draw. I like acrylics and using conté.

When did you first encounter the use of computers?

Commercial Art Student 1:	I had a C-64 (Commodore) at home. I had it for years and got bored with it. C-64s also appeared in the London schools in my last year. 'Play along and learn games.' No serious instructional use. No big deal.
Commercial Art Student 2:	I took a computer course at Althouse. It was a basic level course. It didn't make me feel very comfortable using computers.
Commercial Art Student 3:	I was in grade 10 when I first encountered a computer, in my mother's workplace. The second time was here in Sandi's room.
Comprehensive Art Student 1:	I used a Commodore Pet 2000 in grade 6–7. We used it for word-processing and computer literacy. It was in the hall shared between three classes. I used it once in two years.
Comprehensive Art Student 2:	I have an APPLE II at home. My parents bought it for me to use in school.
Comprehensive Art Student 3:	My neighbour got a C-64. We played games on it. When I was in the sixth grade we had some Pet microcomputers. We used them for spelling and maths games. I also used computers for writing in an enriched English class and used them for music theory lessons in music classes.

What sorts of things have you done outside school using computers?

Commercial Art Student 1:	I played games on my C-64 and learned some BASIC programming. I learned by typing in games from magazines.
Commercial Art Student 2:	I learned to program in BASIC in the teacher education course. We also learned a little word-processing.
Commercial Art Student 3:	No other experience.
Comprehensive Art Student 1:	I have an Atari . . . a game machine. That's a computer of sorts. But I'm not one for video games. That's a waste of money.
Comprehensive Art Student 2:	I have APPLEWORKS and MOUSEPAINT. I used to use the word-processor but I quit because my printer is terrible. Now, I mostly use the APPLE for business-related programs. I used to type in game programs and taught myself BASIC. I also took COBOL as a business course in school.

Comprehensive Art Student 3:   I played games on my neighbour's Commodore. Like Skiing. We used a joystick.

What kinds of projects or tasks does your art teacher assign that require the use of microcomputers?

Commercial Art Student 1:   All the projects we are assigned can make use of the computer to produce some part of the graphics. Sometimes she will give us a specific computer assignment; like a page layout or animation.

Commercial Art Student 2:   I use it all the time to print out text for my graphics. But I have to lay it out by hand.

Commercial Art Student 3:   I'm laying out a catalogue on the computer for a computer company here in London. We've started to learn the animation program and now have an animation assignment . . . with a commercial purpose.

Comprehensive Art Student 1:   She gave an assigned painter and we were supposed to copy their style. Then, I re-created it on the computer with my own touches.

Comprehensive Art Student 2:   The first project was just so we could try it out. We have to learn how to use it before you try anything serious.

Comprehensive Art Student 3:   I was supposed to analyze the form of a painting and do it as modern art. I was doing an analysis of Rembrandt. 'The Night Watch', I think.

Have you ever had any 'technical difficulties' with the ICON computers?

Commercial Art Student 1:   I never had any technical problems on the ICON. I had a bad disk on the MAC. I lost all of my work because I couldn't open a damaged disk. It was a REALLY BAD experience.

Commercial Art Student 2:   No problems. Just general frustration.

Commercial Art Student 3:   I blew up a MAC disk. It was awful. It was a major layout assignment. I couldn't print or save. The technician and Sandi couldn't open the disk. My whole semester's work was gone. Now I back up almost everything.

Comprehensive Art Student 1:   No problems.

Comprehensive Art Student 2:   It stopped once. I lost the cursor and couldn't get it back. I was trying to use the perspective feature. The picture stayed on-screen but it wasn't saved. We had to turn it off and on to start over.

Comprehensive Art Student 3:   Yes. Once I misplaced some of my work. I forgot my log-on and password and used a general purpose log-on to work. I did a drawing on the general purpose log-on and couldn't find it later. Mrs White found the files for me and put them back into my own workspace. I understand what I did wrong.

What programs have you used on the ICON?

Commercial Art Student 1: I have used the MAC and ICON graphics programs in Sandi's classes. The first time we used the ICONS, I went in and looked around at the courseware and the word-processor . . . but I haven't had any time to use them.

Commercial Art Student 2: Just the graphics programs on the ICON and the MAC programs.

Commercial Art Student 3: CRICKET PAINT, MACDRAW, MAC-WRITE, and PAGEMAKER on the MAC. SPECTRICON and IPAINT on the ICON. We played around a bit when we were first using the ICON. There are other programs in there but they are of little use to us.

Comprehensive Art Student 1: Just SPECTRICON.

Comprehensive Art Student 2: Just the graphics program.

Comprehensive Art Student 3: SPECTRICON.

Overall, how do you react to the idea of using computers in the art curriculum?

Commercial Art Student 1: For Sandi's class, they are a TREMENDOUS time saver! The computer is a helpful thing. But I wouldn't do a whole project on the computer. It is just one of a variety of media.

Commercial Art Student 2: I see it as a sign of the times. I think it's just something the students will have to learn how to do. Computers make the work of commercial art easier and faster.

Commercial Art Student 3: It bothers me that there is one computer in our art room and in the computer room there are SO MANY . . . and we can't use them. Because we're art students doesn't mean that we don't know anything about computers. We should get to use those other machines too.

Comprehensive Art Student 1: I'm positive about using the computer . . . but I don't think that it's any more important than doing things by hand. There's a human element to art, that's the most important thing.

Comprehensive Art Student 2: It's a good idea. It could make the production of artwork much faster. It's especially good for drafting and design.

Comprehensive Art Student 3: I think for graphics it is really good. But for the 'fine arts' it isn't as good. For my Rembrandt . . . it just didn't fit. It was hard because of the kind of detail in the original painting.

What benefit do you see for yourself in relation to others from using microcomputers in curriculum?

Commercial Art Student 1: It increases my productivity and speed.

Commercial Art Student 2: I'm here because I want to learn how to control the computer rather than the computer controlling me! The computer enhances the capability of the human being.

Commercial Art Student 3: It gives us an edge over other kids that don't have the computer background. In university and vocationally, that will be important.

Comprehensive Art Student 1: Three things: 1. speed; 2. accuracy . . . ability to try things over till you get it right; and 3. more of an awareness of computers overall.

Comprehensive Art Student 2: It is a lot faster to use the computer to draw. I did that picture last week in forty-five minutes. If I had done it by hand . . . it would have taken lots more time.

Comprehensive Art Student 3: The benefit for me is general knowledge about computers. I would use computers if they were available to me in the home. If I had the money, I'd buy one for myself to use at home.

What are the opportunity costs for you to learn to use the computer in your art class?

Commercial Art Student 1: None that I'm aware of. . . . We have to learn manual drawing skills anyway. Maybe I've become a little overdependent on the computer.

Commercial Art Student 2: Yes. I have to choose now between Specials and the Fine Arts curriculum. I'm uncomfortable with that choice. I want to do fine arts . . . but that leads away from computer use. I think fine arts and commercial art should both be integrated with computer use. Computers have expressive applications and they should be a part of the fine arts curriculum.

Commercial Art Student 3: There are no opportunity costs. Sandi makes us learn everything manually. THEN we do it on the computer. It takes more time on the computer and quality is generally better.

Comprehensive Art Student 1: None.

Comprehensive Art Student 2: Art classes have like a month to do this, and a month to do that. Computers can be just another part of the art class. Just stick it in the middle. If you're done early on your water-colour . . . use the computer.

Comprehensive Art Student 3: No cost to me. We were doing all the same things off the computer. With the computer we are just working in different ways with a different medium.

If you could create your own ideal situation for using computers in the art classroom, what would it be like?

Commercial Art Student 1: I want another MAC for the classroom. There are too many people using too few computers.

Commercial Art Student 2: I think it would help me to see the *practical relevance* of what we are doing first. I learn better if I understand the context. I have an inductive learning style and Sandi structures the projects in a deductive manner. It would help me to see the big picture.

Commercial Art Student 3: Three or four more MACs for us to use in studio. People come up all the time and use the computers during our class. A lot of them are doing résumés. I don't mind that . . . but not during our class time. Students and teachers too! Sometimes teachers will come up and just walk out with our laser printer. Then it will come back and refuse to work for us. If you are a student working on it during class time and a teacher comes along — I NEED IT TOO! What about me? What about what I'm doing? There ARE priorities.

Comprehensive Art Student 1: Maybe a computer art course. I would like to take a more specialized course devoted to art with the computers.

Comprehensive Art Student 2: You could probably get more done with a big central site. It would be a big hassle in some ways . . . but you could start everyone at once and have everyone working at the same time. For learning to use software it would be easier. The teacher could clear up everybody's problems at once instead of two or three at a time.

Comprehensive Art Student 3: I'd have it half and half. I'd have one computer per two people. Then I'd divide the class in half and have half working on traditional art projects and half on the computers. I'd want the computers in the classroom. It is partially psychological . . . but I've tried to work in the library and I just can't get into it. I'd take down the wall too. Personally, it's like being in a closet.

Summary and Conclusions

Like most naturalistic studies, the data illustrating this case is only a tiny fraction of the amount gathered during the fieldwork. This document is a second attempt to produce a suitable report. My error in the initial version was that the study included a much larger amount of the data and assumed that the description alone would tell the story. In fact, that was not the desired outcome and I now have another way to focus the ending of the tale.

The most direct way to address the meaning or significance of this study is to summarize the information in terms of the six issues or questions that were suggested in my earlier paper on methodology (Blomeyer, 1989a). The issues are restated in this document on p. 5. I will address each of them in turn and summarize what this case has to tell us about each of these issues. Finally, I will suggest a practical use for this and other similar case studies about technology, teaching, and learning.

Design Characteristics of Instructional Technology

The interactive applications used by the students and teachers in this study of microcomputers in art curriculum were virtually all computer graphics tools. In particular, PAINT, IPAINT II, and SPECTRICON were the three programs used on the ICON microcomputers by all the students. In addition, a variety of Macintosh-based graphics, word-processing and page layout software (PAGE-MAKER) were used by the vocational art students.

In general, most of these graphics programs used a visual/iconic interface similar to the standard set by the original MACDRAW and MACPAINT programs published by Apple Computer Corporation. The operation of the program is transparent from the appearance of the function selection menus. If the user wants to draw freehand, then he or she selects the menu item represented by a pencil icon. If the user wants to paint, he or she selects a paintbrush icon, etc.

The selection of a graphics tool suggests that some graphic art or illustration is the intended product of the transaction between the person and the micro-computer. The tool does not have an instructional purpose inherent in its design. The instructional purpose must be supplied by a teacher within the context of a class or some other staged educational event.

Graphics programs can be used by very experienced artists or by a student novice. The mechanics of using the graphics programs observed during this study appear easy to master. In particular, the vocational art teacher had a great deal of experience using computer graphics and she was able to demonstrate and model manipulative techniques that the students could then adapt for their own purposes. The general art teacher had less experience as a user of computer graphics but she had learned to use the tools and was able to model techniques and support her students in their own learning process.

The graphics tools used by the teachers and students during this study were clearly emancipatory as opposed to instructional, revelatory or conjectural (MacDonald, Atkin, Jenkins and Kemmis, 1977). They were labour-saving devices. They saved time that would otherwise be spent learning to make graphic art by trial and error. This is not to say that the essential trial and error learning process was changed by the use of computer graphics tools, rather that the time required to correct errors or replicate error-free effort was dramatically reduced. The result of this saving in time was to empower the students and allow them freedom to create visual expressions of some sophistication and complexity.

In terms of the UNCAL typology of learner/CAL interactions (Kemmis, Atkin, and Wright, 1977), graphics production tasks are more like the 'constructive understanding' demonstrated when students use higher-order computer tools to create unique environments or symbolize new knowledge. In terms of the typology suggested by Kemmis *et al.* this is the highest level of interaction or transaction possible between a human being and any technology system. The open-ended design characteristics of these computer graphics programs makes them powerful and non-trivial tools for extending the capacity of students and teachers into the realm of self-expression and creativity.

Curricular and Disciplinary Sources of Lesson Materials

The concept of *lesson materials* for computer aided learning in fine and vocational art education requires some definition. In traditional fine arts education, the lessons consist of learning techniques that the student artist uses to create art using a variety of media and materials. These techniques are learned primarily by demonstration and modelling.

Beneath the 'learning how' there is also a strong tradition for 'learning what', or learning about the historical precedents for techniques and their application. In contemporary *discipline-based art education*, learning about art history and the aesthetic foundations of the visual arts have been elevated to a status nearly equal in importance to learning techniques and using them to make student art.

Vocationally-oriented graphic arts retains much of the emphasis on technique that we find in traditional fine arts education, but the emphasis on the product is changed. Vocationally-oriented graphic art is oriented more toward production of a highly polished and professional-looking graphic product for a purpose to be defined by another person.

Tasks are developed and assigned by the teacher as a surrogate employer. The particulars of any given assignment may be defined in either a very precise or a very ambiguous manner. Both types of assignments will probably be used in class because the vocational graphic artist should be able to respond to either literal or vague suggestions or hints about what is wanted by a potential client.

The assignments or lessons developed by the teachers and project support staff for use with the fine arts and vocational arts students were consistent with the regular non-computer lesson materials used in the same classes. In the traditional fine arts classes, the teacher set up problem definitions that gave direction to student art projects. In one class, the students were charged with creating elaborate Egyptian motif decorations for a school production or 'show'. In another class the students were given an assignment that required them to analyze the work of a selected traditional artist and create a derivative artwork that emulated some of the significant formal or style elements attributable to the artist studied.

In the vocational art classes, the teacher set up assignments or tasks for the students based on her personal knowledge of workplace expectations and the anticipated dynamics of client-artisan negotiations. It was important to the vocational teacher that the students also learn management and negotiation skills so that they could succeed at the business end of the trade as well as produce good graphic art. Art production tasks included advertising layouts, catalogue copy, book cover designs, and a variety of other realistic assignments. However, the problem-solving or application dimension of the vocational projects was distinct and unlike similar projects in fine arts.

In the last analysis, both fine arts and vocational arts teachers made only minor changes in the structure or content of the assignments given to their students on or off the ICON computers. The fine art teacher emphasized the discipline-based approach in her assignments and the vocational art teacher emphasized the application or problem-solving dimension in hers. For both teachers it was necessary to spend some extra time helping the students learn how to use the computer graphics tools.

The real lessons came when the students mastered basic manipulative techniques and began to *use* the traditional or computer-based techniques to produce fine or applied art within appropriate task structures. According to John Dewey:

> When artistic objects are separated from both conditions of origin and operation in existence, a wall is built around them that renders almost opaque their general significance with which aesthetic theory deals. (Dewey, 1934, p. 3)

Pedagogical Characteristics of Art Education

The pedagogy of art education is exemplified by the activity of the two art teachers observed during this study. The teacher first plans a task structure or art project for the student. Then, they communicate the assignment to the student and define or demonstrate any new techniques or methods necessary to follow the task structure. Another aspect of communicating the assignment is that the student is often shown examples of art having the formal qualities that the teacher wishes the student to emulate in his or her own work.

Once the techniques are demonstrated and the task structure is communicated to the student artist, the teaching stops and the learning begins. Now the teacher shifts role and becomes a mentor or facilitator. In an art studio setting, the teacher *circulates* among the students who are engaged in working on their individual projects. The teacher answers questions, makes supportive comments regarding the students' individual work, and occasionally stops to troubleshoot or remediate if visible evidence indicates a technical flaw or some miscommunication of the assignment.

The whole time that the teacher is circulating and distributing his or her attention among all the students in the group they are also scanning the group. Good studio management requires that the teacher to be able to respond to the routine and occasional non-routine situations that are associated with a 'hands-on' setting. Students occasionally get side-tracked and must be directed back onto their assigned tasks. Materials get spilled and messes need to be cleaned up. Students cannot find a critical material and cannot continue with their project until the teacher helps locate the missing item.

The most important aspect of this distributive circulation and scanning behaviour is that the teacher continuously interacts with the students. Anthropologist Dan McLaughlin suggests that teachers can operate in a reciprocal-interactive mode whereby students are active participants in their education or students can be passive and uninvolved as they listen to the teacher lecture (McLaughlin, 1990). In these art classrooms, the teachers comment, but also listen to what the students have to say. The students asks for help and the teachers either respond immediately or cue the required response behind other tasks having immediate priority. In either case, the teachers lets the students know that their request is received and that help is on the way. Interactivity and the judicious distribution of positive attention seem to be the keys to maintaining a good studio or computer lab environment.

The description given here of activity sequencing and standard teacher behaviour in art classes was also typical when both teachers were monitoring and assisting students doing computer graphics assignments. It made apparently little difference whether the students used a traditional art medium or a microcomputer work station. The teachers behaved in a manner that was totally consistent with the ways that I have seen art teachers operate throughout my teaching career. From these observations, and from what the teachers said in their interviews, I conclude that their approach to teaching with the computers is probably influenced by their pedagogical training and background in art education.

Hardware and Site Logistics and Access to Hardware

One of the most significant findings that this research may contribute to our broader understanding of CAL and the curricular integration of microcomputer technology may relate to the two contrasting hardware configurations that were designed into the two cooperating schools. A distributive ICON network was installed in the comprehensive high school. This configuration placed three networked ICON work stations and a printer in each of the cooperating teacher's classrooms. In contrast, a centralized and 'hardened' microcomputer installation having twenty networked work stations, two printers, and a ROBOTEL console (allowing one selected screen to be displayed at all the terminals) was installed in the vocational high school. These distinct hardware installations probably influenced the teachers to operate differently in the two settings.

In the fine arts classes, individual students were chosen by the teacher at the beginning of a newly assigned art project and given the opportunity to work with the graphics programs on the ICON computers. Assignments to the microcomputer work stations were being rotated through the entire class and eventually all the students would get an opportunity to do an art assignment on the ICON.

I observed that regular art projects generally took from a few days to a week for completion. Because all the art projects were self-paced and some students were starting and finishing almost all of the time, students completing a computer art project were likely to be replaced by a new computer artist rather quickly. The turnover was continual and the flow of the class never seemed to shift to accommodate the ICONS in an intrusive manner.

In the vocational art classes, the students were accustomed to using the single available Macintosh work station in a way that was similar to the use of ICONS in the fine arts programme. The major difference was that the students rotated on and off of the single work station when their work required it rather than when the teacher directed it to occur.

The vocational art students were generally older and more experienced artists than the students in the fine arts programme. The vocational art teacher generally gave them wide latitude to decide what tools they would use to execute any particular assignment. If they chose the Macintosh as a tool, then they waited for its availability in class or came in after school to use it.

When the vocational art class used the ICON laboratory it was a different story altogether. First, the ICON lab had to be scheduled for the vocational art class. Then the lesson had to be planned and the class notified about the date and time that they would be going to use the lab. During a period where a new computer graphics tool would be introduced (e.g. IPAINT II), all the students would be able to see the teacher's initial demonstration and use a work station individually to try using the features of the program. In one sense this was an efficient learning situation. In another sense, use of the ICON lab was intrusive and represented a marked departure in the way that the class was normally conducted.

In short, the pacing of the learning events in the ICON lab was more teacher-directed and less responsive to individual variation in skills, background, and learning style. This was mediated somewhat by the vocational art teacher whose personal style and approach to instruction was highly individualized.

One of the ways that a difference between a teacher-centred or student-centred classroom focus could be identified in the ICON lab was the students' reaction to engaging the ROBOTEL. When the teacher or instructor grabbed the students' video screens with ROBOTEL for a demonstration, there was an audible *snap* . . . followed by a sigh as everyone realized that control over their individual work stations had been lost. Often the teacher asked students in the class to demonstrate the computer graphics techniques using the ROBOTEL and control was always returned after the demonstrations ended. But the temporary loss of control over the resource still had a pronounced effect on student engagement and productivity.

Overall, the distributive network site was less intrusive on the classroom routine of the teacher and students than was the case in the centralized ICON site. Visits to the ICON lab seemingly altered the flow of work and the established routine in the vocational art classes. In contrast, placement of ICON work stations in the fine arts studio had no pronounced effect on the work patterns or verbal interaction patterns in the studio setting. There were possible gains in instructional efficiency associated with having a larger number of micro-computers in one place. This was accompanied by a loss in individual task focus and productivity when the ROBOTEL was engaged for group-mode instruction.

Both scenarios had apparent assets and deficiencies. The longitudinal study undertaken as part of the RUCCUS project should eventually produce some substantial data on the instructional outcomes of choosing either a distributive or a centralized network arrangement. Either arrangement may be more appropriate in a specific setting or application. Hardware configurations should be set up too with full knowledge of the options and due attention to local needs.

One of my most significant insights from this case study is that there appears to be an optimal approach common to training both teachers and students to use interactive technology. This approach appears to be based on two primary instructional practices: (1) demonstrating or modelling the appropriate techniques; and (2) letting the students use the techniques under the vigilant support of an experienced and sensitive teacher. To a former music teacher, this should be no surprise at all. Even so, when I realized that *circulating behaviour* was a significant attribute in the teaching practice of Peder Nielsen and both of the art teachers, I thought that I was on to something.

The question is, where did this behaviour come from? Since both art teachers in the study exhibited this as a dominant classroom behaviour (with and without the computer being present as a student tool), it seems naive to conclude that both art teachers learned the circulating behaviour from their in-service mentor Peder Nielsen. Is this highly individualized instructional behaviour a shared pedagogical assumption in physics and also in art education? Or, is it good common sense to assume that self-pacing, individualized instruction is a highly effective way to go about the business of teaching regardless of the subject matter or instructional medium?

One of the devices that Peder Nielsen used in his in-service training classes with the teachers from both schools was the introduction of sample cases wherein some instructional application would be made of a software tool from the ICON tool and courseware library. The particular software application might be an example of word-processing in writing classes or spreadsheet use in social or natural sciences. Peder was very balanced in his approach to demonstrating the use of microcomputer tools in a variety of curricular contexts, but he showed an affinity for the use of tools rather than for drill and practice oriented computer assisted instruction.

In retrospect, it seems that the most important attribute of these demonstrations may be that they were in fact based on contextually embedded cases about the curricular integration of microcomputer technology. There was usually a skill-learning component involved in his teaching cases. Certainly, to use a new instructional technology effectively with students, one must know what button to push . . . but his instruction didn't stop there.

It was common for the teachers in the classes to digress and discuss instructional and logistic issues related to their own intended or projected use of the software tool. They asked Peder's opinion and engaged him in brainstorming and troubleshooting with hypothetical scenarios that they might encounter in their schools. It wasn't until recently that I realized I was watching an application of case method instruction to the transfer of technology. Case pedagogy has been an accepted method of instruction in law, diagnostic medicine, management, economics, technology, and a variety of other discipline bases for many years. In a paper by Dr Margaret Boos from the University of Konstanz in West Germany entitled 'A Typology of Case Studies' (Boos, 1990), we find the following description of case method as a teaching tool:

> As a means for education and training, cases are mostly used by jurists
> or economists. With a case, different ways of applying existing laws or

theoretical models to real life events can be demonstrated. Management programs of numerous American business schools and universities are characterized by a strong emphasis on case method teaching in the tradition of the Harvard Business School. The advantage of this teaching method consists in the fact that theoretical concepts and methods can be introduced in a problem oriented way. Abstract facts are mediated in a way retaining the complexity, interdependency and uncertainty of empirical reality. (Boos, 1990, p. 3)

The line of research followed by this study used observation, interviews, and collection of trace documents, work samples, evaluation forms and other incidental artefacts. The theoretical and organizational model for the study presented here is the case study (Stake, 1988). Given this model as an organizational framework for the enquiry, unique constraints and field conditions effecting naturalistic enquiry tended to make subtle changes in procedures and evolve methodology in much the same way that foreshadowed questions are evolved by subsequent iterations of research and reflection.

Within the framework of this case study, adequate and valid interpretation of the observed events in terms of participants' viewpoints and knowledge structures has emerged as a significant issue. Recently, House, Mathison and McTaggart (1989) have suggested that in educational research the concept of *validity* should be expanded to include 'inferences that practitioners draw from their own experiences'. They go on to suggest that 'practitioners often cannot state what they know in propositional form. Nonetheless, it is the validity of their causal knowledge that is critical for professional practices like teaching' (p. 15).

One of the most important insights gained from the teachers and students observed during this study is that microcomputers were apparently little more than an alternative medium or tool to support the students' activities. The microcomputers were no big deal. With or without them the business of producing student art projects continued in a traditional and predictable manner. Considering the special status we often associate with new technologies in our culture, the view expressed by these teacher-practitioners that microcomputers are 'just another medium' seems to indicate a shift away from more elitist attitudes about technology.

The validity of this discrepant view on microcomputers in curriculum has important implications for guiding the effective integration and use of microcomputers in the schools. Should educators let technology specialists guide the integration and use of microcomputers in the schools or should we listen to our own voices? Will the skills necessary to manipulate and creatively apply interactive technologies be limited to a technological elite in society or will microcomputers become tools for application toward a general increase in the efficiency and general productivity of the society at large?

This particular case study of ICON microcomputers in art education may not answer these questions but due consideration of inferences based on teachers' unique initial experiences integrating microcomputers in curriculum may have the same effect. In describing the qualities that distinguish case studies from other educational research, Bob Stake offers the following:

In my own writing I sometimes talk about 'naturalistic generalization.' I think of this 'way of knowing' as very important, for researchers and for others. We all, of course, also arrive at understandings through experimentation and induction, through what is commonly called 'scientific generalization.' It is not terribly important to decide which is more important. There are ample needs for both modes of acquired understanding.

Most case studies contribute more to naturalistic generalization than to scientific generalization. But however they are useful, I believe they are more useful when careful thought is given to the boundaries of the case, the issues, and the patterns that illustrate the issues. (Stake, 1988, p. 260)

In the situation examined here, method should not be considered as an issue apart from the author's intention to illuminate the issues, case, and the patterns of events critical for understanding this particular application of microcomputers to curriculum. While it is a case *about* the integration and initial use of ICON microcomputers in two Canadian secondary art education programmes, it is really a story *of* people learning to use interactive technologies in support of teaching and learning.

It is the author's intention that this case should illuminate the *causal knowledge* that the participating teachers drew about initial integration of microcomputers with art education and make that knowledge accessible for consideration by other educational practitioners. Although some events in these art classes may not have obvious relevance for developing technology integration strategies in other disciplines, important lessons have been learned.

We hope that by telling the story, we will provide support and encouragement to applications developers, educational planners, teacher educators and other instructional personnel who are working toward achieving integration of microcomputers in the K-12 curriculum. A fitting application of the information gained from this research might be the creation of case materials for use in training teachers to meaningfully integrate microcomputers into curriculum. There is a great deal of work waiting to be done. I hope that we are up to the challenge.

Notes

1 The single class that was observed *not* to use the ICON microcomputers was a low-ability group. The teacher was initially reluctant to supervise the use of microcomputers with students she considered less reliable than her regular classes.
2 Note that the idea of distributive networks and distributive pedagogy has major implications for nearly all the foreshadowed issues carried into the study from earlier research. More will be said about this in the conclusion.
3 Parental permission forms were secured by the RUCCUS project staff before conducting student interviews. Semi-structured interviews were used to permit comparative treatment of the responses. Interview items were developed by the researcher to learn about: (1) students' prior experience with art and with microcomputers; (2) what assigned work they did on the ICONs; (3) technical difficulties they encountered using the ICONs; (4) what particular ICON programs they used; (5) what value they attributed to using the microcomputers in art classes; (6) what costs they attributed to using the microcomputers; and (7) what they might change to create an ideal situation for computer use in an art classroom.

References

BECKER, H.J. (1986) *Instructional Uses of School Computers: Reports from the 1985 National Survey*, Center for the Social Organization of Schools, Johns Hopkins University, Issues 1–3.

BLOMEYER, R.L. (1985) '*The use of computer-based instruction in foreign language teaching: an ethnographically oriented study*', Doctoral Dissertation, University of Illinois.

BLOMEYER, R.L. (1986) 'Instructional policy and the development of instructional computing: maintaining adaptive educational programs', *Educational Considerations*, 13(3), pp. 17–20.

BLOMEYER, R.L. (1989a) Monitoring curricular integration of new interactive technologies', in GOODSON, I. (Ed.) *Curriculum and Context in the Use of Computers for Classroom Learning*, London, Ontario, Research Unit for Computers and Curriculum Studies, pp. 253–96.

BLOMEYER, R.L. (1989b) 'A naturalistic perspective on computer aided learning: guidance for policy and practice in higher education', *Journal of Education Policy*, 4(3), pp. 259–74.

BLOMEYER, R.L. and BRIGHT, G. (1987) 'Policy and practice effecting the instructional use of computers in elementary schools', *Proceedings of NECC '87*, pp. 77–84.

BLOMEYER, R.L. and MARTIN, C.D. (Eds) (1991) *Case Studies in Computer Aided Learning*, Philadelphia, PA, Falmer Press Limited.

BOOS, M. (1990) 'A typology of case studies', University of Konstanz, West Germany.

BRIGHT, G. (1988) 'Using a local area network in a college of education', *Technological Horizons in Education Journal*, 15(8), pp. 90–3.

CLINE, H.F., BENNETT, R.E., KERSHAW, R.C., SCHNEIDERMAN, M.B., STECHER, B. and WILSON, S. (1986) *The Electronic Schoolhouse: the IBM Secondary School Computer Education Program*. Hillsdale, New Jersey, L. Erlbaum.

DEWEY, J. (1934) *Art as Experience*, Capricorn Books, G.P. Putnam's Sons.

GOODSON, I.F. (Ed.) (1988) *The Making of Curriculum: Collected Essays*, Philadelphia, PA, Falmer Press Limited.

GOODSON, I.F. and BALL, S.J. (Eds) (1984) *Defining the Curriculum: Histories and Ethnographies*, Philadelphia, PA, Falmer Press Limited.

GOODSON, I.F., MANGAN, J.M.A. and REA, V. (Eds) (1989) *Curriculum and Context in the Use of Computers for Classroom Learning*. Interim Report 1. London, Ontario, The Faculty of Education, University of Western Ontario.

HOUSE, E.R., MATHISON, S. and McTAGGART, R. (1989) 'Validity and teacher inference', *Educational Researcher*, 18(7), pp. 11–15, 26.

KEMMIS, S., ATKIN, R. and WRIGHT, E. (1987) *How do Students Learn? Working Papers on the UNCAL evaluation Studies* (Occasional Publications No. 5), Norwich, UEA, CARE.

MacDONALD, B. and WALKER, R. (Eds) (1974) *SAFARI; Innovation Evaluation Research and the Problem of Control*. Norwich, UEA, CARE.

MacDONALD, B., ATKIN, R., JENKINS, D. and KEMMIS, S. (1977) Educational paradigms for CAL. In S. Kemmis, R. Atkin & E. Wright, How do Students Learn? Working papers on the UNCAL Evaluation studies (Occasional Publications No. 5), Norwich, UEA, CARE, pp. 24–7.

MALINOWSKI, B. (1922) *Argonauts of the Western Pacific*, London, Routledge, 1922.

McLAUGHLIN, D. (1991) 'Curriculum for cultural politics: literacy program development in a Navajo school setting', in BLOMEYER, R.L. and MARTIN, C.D. (Eds) *Case Studies in Computer Aided Learning*, Philadelphia, PA, Falmer Press Limited, pp. 151–64.

NIELSEN, P. (1989) 'Ministry Guidelines and Board Policies'. In GOODSON, I.F.,

MANGAN, J.M.A. and REA, V. (Eds) *Curriculum and Context in the Use of Computers for Classroom Learning.* Interim Report 1. London, Ontario, The Faculty of Education, University of Western Ontario.

NORRIS, N. (Ed.) (1977) *SAFARI: Theory in Practice*, Norwich, UEA, CARE.

OFFICE OF TECHNOLOGY ASSESSMENT (1982) *Informational Technology and its Impact On American Education*, Washington, DC, US Government Printing Office, November.

SMITH, L. and POHLAND, P. (1974) 'Education technology, and the rural highlands', in STAKE, R. (Ed.) *Four Evaluation Examples: Anthropological, Economic, Narrative, and Portrayal* (AERA Monograph Series on Curriculum Evaluation No. 7), Urbana, Illinois, Center for Instructional Research and Curriculum Evaluation, pp. 5–54.

STAKE, B.E. (1990) 'Plato mathematics: the teacher and the fourth grade student response', in BLOMEYER, R.L. and MARTIN, C.D. (Eds) *Case Studies of Computer Aided Learning*, Philadelphia, PA, Falmer Press Limited, pp. 53–110.

STAKE, R. (1988) 'Case study methods in educational research: seeking sweet water', in JAEGAR, R.M. (Ed.) *Complementary Methods*, Washington, DC, American Educational Research Association, pp. 253–78.

Chapter 4

Appropriate Tools?
IT in the Primary Classroom

Les Watson

Once upon a time the government of the day decided that as part of the National Curriculum for primary schools the study of haute cuisine was essential. Realizing that few primary schools had the necessary equipment to implement this important curricular area the CES (Committee for Education and Science) along with the CTI (Committee for Trade and Industry) offered subsidized resources to schools. The key part of the resource package was ... a half-price camping stove! The stoves were obviously inadequate for the job, but it was felt that they at least provided a starting-point for implementing this important curricular innovation. So as to appear even-handed the scheme offered the two main types of stove which were available at the time. These were the Chestnut stove supported by a series of radio programmes at its launch, and the Roasting Machine. Ancillary equipment was also required to make full use of the stoves such as a set of pans, a range of kitchen utensils, and a gas bottle. Needless to say the two types of stove required different types of gas bottle and these were not transferable between the types of stove. This created some problems, particularly in schools which invested in both types of stove, and eventually led to each LEA favouring one type or the other e.g. some LEAs went Chestnut. A two-day training course for a small number of staff from each school was provided. This aimed to provide them with a basis for using the equipment in school, but in reality just about managed to show them how to light the stove, and made no reference at all to the educational aspects of using the equipment. It was also seen as necessary by the government to provide a range of recipes which schools could use in order to make use of the equipment provided. Consequently a pack was produced and distributed to all schools. A large number of third parties saw a business opportunity in the production of recipes for schools to use in the implementation of haute cuisine in the National Curriculum. The result of this was the production of a vast range of recipes for schools, some of which were of dubious quality, many being alternative ways of preparing the same dish. This added further to the problems in schools, as there was no reliable guidance on which recipes to buy, or how to evaluate recipes prior to purchase.

Slightly later in the saga a new type of stove came onto the market which was more powerful (it had a double burner) and consequently Chestnut and Roasting Machines produced updated versions of their stoves. The race was on to provide more and more power. The casualties in this race were of course the schools. Some schools spent lots of money trying to keep abreast of developments, only to be rewarded with a whole kitchen full of incompatible cooking equipment. Those who couldn't afford to play this game felt quite left out of developments and developed a serious inferiority complex. Needless to say the implementation of haute cuisine in the National Curriculum was pretty patchy and not generally regarded as a success. A body of opinion developed that thought the CES had gone about this project in the wrong way and would have been much better providing adequately powerful cooking facilities in the first place. There were also those who felt that the programme would have stood a better chance if teachers had been provided with a decent stove and a full set of pans at the outset so that they could brush up their culinary skills prior to attempting to implement this as part of the National Curriculum.

Whilst it may be amusing to picture the series of events described above it is sad to note the parallel with the early attempts to introduce the use of IT into the primary school curriculum. It is not surprising that early studies of the use of microcomputers in primary schools[1] found that 'software in use was predominantly drill and practice'. It is also sad to note that the lessons from this early experience have not been learned. The folly continues in many LEAs where the policy is to move old, outdated, inadequate machines down from secondary schools to primary schools and bring new powerful hardware in higher up the age range. There seems to be an assumption that IT in the secondary school requires more sophisticated hardware and software than in the primary school.

The question of what hardware and software primary schools should have can only be answered if we think carefully about what we want the teachers and children to be able to do and how the hardware and software can contribute to the processes we desire to take place. This inevitably involves some consideration of the educational process as it applies to both children and teachers, and the possible contributions of IT to that process. Figure 4.1 shows some important educational activities. The expected outcome of a pupil's experiences in school is usually the presentation of a piece of work, be it written work, artwork, a model, or oral presentation. Preceding this presentation is a period of information gathering, selection, analysis and evaluation. Information Technology can play a significant part at all stages of this process — provided the pupil has appropriate hardware and software.

Alongside the educational processes shown there is a need to make more than a passing reference to the acquisition of knowledge, and the development of understanding! The integration of appropriate content with a suitable approach can provide a stimulating learning environment. However, we cannot expect to develop and enhance skills such as creativity, imagination, and problem-solving in young children with outdated limited hardware and software. Powerful ideas need powerful flexible resources.[2]

Educational activity   **The contribution of IT**

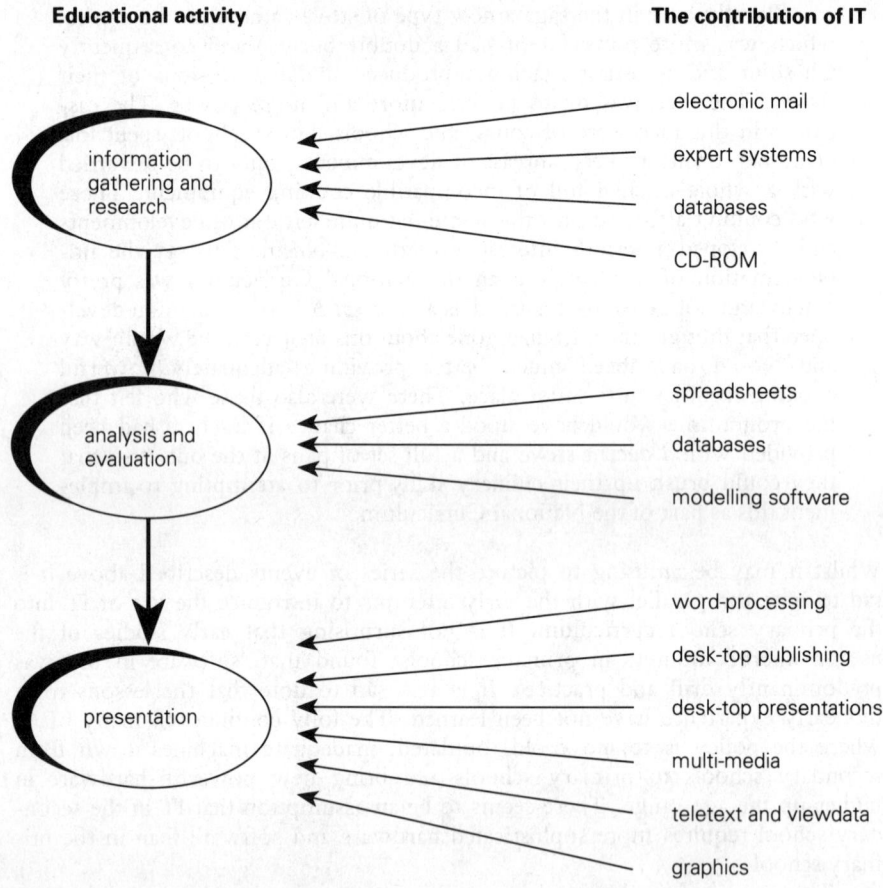

Figure 4.1: The contribution of IT to the education process

> Think of buying a computer as like buying a car. A car just moves your
> body; your computer, though, is the chariot of your mind, carrying it
> through the whole universe. How much is your mind worth to you?[3]

Given suitable facilities to combine one's educational thinking with an agreed
body of knowledge can produce a powerful environment for learning. The
competent practitioner would give his/her annual stock of chalk to have the freedom to *produce their own IT materials*. What we are talking about here in an IT
context is making a computer do what the technologically naive teacher wants
it to do. Given the parallel with the production of printed materials — most
teachers would prefer to adapt work by others or produce their own from
scratch. This is not so easy with IT materials unless teachers are provided with
appropriate software tools. Since 1985 PEG[4] has been tackling this problem
by writing and trialling software which allows teachers to produce their own

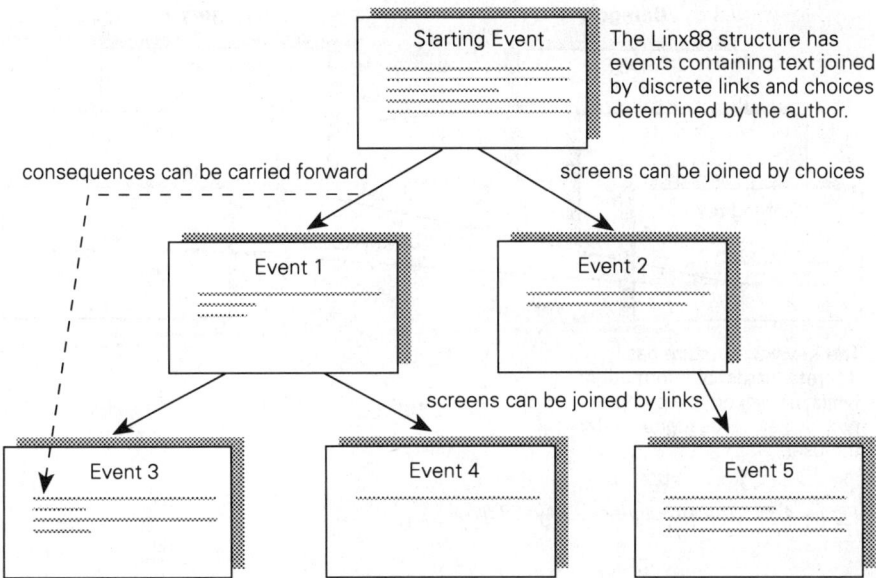

Figure 4.2:   The structure of a Linx88 file

programs for use in their own classroom. This has enabled them to use IT in the attainment of their own curricular aims and objectives. The Cheltenham base of PEG has concentrated its efforts in primary schools using 16-bit microcomputers and the PEG software Linx88 and Keys88. These two pieces of software allow teachers and children to author their own programs.[5]

Linx88[6] is the latest version of a program originally produced by Jonathan Briggs, Jackie Dean and Jon Nichol. It has undergone extensive trials in schools and colleges over the last five years and seen many improvements. It allows the authoring of simulations, adventures and interactive branching stories. The software is menu-driven and requires no special programming skills. The use of the software allows the writing of complex stories. These stories consist of a number of screens of text linked either directly or by choices and may have several different outcomes. Linx88 also allows the consequences of decisions made early on in the use of a story to be carried forward to affect later events. Keywords can be identified on any screen of text and these will be available for the user to 'look up' during the use of the program. Figure 4.2 shows a possible structure for a Linx88 program.

The second program, Keys88, was written and developed by Derek Brough, Jonathan Briggs, Jon Nichol and myself.[7] It was originally conceived as a 'free form' word-processor. The user can decide to have one or more categories of information and type text into these categories. Each item of information can contain words which are identified as 'keywords' and which can be used to form links between items. The user interface for Keys88 is very similar to that for Linx88 also being menu driven. The outline for a possible Keys88 program is shown in figure 4.3.

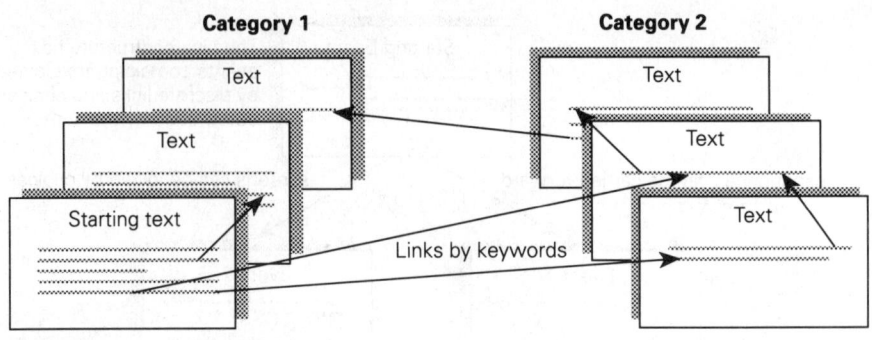

The Keys88 structure has
discrete 'cards' of information
which are linked in a complex
way by keywords identified by
the user.

Figure 4.3:   The structure of a Keys88 file

The curriculum of the primary school should be thought of in terms of activity and experience rather than of knowledge to be acquired and facts to be stored.[8]

In developing problem solving skills, teachers have the important task of helping pupils to tackle problems analytically and to adopt logical procedures in solving them. At the same time, pupils must be allowed to make mistakes and to follow false scents in what is essentially an exploratory process; and the teacher has to resist the temptation to give the 'right' answer or to over direct the pupil otherwise the skill is not developed or practised.[9]

The role of the computer in the schemes of work produced by the PEG Cheltenham group has been to promote a range of activities away from the micro which provide the educational experiences relevant to the curriculum of the primary school. Much of the work has taken a problem-solving approach. The computer has provided a focus for classroom activity whilst placing the emphasis on investigation using traditional sources of information. The emphasis has been moved from being told to wanting to find out. The computer has acted as a stimulus for a range of activities such as writing, artword, drama, and model making. The starting-point for the work has always been the curriculum as is illustrated by the following short case studies of some of the work which has been undertaken.

One of the early projects was an excavation of a Viking village[10] by a group of 7-to-8-year-old pupils. The idea for this application of Linx88 came from my asking the teacher, who had decided that the Vikings would be the topic work for the term — 'If you could do anything with the computer what would it be?' The answer was that he would like the children to be able to excavate a Viking village which he would design to include evidence about life as a Viking such that

Plate 4.1: Pupils of Randwick school discussing a find during the Viking dig.

Plate 4.2: Pupils at Novemarsh school plotting a find in the computer based Roman dig on the map.

children would 'experience' life at that time as well as learn about it. The result was a Viking village with 3120 locations organized on three levels. The top level was the evidence visible on the surface of the site. Pupils could also dig and excavate the site. On doing so they found various artefacts which gave them information about life in Viking times. They were required to keep careful records of their finds. It was not always obvious what a find was and some further research (in the library corner) and the use of deductive skills were required to identify the object. Weekly meetings were held to discuss the class finds and enter them on the master map. The project provided a stimulus for a wide range of classroom activities such as factual and creative writing, artwork and model making.

Starship Longleaze is a simulation of a space journey written in Linx88. The project involved a class of sixty-four 9-to-10-year-old children in a voyage into space, and lasted for a whole term. The children were allocated to crews, but only after they had written a letter of application for a particular job aboard the spaceship. Once the project was started the computer acted as mission control, being a central focus in the classroom. Each group took their turn at the machine, making discoveries and being set a range of tasks such as designing games to keep the crew happy on the long voyage, baking moon rock cakes or researching new recipes and menus to feed the crew. Some pupils were involved in designing the spaceship and others in charting the planets and producing scale models of them. The reading room which is an annexe to the classroom was decorated with views through the windows of the spaceship produced by the children. The class had not realized how much writing is involved in flying a spaceship: there was the ship's log to complete each day, newspapers to produce to provide the crew with in-flight information, and the legends of the planets visited to record for recounting back on Earth. All these tasks were aimed at achieving the objectives set by the teachers such as encouraging the children to work cooperatively, providing opportunities for the use of a range of writing styles, stimulating creative work in art, music and drama, and developing research skills. The project took place as the preliminary guidelines for the National Curriculum in schools were being produced and these were taken into account by the teachers in their planning as shown in figures 4.4 and 4.5.

The Starship Longleaze project was followed by a farming project called Longleaze Farm. This was a simulation of the day-to-day running of a farm which was written in Linx88. The project provided opportunities for a wide range of tasks although its main focus was on teamwork and discussion skills. The class of 9-to-10-year-old pupils formed management teams each of eight members. Each team had the task of running a farm for one term. The topic was chosen to link with National Food and Farming year. Bank loans were provided for each group to set up their farm based on the quality of their application to the teachers in charge. Information on the daily fluctuations in hay prices and rates on the stock exchange were available within the simulation for the 'management groups' to use when making important decisions regarding their business plan. A key feature of the project was the regular board meetings of each group. I visited the school one Friday afternoon to find these meetings going on. Some important decisions were being made by the children as they had just learned of the crash of the bank by which they were financed. I was impressed not only by the quality of the discussion taking place but by the knowledge the children had concerning farm prices and the consequences of actions such as diversifying their operations

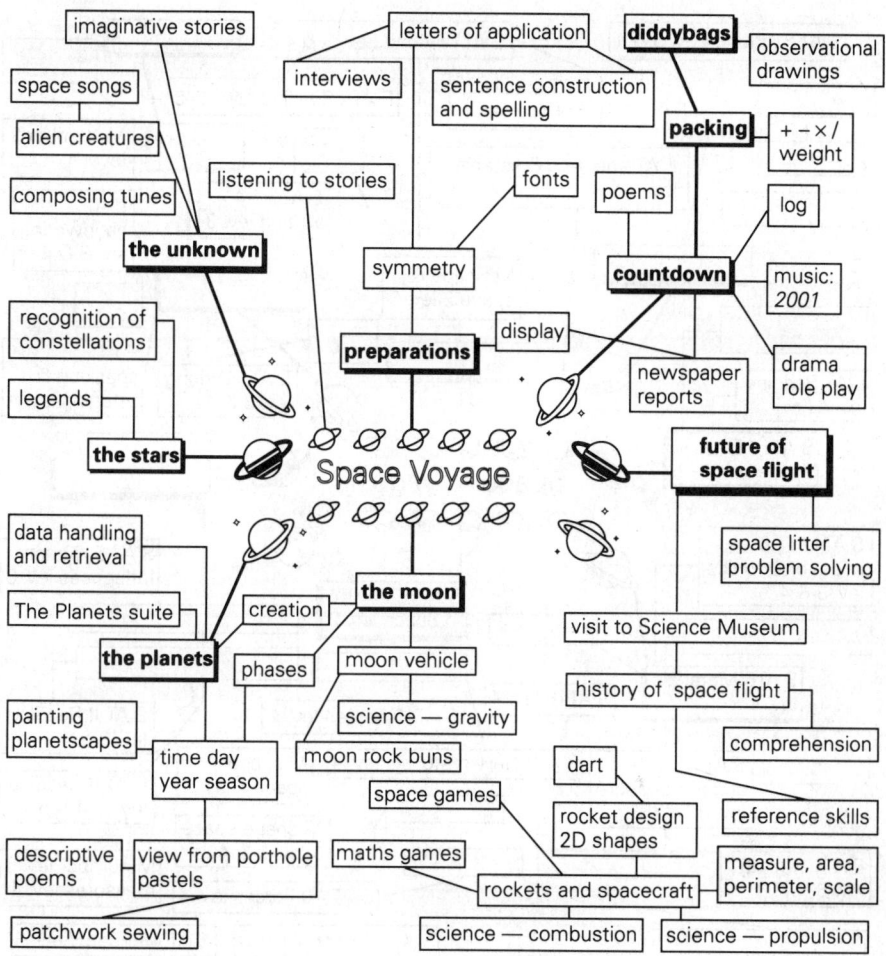

Figure 4.4: A topic web for Starship Longleaze

or selling certain parts of their enterprise. The strict observance of formal proto-col in the meetings was also impressive. The project culminated in each group preparing a prospectus for their business in order to put it up for sale. A local estate agent was called in to comment on the properties and their market value. He was impressed by the children's presentation of their properties and by their realistic valuations.

A group of 7-to-8-year old pupils were involved in solving a mystery writ-ten in Linx88. They had to apprehend the criminal who had stolen the jewels from the manor at Dimville. Before they could tackle this they had to construct a map from information held in a Keys88 database. This was linked to a schools TV programme on map making and direction finding. Their map-making skills were put to a stringent test by the combination of these two programs as it was impossible to track down and apprehend the criminal unless the map of Dimville

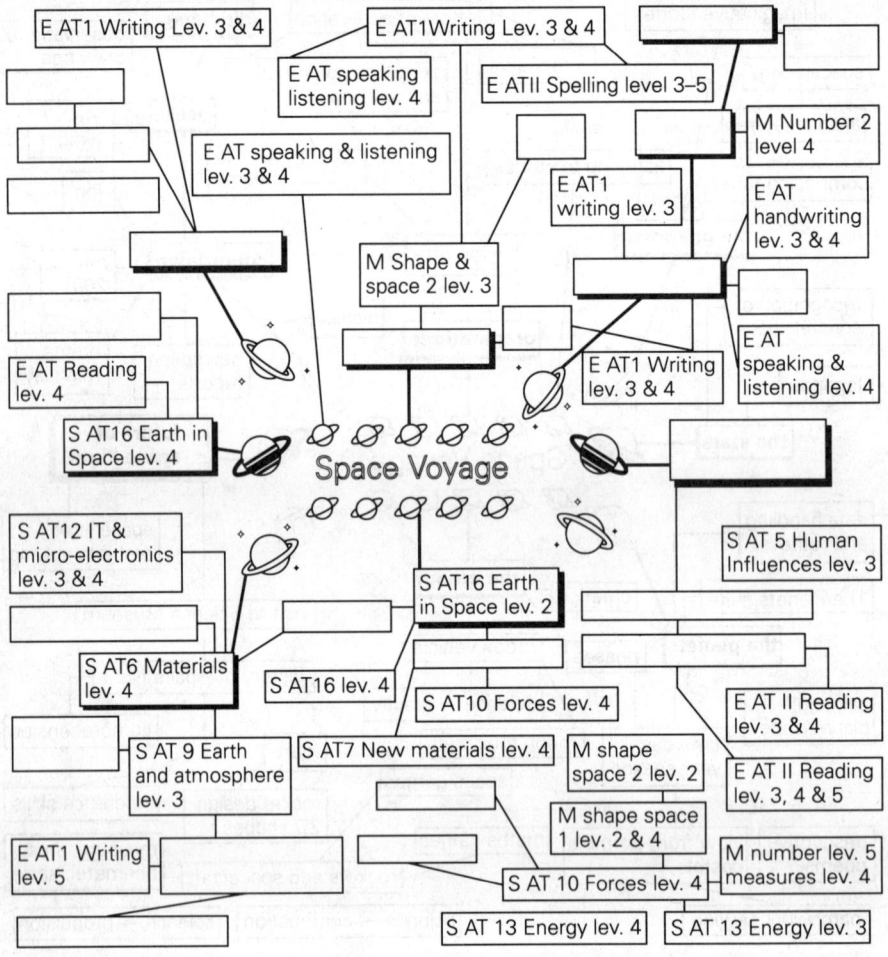

Figure 4.5: Relating Starship Longleaze to the National Curriculum

was correct as the mystery was written as a series of directions which had to be followed. Plate 4.5 shows some of the children with a laptop computer using their map to solve the mystery.

Chedworth Roman Villa was a Linx88 program which formed the basis for a study of the Romans by a class of 7-year-old children. The program itself was a simulation of the excavation of the Roman villa at Chedworth in Gloucestershire. The emphasis in the work was on deduction and evidence. The children were provided with clues about what they had found during the excavation rather than actual objects, and so had to work out what the objects were and their significance. The starting-point for the building of the simulation was a visit by the teacher to the Roman villa. This included a chat with the manager of the site and provided an insight into the problems of archaeological investigation. The ideas she picked up from this visit along with the actual layout of the villa were

Plate 4.3: Pupils on the Starship Longleaze project with a game that they had designed to keep the crew busy on the long journey.

Plate 4.4: Investigating space.

Plate 4.5: Using a laptop computer with Linx88 to solve a crime in the village of Dimville.

then used to produce a Linx88 program which the children could use. During their investigation of the site within the computer the children were involved in research of life in Roman times, interpreting data gathered, production of art-work in the form of Roman mosaics, model making — Roman standards, as well as a comprehensive study of the Roman period.

An open-ended project with a group of 7-year-olds called Creapsville involved them in a detective mystery. The mystery was written as a Keys88 program. There had been some strange goings-on in the village of Creapsville and the lady of the manor advertised in the local paper for someone to investigate them. The 7-year-olds who took part in this work had to write applications for the job and were then involved in trying to explain the information contained within the Keys88 database which had been produced by their teacher. The children had to make up a map of the village as they investigated the strange happenings and to not only write reports of their findings but also attempt to explain them. Were they supernatural, extraterrestrial, or criminal? In fact the teacher had made sure that the evidence was inconclusive. Consequently it could be interpreted in a variety of ways and gave the children an opportunity to try to provide evidence for their arguments.

The examples outlined so far have all been produced by teachers for children to use. In a topic on Human Growth and Development, a group of 7-year-olds produced a text database using Keys88. The work was linked with a series of TV programmes on sex education. The children gathered information from a number of sources including the TV programmes, books, and a range of school visitors such as the local doctor and a midwife. They then wrote a short piece of text on one aspect of the work and entered it into a Keys88 database, identifying the text by a keyword. As explained earlier Keys88 then creates links between these keywords allowing a user to browse the database looking up information on words that they wish to follow up. The building of the Keys88 database was only one of a range of activities which took place in the classroom and served as an additional focus of the knowledge being acquired by the children as well as a reference point containing a summary of the knowledge of the class. As this is a recurring topic in the school it is likely that the database will be used with and extended by other children.

None of the examples above could have been produced without the right sort of resources. This may seem obvious but what may not be so obvious is that resourcing is a complex issue. A variety of resources are required. The software and hardware resources are vital. The hardware and software used by the teachers above is powerful and not generally commonplace in primary schools. The fact that the schools working with PEG Cheltenham have produced such excellent examples of good classroom practice highlights the need for primary schools to be given a high level of IT resources. However, these can only be of use if provided in conjunction with time — time for training and time for practice.[11] Accessibility of the equipment and ownership of the ideas are also extremely important. Adopting this software and this approach to using IT in the primary curriculum means adopting a certain approach to education and to classroom practice. For some this may involve a change in their current ideas and working practices; such changes require time for practice, experiment, reflection, and evaluation.

Notes and References

1 JACKSON, A., FLETCHER, B. and MESSER, D.J. (1986) 'A Survey of Micro-computer Use and Provision in Primary Schools', *Journal of Computer Assisted Learning*, 2, 1.

2 The powerful ideas are those produced by imaginative, creative teachers in the design of their approach to topic work. The flexible resources of the software allows the full expression of these ideas, along with hardware that can handle the quality and the complexity of data. The adaptation of software and hardware for educational usage is a central feature of the PEG enterprise. Indeed, PEG is best regarded as an enabling force to enhance teaching and learning through the impact of IT. It makes the powerful tools of IT accessible to non-computer-literate teachers after a comparatively short period of in-service training. PEG software is the product of computer scientists and educationalists working together. The software is extensively tested and used by real teachers with real pupils in real classrooms and is moulded over time, through feedback, to fit their respective teaching and learning needs as closely as possible. PEG, for example, is the result of cooperation between a lecturer, fourteen teachers and over 400 pupils. PEG is a teacher-pupil led technology movement.

3 Ted Nelson, in SHUSHAN, R. and WRIGHT, D. (1989) *Desktop Publishing by Design*, Microsoft Press.

4 PEG is an association of educationalists and computer scientists based at Cheltenham and Gloucester College of Higher Education, Exeter University, Imperial College and Kingston Polytechnic.

Interested readers can find out more about PEG either by contacting the author at Cheltenham and Gloucester College of Higher Education, PO Box 220, The Park Campus, Cheltenham, Gloucestershire GL50 2QF; or write to PEG Exeter, The School of Education, Exeter University, Heavitree Road, Exeter EX1 2LU.

The only other group similar to PEG is MODUS, which is based at the Advisory Unit, Hatfield, and is concerned with devising and implementing expert systems in schools. The fact is that much that is currently being done in IT developments in primary schools serves only to resurrect and reinforce outdated fact-based practices. PEG attempts to liberate and emancipate pupils and their teachers, allowing the former to participate fully in self and discovery learning.

PEG tools have numerous applications which cover many important areas of the National Curriculum. PEG tools open the way for a suite of teacher-produced programs based on classroom experience and requirements, programs whose writing would previously have needed a professional computer programmer. PEG tools can be used to produce models or micro-worlds of a whole range of situations which pupils encounter in their learning. A model identifies the essential elements in a situation. Most models are developed for specific situations and the descriptive model becomes a micro-world when the computer gives it a dynamic, living dimension. It is participation in this micro-world that provides a high level of motivation for children and this can be harnessed and can stimulate a wide range of cross-curricular activity, often resulting in a greater level of achievement.

5 An indication of this range of activities is to be found in the Case Studies section of the Resource Pack, available from PEG.

6 Linx88 is a type of software known as authoring software. The author types information into the computer; the computer then arranges this into a program for others to use. Teachers do not need to know anything about computer programming, but they do need to have thought things out. You can use Linx 88 for the writing of stories, simulations, classifying things, storing expert knowledge, and many other things. Linx88 can be used in two modes: as an author; and as a user. Anything written in Linx88 has the advantage that it can be played by the author or by other people, and it is interactive: decisions which players make as they progress through the program can affect events at a later stage.

7 When pupils develop their own models they deepen their understanding of a topic through identifying the essential elements in a situation and discovering, researching, organizing and structuring the information in the form of a static model or a living, working micro-world. Linx88 and Keys88 aim to apply this principle across the curriculum, to English, the arts, humanities and social sciences, science, mathematics and technology, as well as personal, social and moral education. Content-free programs have two main roles: they provide teachers with the tools with which they can create their own programs for teaching, and also give pupils a medium through which they can show what they understand of a problem or topic. The aim is to release teachers from dependence upon commercially produced programs which may well not suit their particular needs. Pupil programming using Linx88 and Keys88 places the emphasis on processes. Pupils will realize that these activities which require high levels of thought, originality and creativity require careful planning and structuring. Linx88 and Keys88 have been used to produce a range of types of files such as simulations, adventure games, branching stories, classification programs, detective mysteries, and textual databases.

8 HADOW REPORT (1931) *The Education of the Adolescent.*

9 *The Curriculum from 5 to 16*, DES, 1985.

10 WATSON, L. (1988) 'Knowledge bases in primary school', in Proceedings of the International PEG conference, Copenhagen, Denmark; WATSON, L. (1988) 'Key clues', *Times Educational Supplement*, 17 July 1988.

The Resource Pack details how PEG tools might be used and, it is hoped, will make PEG better known. However, most teachers still suffer from a lack of IT knowledge and a lack of IT confidence. PEG is attempting to specify and produce appropriate classroom tools and support teachers in their employment of these.

11 It is important to stress the 'integrated' nature of the resource needs. Appropriate hardware, software, training, support and time to implement knowledge and techniques are all needed. What is important is that they are each available as any one missing would greatly restrict the use made of the materials. Quality is crucial. The quality of hardware and software can be illustrated by the analogy of the cooking stove — you cannot cook a soufflé on a camping stove because fried eggs are probably the limit. Important, too, is the quality and enthusiasm of the people: teachers with a traditional approach to education (viewing it as facts to be acquired rather than the skill development and experience of the pupils) have not generally taken to PEG techniques and ideas.

Chapter 5

Word-Processors and Collaborative Writing

Graham Peacock

Introduction

One of the effects of bringing word-processors into primary classrooms has been to encourage teachers to develop collaborative writing more than they might otherwise have done. Cautioning against overzealousness Chandler (1986) wondered if we are being seduced by an attractive toy. In using computers to encourage collaborative work are we doing so uncritically and neglecting the cheaper and simpler ways of encouraging collaborative writing?

There is nothing particularly new about collaborative writing in the class-room (Chandler, 1984). But the public nature of the word-processor screen seems to make it a natural way to encourage children to write together in groups. At first sight there does seem a greater level of interaction within a collaborative word-processor group compared with a group writing with a pencil but does this impression bear close examination? Daiute (1985) observes that 'although any writing environment can be designed to include discussion and sharing, the class-room with computers may be most appropriate for interaction' (p. 19). Daiute goes on to suggest that since computers display the text upright, group reading is encouraged as much as group writing.

But does the word-processor actually improve the way that groups collabor-ate or is it just that we are unused to seeing collaborative writing of any kind in classrooms? What sort of interaction is taking place within the group? Could the results that are enthusiastically reported for collaborative writing using word-processors be replicated if pencils were used instead?

Potter (1987) reported that few studies have sought to compare the two writing implements. So in the light of these issues a small-scale observation proj-ect was initiated. The objective of the study was to find out the extent and type of interaction between groups of children when writing as a group using a word-processor compared with the same children's interaction when using pencil and paper.

When using a word-processor do children:

   (i)   share ideas and suggest words more freely;
   (ii) review and alter their work more;

(iii) take more care with punctuation;
(iv) produce work of greater length and quality;
 (v) type as quickly as they write?

Method

Systematic observations were made of children at work in collaborative groups using either a word-processor or pencil. An observation schedule based on Baker (1986) was used which recorded the dominant activity for each member of the group every twenty seconds. The categories of activities included:

1 typing or writing;
2 suggesting new words or new directions that the writing might take;
3 orally responding to suggestions;
4 reading aloud from the screen or paper;
5 assisting with spelling or layout;
6 being off-task;
7 silently reading the screen or paper.

The groups of children worked in their normal classrooms. The writing tasks were, as far as possible, those in which the rest of the class was also engaged. All the children were used to some collaborative writing but normally they wrote individual pieces of work.

In addition to watching the children writing, twenty finished pieces of writing were collected. Ten of these pieces were done using pencil and ten were done using a word-processor. They were made indistinguishable by typing both sets of work.

The children were from two schools. One of the schools is in a decaying industrial area and the other in the centre of a large council estate. A total of twenty-seven children operating in twelve different groups were observed. The children were 6 to 7 years old from a first school (5–8 years) and 11 to 12 years old from the top class of a middle school (8–12 years). The children in both schools had little previous word-processor experience. They received about fifteen minutes' instruction before beginning to write in earnest. The younger children used the programs Writer and Folio. The middle school used Pendown.

Findings

(i) Suggesting or Responding to New Words or Ideas

In the categories of suggesting new words and responding, the figures for the first school were almost identical for both media. The older children seemed to inter-act rather more when using a pencil than when word-processing. The figures are rounded averages of the number of occasions the behaviour was noted within the group in a ten-minute period.

	First school	Middle school
Word-processor	13	22
Pencil	13	26

(ii) Reading Aloud from the Screen or Paper

The frequency with which the children read aloud from either the screen or paper was identical. On average the first school children read aloud four times every ten minutes. The middle school pupils read aloud twice every ten minutes.

(iii) Interactions Concerned with Spelling and Layout

The number of occasions that the children were observed helping the scribe or typist with suggestions about layout, punctuation and spelling were noted. The figures refer to the number of occasions recorded in a ten-minute period.

	First school	Middle school
Word-processor	12	7
Pencil	6	1

(iv) Concentration on the Writing Task

The amount of time the children were off-task is presented as the average per child in a ten-minute period.

	First school	Middle school
Word-processor	65 seconds	0 seconds
Pencil	129 seconds	43 seconds

The time spent silently watching the paper or screen but making no audible or visible contribution was similar for both age groups. The writing method made very little difference.

(v) Length and Quality of the Writing

The average number of words written by the children in ten minutes was:

	First school	Middle school
Word-processor	19	83
Pencil	25	116

The average length of the finished work done by the first school children using the computer was greater than that done using pencil. On average, their work was 92 words long using a word-processor but only 74 words when pencil writing. However, the computer group took a great deal more time over their work. Six panels of teachers judged the quality of the communication of the scripts. They judged the word-processed work to be of slightly higher quality than the pencil-written scripts.

The amount of redrafting that the children did was beyond the scope of this enquiry. All the children who were asked thought that their work looked best when printed. Teachers all thought that the children had a very positive attitude to their writing when done with the word-processor.

Discussion

In analyzing these results two distinct types of writing activity can be described. The first type is where the children are actively cooperating to create the writing. This includes suggesting new words (category 2 of the schedule), responding to suggestions (category 3) and reviewing the writing by reading aloud (category 4). It is suggested that children were interacting about the content of their work at these points. The second type of activity concerns the technicalities of presentation and suggestions regarding spelling or punctuation (category 5 of the schedule). These interactions are concerned less with the content and more with the form of the finished product.

Creative Interaction

The fact that there did not seem to be a dramatic difference between the sort of creative interaction witnessed when the children were word-processing compared with when they were using a pencil was surprising. The results for the younger children were strikingly similar. It was apparent that children of this age find the act of writing very demanding whatever the medium. They used the word-processor in much the same way as they used pencil and rubber to make local changes to spelling and individual words. The older children were clearly more at home with a pencil and they interacted creatively at a significantly higher rate when using the pencil. Of course, the older children have been using pencil for about six years whereas their exposure to the computer has been very limited indeed.

Reading the text aloud by one of the group seemed to indicate the degree to which the text was being reviewed. The finding that the text was read aloud with precisely the same frequency irrespective of the writing medium was surprising. Daiute (1985) and others have commented on the greater physical ease with which the screen can be viewed compared with paper. However, if we take into account the slower speed of typing, it is clear that on a word-processor the writing is reviewed aloud in shorter chunks. The fact that a screenful of words with Writer or Folio is quite short may also play a part in this.

Technical Changes

These observations suggest that when children are using a word-processor they interact more concerning technicalities, such as spelling and punctuation, than when writing with a pencil. The fact that someone was always typing and others were frequently helping to correct spaces and spellings and pressing keys made the computer groups appear very busy. This amount of activity could easily be mistaken for collaboration at a higher level if looked at casually.

Access to Computers

The children were new to word-processing and this novelty could account for their greater concentration as shown by the short period they were off-task. When writing collaboratively with pencils, on the other hand, the children spent longer just watching the scribe or off-task.

The speed of typing was surprisingly fast considering the relative lack of keyboard experience. It must be anticipated that within a short time the younger children would be typing as quickly as they can write. This assumes that they could get sufficient word-processing time which is unlikely given the scarcity of computers in classrooms.

A survey in the Times Educational Supplement (Wellington and Macdonald, 1989) reveals that in primary schools the average number of children to one computer is about sixty-nine. Clearly, the amount of time any one child could spend word-processing must be small. So the chances for developing the skills necessary to type at speed and use the full potential of word-processors must be limited. To make matters worse, in most classrooms the computer is available for word-processing for only part of the school day. The computers that are available are used for a variety of purposes ranging from LOGO to structured reinforcement. There are occasional instances, such as may be found in special schools for example, where the amount of time available to each pupil is considerably greater than the average. One instance of this is decribed by Collins (1986). But these are exceptional.

It is not surprising that with time for word-processing being so precious teachers have pragmatically decided to maximize the access to word-processing experience by getting their children to work in groups. This point is made by Eraut and Hoyles (1989, p. 13): 'Scarcity of computers is likely to make working in groups a practical necessity for many years ahead.' They also observe that 'the potential of groupwork is rarely exploited and collaborative learning in such groups happens more by chance than design.'

It is interesting to speculate about what would happen if each child had access to a machine. Would there be a move towards more individual work with word-processors? As Dunn and Morgan (1987) point out, cooperative writing projects are not easy to organize.

Implications for Practice

On the basis of this evidence, if a teacher wants to encourage collaborative inter-action in writing there is little point in just sitting a group of inexperienced children around a screen. That by itself does not seem to start them sharing ideas and talking about new directions for the work.

The unstructured approach where children learn to use the word-processor by doing tasks similar to those for which they normally use a pencil may not be suffiient. Eraut and Hayles (1989) and Dunn and Morgan (1987) all comment on the need for a thoughtful approach if the potential of computer groupwork is to be realized.

There have been many reports of interesting practice. Clough (1987), for instance, encourages groups of children to read other groups' word-processed science reports. Clough's approach is highly structured and uses the word-processor's ability to encourage review and redrafting following constructive comment from peers. Marshall (1987) also suggests ways of presenting collaborative writing work which could only be done using a word-processor. In both cases the groupwork approach was an integral part of the planning of the task.

Researchers like Baskerville (1985) and Keane (1986) have pointed out that children find the word-processor motivating; but is this the result of novelty? The results from this small-scale study indicate that word-processors do encourage children to pay more attention to spelling, and earlier studies indicate a more positive attitude to the finished product. Clough has also indicated that where the teacher encourages the children to see the need for review the word-processor is probably the best tool for the job.

If the attention paid to collaborative writing at the word-processor results in a more thoughtful approach to group writing tasks whatever the medium, it will be worthwhile. However, if there is an uncritical response to the word-processor and an assumption that it will by itself usher in a golden age of writing then we will be missing an opportunity to examine the way that children write. In this limited study the high level of discussion around the computer appeared to be little more than concern over the finer points of already fixed writing.

References

BAKER, N. (1986) unpublished B. Ed. dissertation.

BASKERVILLE, J. (1985) 'Word processors and the development of children's written language', *Microscope*, No. 14.

CHANDLER, D. (1984) *Young Learners and the Microcomputer*, Open University Press.

CHANDLER, D. (1986) 'Writing in the third person', *TES*, 24 October.

CLOUGH, D. (1987) 'Word processing in the classroom and science education'. *Primary Science Review*, 5, pp. 4–5.

COLLINS, D. (1986) 'Music and the micro: the improvement of self image through creative achievement'. In HOPE, M. (Ed.) *The Magic of the Micro*, Council for Educational Technology.

DAIUTE, C. (1985) *Writing and Computers*, Addison Wesley.

DUNN, S. and MORGAN, V. (1987) *The Impact of Computers on Education*. Prentice-Hall.

ERAUT, M. and HOYLES, C. (1989) 'Groupwork and computers', *Journal of Computer Assisted Learning*, 5, 1, pp. 12–24.

FOLIO, Tedimen Software, Southampton SO9 7BD.

KEANE, P. (1986) 'Writing: a group and a computer', in HOPE, M. *The Magic of the Micro*, CET.

MARSHALL, D. (1987) 'Practice makes perfect', *Educational Computing*, 8, 7, pp. 35–40.

PEACOCK, G. (1986) 'An interim report on the introduction of a word processor in two inner city schools', *Microscope: The Journal of MAPE*, No. 19.

PENDOWN, Logotron, Cambridge CB1 2LJ.

POTTER, F. (1987) unpublished paper given at BERA conference, Manchester.

WELLINGTON, J. and MACDONALD, G. (1989) 'The parents pay', *TES*, 17 March.

Chapter 6

What Can't Speak Can't Lie: Computers and Records of Achievement

Christopher Pole

Introduction

> Relationships between teacher and pupil in this school have improved considerably since we started negotiating Records of Achievement. I mean a lot of the children say a lot of very confidential things in the negotiations and you create an air of trust and confidentiality which you never created between pupil and teacher before. (David Fox, Head-teacher, Benton High School)[1]

This unequivocal celebration of Records of Achievement is made by a head-teacher who, over a period of five years, has introduced a Record of Achievement process throughout his secondary school. The Record of Achievement is the main means of reporting and recording pupil progress to parents, employers, members of staff and the pupils themselves. More than this, however, the Record of Achievement acts as an important diagnostic tool in the formative development of the pupils in the school. At the centre of the Record of Achievement process is dialogue or discussion between teachers and pupils. The dialogue, during which teachers and pupils discuss not only academic achievement, but also out-of-school activities and home life, and agree on a set of goals or targets for the pupil, is seen as a highly personal act which relies on rapport and the quality of the relationship between teacher and pupil.

In the view of the head of Benton School, the teacher-pupil discussions have been instrumental in fostering an air of trust between the two parties and generally better teacher-pupil relations. What is interesting is that claims relating to interpersonal qualities of trust and confidentiality should be made in relation to a process of dialogue and discussion which is mediated and shaped by a computer.

The subjects for discussion between teacher and pupil are defined by a specifically designed software package which requires teachers and pupils to select appropriate statements from a database (see Appendix) and to enter details of any agreed action which has resulted from discussion of the statements. The computer is therefore instrumental in defining, shaping and aiding the discussion, in identifying areas for the pupils' development and in formatting final reports for parents and employers. To achieve all of this there is a requirement for the software to be not merely efficient but sensitive to individual needs and sufficiently flexible to accommodate a wide range of different pupil abilities and achievements.

Traditional perceptions of computers as cold, super-efficient machines without soul or conscience would certainly not encompass notions of the computer as go-between, as arbiter or as a facilitator of dialogue between teachers and pupils. In the opinion of the head of Benton School and some of his staff, however, this is certainly the role which computers play in the Record of Achievement process. Computers have provided a basis for discussion, have enabled teachers and pupils to learn more about each other and have generally helped to improve teacher-pupil rapport. This chapter offers a critical examination of the computer in the Record of Achievement process by examining the experiences of Benton staff and pupils as they have worked with and developed their Record of Achievement process. It will consider what is a new use of Information Technology in schools and look at its contribution to the formative process of reporting and recording.

The Development of Records of Achievement

Although ideas about the merits of some kind of Record of Achievement in schools have been traced back to the early part of this century (Broadfoot, 1986) their development has been located largely within the post-war history of education. Initial schemes developed by Stansbury in the 1960s (cf. Stansbury, 1984) and the Scottish Council for Research in Education (SCRE, 1977) were followed in 1984 by support for Records of Achievement from the Department of Education and Science by means of their statement of policy on Records of Achievement (DES, 1984) which in turn led to the generous funding of a large national pilot scheme in secondary schools (cf. PRAISE, 1987, 1988). The general intention behind all of the early schemes, and indeed behind present initiatives, is that a method of recording and reporting pupil progress and achievements be developed which goes beyond the traditional end-of-term report, by contributing to the formative development of the pupil.

When the early Records of Achievement or pupil profile schemes were first introduced in the 1960s relatively few schools owned computers, and even in those which did, staff probably never dreamt of using a computerized system for reporting and recording pupil progress. Since the 1960s, however, this new form of reporting and recording has begun to employ new technology and now, thirty years on, computers are at the centre of the formative Record of Achievement process in many schools.

Two Types of Program

The types of computer program developed for Records of Achievement processes may be divided broadly into two categories; one which is termed 'Comment Bank', the other 'Open-Ended or Free Prose' (cf. Skinsley, 1986; Molyneux, 1987; John, 1989). Both types of package have been designed to aid discussion between teacher and pupil, to facilitate the production of a statement which is agreed by both teacher and pupil, and to reflect the progress and performance of the pupil. In this sense, the computer programs may serve a formative purpose in helping teacher and pupil to identify areas for further development, and a summative purpose in producing a statement which reviews the achievements of the pupil over a given time span. The systems do not take away the need for human interaction, leaving pupils plugged into machines baring their souls to a floppy disk. With both types of program, the technology is there to enhance pupil-teacher dialogue, not to bypass it.

As the term suggests, Comment Bank programs involve the pupil and teacher in the process of selecting comments which accurately describe the achievements of the pupil (see Appendix).

Comment banks use database programs from which comments are pre-specified and may be grouped in order to address particular skills (e.g. reading) or personal qualities (e.g. cheerfulness) or to address specific school subjects (e.g. maths, English, PE, languages, etc.). Teacher and pupil call up the groups of comments on the screen and with discussion select those which are felt to be most appropriate for the pupil. In theory, selection involves both teacher and pupil as equal partners. Agreeing which comment should be selected from the bank may, therefore, involve negotiation where teachers and pupils have differing views of pupil achievement.

After selection of appropriate comments these may be printed out individually or, in the case of some packages, they may be linked together to form a prose statement. Collectively, the comments should provide an accurate picture of the pupil which has been reached as a result of discussion between pupil and teacher.

Free prose or open-ended systems seem to have been less common for Records of Achievement purposes than comment banks, but have nevertheless been adopted by some schools[2] (PRAISE, 1988). The systems use word-processing programs and allow free entry of text by teacher and pupil. Specific headings may be programmed by teachers to guide pupils in their entries and to aid them in summarizing their achievements. In essence, the free prose system offers a form of self-reporting to pupils, with the pupil-written reports providing the basis for discussion and negotiation with teachers, and ultimately the production of an agreed joint statement.

The development of computer programs to facilitate teacher-pupil discussion and to reduce the amount of time taken to conduct such discussions accompanied the general development of Records of Achievement in schools. Based on their analysis of data collected from schools involved in the national pilot scheme, James and Stierer (PRAISE, 1988) suggest that schools introduced computer packages to the Record of Achievement process for a variety of reasons. Teachers expected computer programs to produce a more cost-efficient and cost-effective recording process. In addition, teachers in several local education authorities expected computers to speed up the process of discussion by offering 'ready-made' statements about progress and performance (grades, marks for class work, examination results, etc.) which could be retrieved and discussed during a negotiation session. Furthermore, exponents of computer-assisted Records of Achievement expected the process to be quicker, more efficient and cheaper in the production of standardized summative statements which could be presented to parents and employers.

Experiencing the Computer and Records of Achievement

Whilst many schools throughout the country may have developed comment bank or free prose packages for Records of Achievement, there exists no systematic evaluation of the experiences of those involved with their development and use. However, as part of a Local Education Authority research project (Pole, 1989) which looked at all aspects of Records of Achievement within the context of one Midlands secondary school, consideration was given to the views and experiences largely of teachers but also of pupils who had used a comment bank program as a central part of their Record of Achievement process. This chapter arises from that project and describes teachers and pupils' experiences of a computerized Record of Achievement system. In particular it raises a number of important issues which are central to the debate about the capacity of computers to respond to and cope with individual reports on pupil progress and performance.

The school, which is referred to as Benton High, is a rural secondary school with less than 300 pupils on roll. The headteacher, David Fox, and many of the staff, are keen supporters of the Record of Achievement concept and place particular importance on the teacher-pupil discussion sessions.

The discussions are referred to as negotiations and involve teachers and pupils agreeing to the selection of appropriate comments or descriptors from a computerized comment bank which then go to form the pupils' Records of Achievement. The computerized comment bank constitutes an integral part of the dialogue between teacher and pupil. Pete Robbins, the deputy head, explained that the computer is always present during negotiation sessions:

> So we've got this thing called the negotiation room, and the majority of negotiations go on there. You know we've got easy chairs in there and there's a potted plant in there, and there's a table, but there's always the computer and hopefully it's conducive to the negotiation environment.

As far as the senior management of the school is concerned, the computer makes a positive contribution to teacher-pupil dialogue, and consequently to the success of the Records of Achievement in the school. The computer is synonymous with discussion and negotiation. Furthermore, the gradual development of user-friendly software and its integration with the reporting and recording process has led to a policy decision that all negotiation sessions for fourth and fifth years should be conducted with the computer, and all summative documents will be produced by it in a standard form.

Pupil Experiences

For most pupils in Benton School the use of a computer was commonplace. Most pupils had experience of using computers through their lessons and in many cases at home. Its use during negotiation sessions was usually accepted without comment. On only one occasion during more than fifty interviews conducted with pupils, as part of the research project, was dislike of the computer during negotiation sessions brought to my attention. Much more common were comments from pupils which supported the use of the computer in Records of

Achievement. The following conversation which I held with two fifth-year pupils, Daniel and Thomas, was similar to many with Benton pupils, both boys and girls:

Researcher: What about the computer, using that, because you will have done profiles with the computer and without the computer. What difference does the computer make?
Daniel: The computer's quicker.
Thomas: Yeah, that's about it.
Researcher: How do you mean, quicker?
Daniel: Well, you don't have to do writing and ring everything, all you have to do is select it and press return.
Researcher: Right, do you enjoy working on computers?
Daniel: In profiles I don't really mind either way.
Thomas: I like computers anyway.
Researcher: So it's quite normal for you to be working on a computer then?
Thomas: With so many around in the school you get used to it.

The fact that computers were part of everyday school life for these two pupils and many others, meant that it was not unusual that they should be used in the Record of Achievement process. What is interesting is the boys' comments about the principal role of the computer being to speed up the process by requiring them merely to press the keyboard rather than write. The boys made no comments about the computer either enhancing or obstructing the dialogue with the teacher. It would seem that computers had become an accepted part of the Record of Achievement process, and, as the deputy head had implied, were part of the furniture of the room in which the one-to-one pupil-teacher discussions took place.

Conversations with pupils also revealed that computer work formed an important part of many lessons in Benton High School. For example, pupils used computers not only in maths and science subjects but also in English where they were used for writing poetry and for literature appreciation lessons and also in history where database work and examination of the content of historical documents, stored on computer, was carried out. The frequency with which pupils encountered computers in the school, and the fact that many had their own at home, seemed in most cases to make its use during negotiation sessions no different from its use in other situations throughout the school.

In some respects, however, there are important differences in the expansion of computers into Records of Achievement from their expansion into other areas of schooling. The emphasis which the Record of Achievement process places on communication and in particular on the dialogue which occurs between teacher and pupil imposes a responsibility on computer software to enhance that communication without removing any of the important interpersonal aspects on which the process rests. Dangers would seem to lie with the introduction of software which made the pupil-teacher discussion sessions merely a mechanistic exercise. In such a situation, following the correct computer-led procedures, entering the right kind of data in the correct format into the right place may become an end in itself. Consequently, the procedures of the computer would detract from the most important aspect of the Record of Achievement, the pupil-teacher discussion. Striking the balance between systems which are cost-effective and efficient in terms of time, yet leave the teacher and pupil in charge of the process, may in some cases prove difficult (PRAISE, 1988). However, Pete Robbins, the deputy head at Benton High School, believes that with the system which they have developed the process has been streamlined, but at the same time, the computer can actually enhance teacher-pupil discussion by helping to break down some of the barriers which may exist between the two parties. He explained:

> . . . The computer itself helps in negotiations because it's this third person and it won't tell any tales and often because people feel embarrassed or whatever, they can actually .. they feel as though there's another person there. They look at the computer when they're talking you know and so the eyeball to eyeball, it's very good and often I have kids .. actually they will put in the information to the computer rather than me do it, that was the idea we would negotiate and put the information in as it came in. The pupil would then look at the screen and they would then say, 'yes, I would like this to be used. . . .'

For Pete Robbins the presence of the computer can often be useful in overcoming any interpersonal difficulties which may exist between teacher and pupil. In effect it takes on its own persona and makes a positive contribution to the negotiation session. In his view the computer is able to contribute to the development of a rapport between teacher and pupil. The fact that they are both able to look at and communicate with the computer and yet the computer is unable to answer back, may help them to overcome any personal difficulties at first, before moving on to establish a more open relationship.

Phil Skelton, a Benton teacher, who has been involved in the use and implementation of the computer software for Records of Achievement in the school, is a keen supporter of their use. Whilst stressing the importance of the personal teacher-pupil relationship in the Record of Achievement process, he describes his experience of a negotiation session using the computer, in terms of freeing the pupil from the possible strain of the one-to-one situation. He says:

> I actually found what I was doing was, I was looking at the screen and talking at the screen and the kid was talking at the screen and they were talking about an indeterminate type of thing which wasn't directly threatening them or involving them and they could talk much more freely about the screen.

Phil Skelton believes that most pupils feel at ease when using a computer, not only because of their proliferation in schools, but also because of what he describes as 'the television culture', which means that most children are used to looking at and responding to screens. In this sense the use of the computer in a one-to-one discussion session is not greatly different from situations which pupils experience both at school and at home.

Staff Experiences

Although most pupils at Benton High School felt at ease when using computers and often had experience of them in a variety of situations, the same could not be said for all the staff. Several teachers expressed a dislike of using the computer and admitted to some uncertainty over the procedures necessary for its effective use.

In the view of Phil Skelton a lack of confidence amongst teachers when using the computer could inhibit the teacher-pupil dialogue. He explained:

> The downside comes with those people who aren't at ease with computers and we do have members of staff like that, who feel threatened by them and that puts them under pressure, because they wonder is this machine going to crash, have I hit the right button, have I just deleted everything off the disk and I'm sure that that, certainly initially, detracts from it.

In such a situation it seems likely that the mechanics of operating the computer would become more important than the teacher-pupil dialogue. Rather than acting as a tool to facilitate negotiation and discussion the successful use of the computer may become an end in itself, taking attention away from the dialogue.

The head of Benton School was aware that some staff were reluctant to use the computer during negotiation sessions and felt that this reluctance was based on fear. He was quick to stress, however, that the level of reluctance and fear decreased substantially as teachers became more familiar with the technology. He stated:

> I think that's very true, I think the amount of fear in that respect that you've come across in your discussions, is about 10 per cent of what it was when we began. Because it was a major concern with everybody then, a real major concern, it's not now a major concern. I think that as time goes on and we get more and more used to dealing with this technology it will get less of a problem.

The head also drew attention to fear which may occur when pupils have a greater knowledge and understanding of computers than their teachers. He explained:

> I think actually, that a bit of this fear on the part of the staff is the understanding that the kids are more able to deal with computers than they themselves are, you know, and whereas in a negotiation situation where there is a computer, a member of staff has got some apprehension about it, there's no apprehension on the part of the pupil.

Where this occurred the teacher may have felt threatened or challenged by the computer or indeed by the pupil with the greater knowledge. The reversal of the traditional teacher and pupil roles may have resulted in adverse effects for the one-to-one discussion as the teacher strove to reassert his/her authority.

One Benton teacher was particularly vociferous in her dislike of computers not because of a lack of confidence in using the software, but because she felt it took time away from real discussion with the pupils. She recalled her experiences thus:

> I don't like computers. I really don't like negotiating with a computer, there to be honest, because when we started we didn't have the computer

and we sat facing the child and we talked, now we've got to look at the computer and we say, are you number one so and so, what do you think you are, and I don't think that we are really talking to the pupils about their problems, we are talking about numbers on a screen and if the staff think that they are 1.3 and they say they are 1.3 and you say oh they must be 1.3 and you just put it down and you don't really look at the descriptors properly like we used to but that takes an awful lot longer.

This teacher's objections to the computer seem to stem from the format used to identify individual descriptor statements, which, in her opinion, results in a neglect of the real issues for discussion and a concentration on the number codes given to the descriptor statements[3] (1.3, 1.4, 1.5 etc.). At the same time she raises the important question of the physical presence of the computer. Whilst one member of staff, quoted earlier, felt the presence of the computer could often be useful in breaking down barriers between teacher and pupil, this teacher draws attention to the fact that teacher and pupil no longer sit facing each other. Both parties now look at the computer. Lack of eye contact and facial expression could perhaps act against establishing an effective rapport between teacher and pupil.

The teacher was not alone in her belief that the use of this particular computerized format actually worked against effective teacher-pupil dialogue. Although some of the difficulties which she encountered may have stemmed from her dislike of computers, other members of staff, who had considerable involvement with computers through their subject teaching, also expressed doubts over their role in the Records of Achievement process. For example, one interview with a maths and computing teacher brought to light the following concerns:

Teacher: . . . now that I think about it, perhaps one or two interviews would be different if the computer wasn't there.
Researcher: In what sense?
Teacher: In the sense that there would be more time for discussion, more time for any specific concerns or queries that arise. It hasn't quite got to the stage of being a production line, although I could foresee a situation with certain approaches to doing it, that with some people it would be.

It seems ironic that the development of a computer system to streamline and enhance the Records of Achievement process should be perceived as reducing the amount of time available for its most important component, the teacher-pupil discussion. The teacher quoted above raises important questions about the depth of conversation and the capacity to discuss concerns which are specific to the individual in the context of the computerized negotiation session. He seems to suggest that the mechanistic nature of the process precludes personal dialogue, as teacher and pupil work their way systematically through the computerized comment banks. Evidence that teachers in the school have become used to referring to the individual descriptors in the computerized comment bank can be seen from the comments of one member of staff. During a general discussion about Records of Achievement he clearly felt comfortable in referring to descriptor statements in terms of the computer numbering system applied to them. He commented:

... suppose they [the teachers] had all gone for three. Suppose they [the pupils] had 2.2, 2.3, 2.4 and they [the teacher and the pupil] had given themselves 2.7. Well I'd say your opinion of yourself doesn't match what most of the teaching staff see you as.

The ease with which this teacher slips into using 'computer terminology' is perhaps indicative of the extent to which, in his case at least, the computer process leads the conversation. Where pupils also have great familiarity with the computer numbering system it would seem likely that pupil-teacher discussion sessions could become merely a discussion of numbers rather than issues.

It would appear that striking the balance between streamlining the process and facilitating effective teacher-pupil dialogue is the key to the successful use of the computer. In addition, the development of staff confidence and familiarity with the computer is also likely to be imperative for their integration with the process. Whilst teachers remain fearful of computers, this may be one area where staff feel challenged, or in some cases threatened by the pupils. The need for effective in-service training for staff to overcome some of this fear and to ensure that they are confident in using computers may perhaps go some way towards developing a computer system which complements the Record of Achievement process.

Supporting or Leading the Process

The experiences of staff and pupils at Benton School give rise to a number of interesting issues relating to the role of computers in the Record of Achievement process. Perhaps the most important of these is the extent to which the use of a computer comes to dominate the Record of Achievement process. Whilst arguments about the amount of time which is to be saved by computerization may be convincing, the risk of turning the process into something akin to a production line must, at the same time, be confronted. If it is accepted that Records of Achievement are about individual pupil progress, motivation and performance (DES, 1984) then surely it is important to examine any computer program in the light of its capacity to treat pupils as individuals and to permit effective pupil-teacher dialogue. Molyneux (1987) describes how the use of a computer program, together with a BBC single disk-drive and printer, made profiling within a Hampshire College far quicker and easier. He states:

> The end result was a program that enabled the CPVE staff at the college to profile up to 150 students on one disk at greater speed and provide each student with a printed update of his/her profile immediately after each profiling session. (Molyneux, 1987, p. 10)

For Molyneux computers are about speed in profiling. He fails to comment, however, on the impact of this quick streamlined process on the students or the capacity of the process to deal with individuals. In his discussion of the computerized process, speed appears to be the principal aim. Whilst it is important to recognize that involvement with the Record of Achievement process is likely to be only one of the many things which competes for time from the teacher (Pole, 1989; PRAISE, 1988), it should also be recognized that Records of Achievement are about pupils and are for pupils. In this respect devising a computer program which is able to streamline the process but remain user-friendly and pupil-centred is probably the key to its successful use in a Record of Achievement process. The use of the same pre-specified statements for a whole group, year or school of pupils may be quick but may also result in pupil profiles which fail to distinguish effectively between individuals, producing a cloning effect. In the experience of one teacher interviewed in the course of my work this proved to be one of the principal drawbacks of the computerized comment bank system. He explained:

> You could take seventy kids and the discrimination between those kids for the summary document of record, unless you are a very discerning reader, is negligible.

Again, it would seem that questions of compatibility between personal pupil profiles and computer comment bank statements are of central importance to the development of a Record of Achievement scheme which gives primacy to the individual pupil.

Efficiency and Surveillance

Many practitioners with experience of computerized profile and Record of Achievement systems (cf. John, 1989; Molyneux, 1987; Skinsley, 1986) have emphasized the benefits to be gained from a computerized Record of Achievement system which relate to storage and retrieval of information. In short, they argue that computerized Records of Achievement cut down on the amount of storage space required to file information on pupils who may have left the school and facilitate easy updating of information on present pupils throughout the school year. Whilst this may be particularly useful for teachers and schools with large numbers of records to store and process, Hargreaves *et al.* (1988) raise issues of social control in relation to excessive collection of information by schools about their pupils. He questions whether Records of Achievement and pupil profiles are in fact an invasion of privacy, which could, intentionally or unintentionally, be used as tools of control or surveillance not only by schools but also by the police, social services and other agencies.

Computerized information which relates to individuals is now covered by the Data Protection Act. The Act entitles individuals to a copy of the information which forms the personal data held about them by a data user. In addition it gives the individual a right to take action to have inaccurate personal data corrected or erased and to seek compensation for damage caused by inaccurate personal data or by loss or unauthorized destruction or disclosure of personal data (Office of the Data Protection Registrar, 1989). However, in order for the Act to provide effective protection for pupils, individual teachers need to be aware of the implications of the Act in relation to computerized Records of Achievement.

Conclusion

The experiences of pupils and teachers at Benton High School are important in highlighting some of the practical implications of using computers in conjunction with a Records of Achievement scheme. Above all they demonstrate the need for careful thought about the introduction and development of computer packages for an aspect of schooling which may remain highly personal to pupils. The fact that recording and reviewing pupil progress in the context of a formative Record of Achievement rests on human interaction and effective teacher-pupil rapport (PRAISE, 1988; DES, 1989), emphasizes the need for user-friendly computer packages which support the process rather than lead it (Pole, 1989).

Individual pupil-teacher discussion for Records of Achievement are time-consuming (Munby, 1989; Hall, 1989; PRAISE, 1988; Evans, 1988). Finding this time may be one of the biggest obstacles to Records of Achievement. However, the discussions are time-consuming for good reason: to enable teachers and pupils to establish a good relationship and to engage in honest and open dialogue. Whilst there may be some advantages in using computer software to speed up the Record of Achievement process by structuring and standardizing the discussion sessions, the experiences of pupils and teachers from Benton High School highlight some of the possible disadvantages. An overemphasis on computerized comment bank phrases, for example, may result in a failure to discuss important issues and in the production of bland summative statements which fail to distinguish between pupils. Furthermore, concern to enter data in the correct format and to press the correct keys may take precedence over talking through important issues.

The experiences of the Benton teachers and pupils emphasize the need for balance in the application of computerized Records of Achievement systems. They show that Records of Achievement are about teacher-pupil relations, about human processes. In this context computer software must be more than efficient, it must be sensitive and accommodating to individual pupil needs. The data suggest that the complexity of such relations and processes may perhaps go beyond the capacity of ordered and logical software. To ensure that computers serve and support the Record of Achievement process and do not lead or direct it, primacy must remain with dialogue.

The positive experiences of Benton teachers and pupils suggest that specifically designed software can enhance the Record of Achievement process and aid teacher-pupil rapport. The negative experiences show, however, that within one school many different views of computers and of Records of Achievement can exist. They also show that computer enhancement of Records of Achievement is best achieved where teachers and pupils understand the systems, are confident in their use and have control over them. Above all they show that effective reviewing and recording of pupil progress can only occur when teachers and pupils know and understand each other.

Notes

1 This and all other quotations in this chapter are taken from tape recorded interviews conducted with staff and pupils of Benton High School.
2 For example, Nasturtium Tertiary College, which was included in the national evaluation of Records of Achievement, developed such a program (PRAISE, 1988, pp. 63–4).
3 Each descriptor statement is attributed a number (see Appendix). During

negotiation sessions, it is, therefore, easy for pupils and teachers to refer to the statements only by their number.

References

BROADFOOT, P. (Ed.) (1986) *Profiles and Records of Achievement: A Review of Issues and Practice*, London, Holt.

DEPARTMENT OF EDUCATION AND SCIENCE (1984) *Records of Achievement: A Statement of Policy*, London, DES/Welsh Office.

DEPARTMENT OF EDUCATION AND SCIENCE (1989) *Records of Achievement: Report of the Records of Achievement National Steering Committee*, London, DES/Welsh Office.

EVANS, M. (1988) *Practical Profiling*, London, Routledge.

GARFORTH, D. and MACINTOSH, H. (1986) *Profiling: A Users' Manual*, Cheltenham, Thornes.

HALL, G. (1989) *Records of Achievement: Issues and Practice*, London, Kogan Page.

HARGREAVES, A. *et al.* (1988) *Personal and Social Education: Choices and Challenges*, Blackwell.

JOHN, M. (1989) 'Good reports', *TES*, 8 September.

MOLYNEUX, G. (1987) 'Profiling with the assistance of BBC disk program', *TVEI Insight*, No. 9, June.

MUNBY, S. (1989) *Assessing and Recording Achievement*, Oxford, Blackwell.

OFFICE OF THE DATA PROTECTION REGISTRAR (1989) *Guideline 5. Data Protection Act 1984. Individual Rights*, DPR, Wilmslow, February.

POLE, C. (1989) 'A case study of Benton School', unpublished CEDAR report, University of Warwick.

PRAISE (1987) *Pilot Records of Achievement in Schools Evaluation: An Interim Report*, DES/Welsh Office.

PRAISE (1988) *Records of Achievement: Report of the National Evaluation of Pilot Schemes*, DES/Welsh Office.

SCOTTISH COUNCIL FOR RESEARCH IN EDUCATION (1977) *Pupils in Profile*, SCRE Publication 67, Edinburgh.

SKINSLEY, M. (1986) 'Profiling using the computer', *Bulletin of Physical Education*, Vol. 22, No. 3.

STANSBURY, D. (1984, Reprint) *Principles of Personal Recording*, Totnes, Springline Trust.

Appendix
Record of Achievement List of Descriptors

Personal and Social Qualities

1.0   Cheerfulness
1.1   ☐   Remains cheerful in the face of difficulty.
1.2   ☐   Soon regains cheerfulnes after any setback.
1.3   ☐   Except for the occasional 'low' is cheerful.
1.4   ☐   Is easily depressed when faced with problems with either schoolwork or relationships.
1.5   ☐   Rarely appears to be happy and cheerful in school.

2.0   Helpfulness
2.1   ☐   Sees where help is needed and readily gives it.
2.2   ☐   When he/she does see that help is needed he/she gives it.
2.3   ☐   When asked for help he/she gives it.
2.4   ☐   Is reluctant to give help to others.
2.5   ☐   Never volunteers to give help to others.
2.6   ☐   Avoids being helpful if possible.

3.0   Open-Mindedness
3.1   ☐   Understands and respects other people's points of view.
3.2   ☐   Is prepared to reflect upon the opinions of others.
3.3   ☐   Is prepared to listen to the opinions of others.
3.4   ☐   Rarely gives proper consideration to the opinions of other people.
3.5   ☐   Is not prepared to listen to, nor to consider the opinions of other people.

4.0   Responding to an emergency
4.1   ☐   Keeps a cool head and takes the lead in an emergency.
4.2   ☐   Keeps cool and gives a helping hand in an emergency.
4.3   ☐   Carries out instructions calmly in an emergency.
4.4   ☐   Has never been involved in an emergency but believes he/she will remain calm.
4.5   ☐   Is inclined to panic easily.

5.0   Perseverance
5.1   ☐   Always tries to see a task through.
5.2   ☐   Tries to complete tasks which interest him/her.
5.3   ☐   Needs encouragement to see a task through.
5.4   ☐   Shows little determination in dealing properly with tasks.
5.5   ☐   Shows little inclination to see a task through unless closely supervised.
5.6   ☐   Unable to persevere with a task for any length of time even when given encouragement.

6.0   Punctuality
6.1   ☐   Is punctual.
6.2   ☐   Is occasionally late to school and to lessons.

6.3 ☐ Is often late.

6.4 ☐ Lateness is a very serious problem.

7.0   Reliability

7.1 ☐ Can be depended upon to carry out what he/she has undertaken to do.

7.2 ☐ Can usually be relied upon to carry out any task that he/she undertakes.

7.3 ☐ Has shown himself/herself to be unreliable on a number of occasions.

8.0   Self-Assurance

8.1 ☐ Is realistically confident about the skills he/she possesses.

8.2 ☐ Is confident in familiar work situations.

8.3 ☐ With support is confident in familiar work situations.

8.4 ☐ Is confident in the company of his/her peer group.

8.5 ☐ Is reserved and diffident in the company of adults.

8.6 ☐ Shows little confidence in his/her own abilities.

9.0   Sociability

9.1 ☐ A popular and central figure with a wide circle of friends.

9.2 ☐ Forms and maintains good relationships with fellow pupils and adults.

9.3 ☐ Whilst getting on well with a small group of friends he/she finds it difficult to form relationships with other people.

9.4 ☐ Is able to mix well with fellow pupils but prefers to be alone.

9.5 ☐ Relationships with others can be spoilt by a lack of self-restraint.

9.6 ☐ Has only one or two friends.

9.7 ☐ Has great difficulty in relating to anyone outside the immediate family.

10.0   Sense of Responsibility

10.1 ☐ Has a mature and responsible attitude to self and others.

10.2 ☐ Takes the responsibility for the consequences of his/her own actions.

10.3 ☐ Sometimes needs reminding of his/her own responsibilities.

10.4 ☐ Occasionally behaves in an irresponsible manner.

10.5 ☐ Often behaves in an irresponsible manner.

Work and Study Skills

1.0   Working with Others

1.1 ☐ Recognises the needs of the groups and is prepared to take a positive lead.

1.2 ☐ Well motivated in group activities.

1.3 ☐ Is prepared to work with others when given a task.

1.4 ☐ Prefers to work on his/her own whenever possible.

1.5 ☐ Finds it difficult to work with other people.

1.6 ☐ Can be disruptive in a working group situation.

1.7 ☐ Is compelled to work alone so that group work can progress unhindered.

2.0   Ability to work Independently

2.1 ☐ Shows outstanding capacity for organising his/her work and time effectively.

2.2 ☐ Shows a considerable capacity for organising his/her work and time effectively.

2.3 ☐ Always works to his/her maximum potential regardless of supervision.

2.4 ☐ A minimum of supervision is required to enable him/her to complete work.

2.5 ☐ Homework tasks are generally completed satisfactorily.

2.6 ☐ Though not regularly completed, homework tasks are of an adequate standard when produced.

2.7 ☐ Needs help and/or motivation in order to fulfil a task set although he/she can sometimes work without supervision.

2.8 ☐ Does not show much inclination to spend time in organising his/her work effectively.

3.0   Listening

3.1 ☐ Listens and responds to ideas and detailed instructions with a high level of understanding.

3.2 ☐ Accurately recalls what is said to him/her and acts upon it.

3.3 ☐ Listens to brief instructions and carries them out accurately.

3.4 ☐ Is sometimes inattentive and misunderstands instructions.

3.5 ☐ Rarely listens carefully to what is being said and as a result his/her response is inadequate and/or inaccurate.

4.0   Oral Explanation

4.1 ☐ Presents a lengthy, fluent, reasoned argument.

4.2 ☐ Clearly explains a complex process.

4.3 ☐ Explains a process clearly and accurately.

4.4 ☐ Explains what he/she is doing.

4.5 ☐ Has a very limited vocabulary and finds it difficult to explain clearly what he/she is doing.

4.6 ☐ Is very reluctant to attempt oral explanation except in very informal situations.

5.0   Talking with Others

5.1 ☐ Speaks confidently and persuasively in a group.

5.2 ☐ Is an intelligent, amusing, conversationalist who expresses himself/herself interestingly on a number of different topics.

5.3 ☐ Makes effective contributions to group discussions.

5.4 ☐ Has no difficulty in expressing himself/herself in a variety of situations but does not always do so fluently.

5.5 ☐ Asks clearly what he/she needs to know.

5.6 ☐ Is reluctant to participate in classroom discussion and does not find personal conversation easy with adults.

5.7 ☐ Replies coherently if he/she is spoken to.

5.8 ☐ Finds difficulty in expressing himself/herself clearly and is particularly unresponsive in formal conversations.

6.0   Reading

6.1 ☐ Reads and understands material presented in a variety of written forms.

6.2 ☐ Follows successfully a series of written instructions and uses when necessary everyday reference sources, e.g. dictionary.

6.3 ☐ Reads and understands basic instructions, notices and messages.

6.4 ☐ Reads and understands simple written material with assistance.

6.5 ☐ Is unable to use alphabetical lists or to organise written material properly.

6.6 ☐ Finds difficulty in understanding any kind of written material even with assistance.

7.0   Writing

7.1 ☐ Writes accurately and appropriately for a wide variety of purposes.

7.2 ☐ Writes with an acceptable standard of accuracy in spelling, punctuation and grammar.

7.3 ☐ Writes clear factual explanations.

7.4 ☐ Uses a vocabulary which is adequate for everyday written work.

7.5 ☐ Writes short directions, instructions and messages.

7.6 ☐ Writes short messages.

7.7 ☐ Has a very limited vocabulary and has difficulty spelling and punctuating even simple written work.

7.8 ☐ Needs assistance to produce even the simplest written work.

8.0   Memory

8.1 ☐ Accurately recalls complicated ideas and gets them in the right order.

8.2 ☐ Recalls the details of a process in the right order.

8.3 ☐ Recalls regular routines but needs reminding about those that are less familiar.

8.4 ☐ Finds it difficult to remember facts, instructions or routines.

8.5 ☐ Soon forgets any information given formally or informally.

9.0   Making Judgments

9.1 ☐ Makes well-reasoned judgments based on all the available evidence.

9.2 ☐ Recognizes bias and unsupported arguments.

9.3 ☐ Normally distinguishes between fact and opinion.

9.4 ☐ Finds it difficult to distinguish between fact and opinion.

9.5 ☐ Sometimes shows bias and makes ill-founded judgments.

9.6 ☐ Does not usually make objective judgments.

10.0   Using Evidence

10.1 ☐ Makes interpretations and predictions based on observed evidence.

10.2 ☐ Is prepared to look for explanations of observed evidence.

10.3 ☐ Makes accurate observations.

10.4 ☐ Has difficulty in making accurate observations.

10.5 ☐ Does not easily distinguish between relevant and irrelevant evidence.

10.6 ☐ Has difficulty in using evidence appropriately to support an interpretation or point of view.

11.0   **Visual Interpretation** (symbols, charts, tables, drawings)
11.1 ☐ Expresses complicated ideas in visual form.
11.2 ☐ Understands ideas represented in visual form.
11.3 ☐ Finds it difficult to understand ideas represented by symbols, charts, tables or drawings.
11.4 ☐ Understands everyday signs.
11.5 ☐ Has difficulty in understanding any form of visual display.

12.0   **Creative Skills**
12.1 ☐ Design work shows originality and appreciation of the potential of a number of different materials.
12.2 ☐ Is particularly interested in creative activities in a variety of media.
12.3 ☐ Design work is original and exciting but poor application spoils the quality of the final product.
12.4 ☐ Responds enthusiastically when guided towards creative activity but is not greatly interested in expressing own ideas.
12.5 ☐ Has shown only occasional interest in most creative activities.
12.6 ☐ Displays little interest in becoming involved in creative activity and his/her work lacks originality and imagination.
12.7 ☐ Attempts practical work conscientiously, but copies rather than creates.

13.0   **Manual Skills**
13.1 ☐ Works with dexterity and precision.
13.2 ☐ Consistently produces an acceptable standard of work.
13.3 ☐ With guidance works accurately.
13.4 ☐ Finds it difficult to produce accurate work manually.
13.5 ☐ Is rather clumsy and this is reflected in the low standard of work produced.

14.0   **Numerical Skills**
14.1 ☐ Consistently solves complex problems by a variety of methods.
14.2 ☐ Solves problems involving the use of decimals, fractions and percentages.
14.3 ☐ Copes successfully with those problems which can be solved by using calculations with whole numbers.
14.4 ☐ Recognizes and uses place value correctly.
14.5 ☐ Can solve problems requiring simple addition, subtraction or multiplication.
14.6 ☐ Requires help to solve accurately simple problems involving whole numbers.
14.7 ☐ Has considerable difficulty in working accurately with numbers even with assistance.

Chapter 7

The Training Materials Network

Nicholas Peacey

Introduction

The Training Materials Network was a three-year project funded by the European Social Fund (ESF) and the Department of Trade and Industry (DTI); it was undertaken by the Information Technology Consultancy Unit (ITCU) of the Notting Dale Technology Centre in 1984. The aims of the project were to develop and implement a communications system that would enable the exchange of learning materials between a group of Information Technology Centres (ITECs).

ITECs had been established in the early 1980s by the DTI as a response to the urgent need to train young people in IT. The original aims of the ITEC programme were threefold: to train young people in IT; to provide access to new technology to the local community; and to support the development of local enterprises. Because of funding pressures, training became the main, and in some cases the only, activity in most ITECs.

By 1984, 175 ITECs had been established. Each had its own organizational form and group of sponsors. Some were under local authority control, others were set up as limited companies with industrial sponsors, and some had charitable status. No formal system for coordinating the whole group of ITECs had been provided, and the only support that was made available to ITECs was the ITCU, a small unit based at the Notting Dale ITEC and funded by the DTI.

The Problem Space

At this time, there was no clear curriculum for Information Technology, and very little in the way of learning material was available. ITCU had previously produced some basic materials for the teaching of electronics and programming, and had begun to develop a syllabus for ITECs in collaboration with the City and Guilds Institute. However, it was evident that much more was needed, since the technology was changing rapidly, and new learning materials needed to be continually written to respond to these developments.

Inevitably, trainers in the ITECs had to write much of their own material, and because of the lack of coordination between ITECs, there was much duplication of effort. The resources simply did not exist to properly support the creation and distribution of the learning materials needed by ITECs.

It was as a response to these problems that the Training Materials Network aimed to develop a communications system which would allow a group of ITECs to collaborate on the production of learning materials, and then to exchange them electronically, thus helping to prevent the duplication of effort, and making a wider range of materials available to students than would otherwise have been possible.

This paper describes the design and implementation of the system. It also describes the social and technological contexts within which the project had to operate, and finally, provides an analysis of the successes and failures of the eventual system.

Specifying the System — Constraints

Several issues had to be considered in the design of the system. Some of these were technical, but most were social or philosophical. The project was constrained in that the network had to be implemented on machines that were already in existence in ITECs; more important, however, was the need to provide a system that gave ITECs a sense of ownership and control of the network. Only then would ITEC staff be prepared to contribute their own materials to the network as a whole. It was also important that high-quality materials could be delivered through the network, including pictures and diagrams. The system had to be easy to use, and decisions had to be made about whether students should have access to the network.

At that time, electronic communication services that were widely available, such as Prestel and BT Gold, were centralized. Prestel was perhaps best described as a large central library, and BT Gold as a large post office that required one to pick up one's mail — a 'poste restante' service.

The Training Materials Network could have adopted a centralized model by establishing a single, central computer to provide the service for ITECs. Using this model would have meant that all materials written by ITECs would have to be delivered to a central location by the participating ITECs and then indexed by the project team, before being made available to other ITECs.

There were several reasons why this 'poste restante' option was rejected:

1 control over the materials would be lost by the author;
2 sending the materials to a central location would involve authors in some expense;
3 larger-scale technology would be required to set up a centralized service;
4 the service would require continuing funding to survive, or would have to charge users to enable its continuation.

The alternative was to look at a distributed service, based in the premises of the participating ITECs. This would involve the creation of a number of small libraries of materials, one at each ITEC. Each 'library' would contain materials written by the staff at the ITEC, and would be indexed by them. However, the indexing structure would have first been agreed by all ITECs. All the indexes would be merged to form a global index of all the materials on the network, and a copy of the merged index would be kept at each site. In other words, it would be like a lot of local libraries including references to books at other libraries in their card indexes, with a note stating where the books were located. Students would have immediate access to the materials stored at their own ITEC, but would also be able to find out what materials existed elsewhere, and request a copy of the particular item to be sent to their ITEC.

This approach, while posing more technical difficulties, avoided the problems of the centralized option. Authors retained control over their own materials, since they were kept on their own machine at their premises; installing them in their 'library' did not cost anything; small-scale technology was adequate to setting up these small 'libraries'; and, most importantly, the service did not depend on a central organization and funding for its continued existence. With the former option, if the centre closed, the service ended; but with the latter option, any single ITEC could close but the network would continue to operate with the remaining ITECs.

The distributed option was therefore chosen. It should be noted that to the best of the project team's knowledge, such a distributed system had not been implemented previously.

In 1984, the most common computer in use in ITECs was the BBC micro. Many ITECs had purchased networks of BBCs as their training machines; the IBM PC had only just become available and was prohibitively expensive at that time.

An important thing in favour of the BBC as the target machine for the project was that a rather unique communications software package had just been written for it. The software was called the Communitel Viewdata System, and had been developed by another part of the Notting Dale Technology Centre. It subsequently formed the core of the Training Materials Network. Communitel enabled any BBC owner to create their own Prestel-type database, and then to make this information accessible to others by connecting their computer to a telephone socket via a modem. (Modems convert computer signals into sound and back again). Anyone with a computer and modem could then dial into the system and read the information 'online'.

It also included a 'telesoftware' feature that meant callers could transfer computer programs and other files from the 'host' system for use later. It was thus possible for BBC micros to be used to communicate directly with each other, allowing direct exchange of information and software without having to pass through a central service such as Prestel.

Communitel provided the basis of the technology that was needed to implement a distributed network, but more development was needed to enable a number of host systems to work easily together as a network, and also to allow the quick transfer of learning materials to be included on the hosts *in the form in which they were written*. These were not trivial problems.

Authoring Technology

Communitel emulated Prestel, in that their screen layouts were the same. The Prestel or viewdata screen allows for twenty-four lines of text, with forty characters on each line. Seven colours are allowed, as are some very crude 'mosaic graphics'. Clearly, this layout was not suitable for many learning materials. A more appropriate design would be to use an A4 layout that could include high-resolution diagrams.

It was straightforward to write a text-only learning module on a BBC word-processor, make it look reasonably nice by including printer commands in the file, and then convert it into a transferable file (telesoftware), thus allowing callers to download it over the phone. Including graphics in the materials was much more difficult for two reasons: firstly, no easy-to-use graphics editor existed for the BBC micro; and secondly, graphics files were much larger than text files, and took a long time to download, incurring heavy telephone charges for the caller.

It took nearly three years before this problem was properly resolved, and the project went down several blind alleys. By this time, the project team had acquired one of the early Apple Macintoshes, and it was immediately evident that high-quality materials could be easily produced using already existing Macintosh software, since it came with a good word-processor (MacWrite) and graphics editor (MacPaint). However, the project was already committed to BBCs as the delivery system for the materials, and there was no prospect of similar graphics software appearing on the BBC, because of its lack of power. The solution was to write software that helped the two machines to work together, as follows:

1 text and graphics files could be transferred from the Mac to the BBC via a serial port cable connecting the two machines;
2 the Macintosh graphics files were then converted into a form that would display on a BBC screen;
3 the graphics files were then 'compressed' so that they were much smaller and thus quicker to download;
4 the text and compressed graphics files were then combined to form the final learning unit as a single file, stored on the BBC.

These final files could then be converted to 'telesoftware', to be included on the Communitel host as files for exchange. They were quickly and cheaply down-loadable, and could be printed directly from a BBC micro.

Linking the Hosts

Whilst the Communitel software enabled ITECs to set up their own online host containing their learning materials, the problem of indexing remained. How would anyone know which ITEC had which materials?

To deal with this, the project team developed an index 'shell' which consisted of general topic categories. Each ITEC was given a copy of this shell, which they installed on their hosts. Every new learning unit was added to their copy of the shell by editing a small part of it as soon as the unit was installed, and a copy of this alteration was electronically sent to all the other ITECs.

Using the library metaphor, this meant that ITECs classified their materials using common categories; and every time they amended or added a card to their index, they posted copies of it to all the other ITECs. Software was written to make the amending of indexes as easy as possible, with the long-term aim of fully automating the process, so that the act of amending an index entry triggered a program that called up all the other hosts and amended their indexes as well.

Providing Access for Students

The final piece of the jigsaw was to provide easy access to all of the materials for students. This was achieved by writing a 'search' program that worked in the following way.

Students would log on to one of the BBCs at their ITEC. This would immediately present them with a menu of learning topics from which they could select a topic by pressing a single key. The next screen would give them a menu of all the learning materials on that topic that were available at all the ITECs.

They could select the unit they were interested in with a single key press, and would then be given a brief description of the learning unit. To print the unit, they would need to press a single function key, causing the BBC to find the learning unit, leaving the Viewdata indexing mode, and display it, either on the screen or on a printer. Pressing another key would then return them to the index, to the place they had just left, and they could then continue looking for other materials they might possibly need.

If the chosen unit was not stored locally, then selecting it would instead establish a telephone call to the ITEC where it was stored, find it, download it, and store it for later printing. The long-term aim was to make all of this as transparent as possible to the user, so that all that they would know was that they looked through an index, selected a learning unit, and got it. As it was, the software dialled the appropriate ITEC automatically, but the user then had to enter their name manually. A key press then took them directly to the place in the index where the desired unit was entered, and another key press downloaded the module. Yet another key logged them off the remote host and returned them to their local system.

The complete system took some three years of development, and was as automated as the technology would allow. At the end of the project a working system existed, but it was felt that this prototype needed to be rewritten for more powerful technology, allowing more automation and an easier interface for the authors.

Implementation

In parallel with the technological developments, the project team spent a great deal of time preparing the ground for the installation of the network. The success of the project would be measured by the materials it ultimately delivered, and there was pressure from the DTI to have some new materials available by the end of the first year. It was important to involve ITEC staff in producing new materials before the network became operational so that it would have some content as soon as it was launched. This required careful nurturing, since many ITEC supervisors came from an industrial background with little if any teacher training, and lacked the confidence to 'publish' their materials.

The team responded in two ways. A considerable part of the first two years was spent on writing learning materials centrally, which were installed on the ITCU host system; and a number of workshops were run for ITEC staff on how to access the ITCU host, download and print the materials. In this way a model was provided on which ITECs could base their own hosts.

Secondly, workshops were given on the writing of learning materials in order to raise the confidence of ITEC staff in their writing ability, and the quality of materials that they could produce. While these workshops were relatively successful, the team was too small to make a significant impact on the needs of what amounted to over a thousand ITEC trainers in every part of the UK.

This initial phase took some two years, during which much of the software was designed for the network. As time went by, changes in technology began to affect the potential viability of the project. By 1986, most ITECs had changed over to PCs as their main learning machines, and many had begun to dispose of their BBC micros. It was too late for the network software to be rewritten for the PC, and efforts were made to convince ITECs that it was worth retaining their BBCs as training material delivery machines.

The greatest problem that faced the project, however, was human rather than technical; ITECs were concerned that there was no guarantee that there would be an equitable exchange of materials, and that they might be contributing their own materials and getting nothing in return. At a time of reduced funding and increasing pressure on ITECs to become self-financing, some saw learning material development as a potential money generator, and were reluctant to enter into free exchange with other ITECs, since they represented a potential market. Strangely enough, financial pressures were making many ITECs more insular, rather than causing them to look to each other for support.

The last year of the project was spent in establishing the prototype network. Six ITECs were invited to become the members of the initial network, and were helped to set up Communitel hosts along with the software written specially for the project. Time was spent with the staff of these ITECs in discussing the content of the materials that they would contribute, and helping them with the design of these.

Because of the financial pressure on ITECs, it became clear that ITEC staff would have to be paid for their contributions if the prototype network was to have any chance of success. An application was made to the MSC's Learning Technology Unit to fund the six ITECs to write ten learning units each, to be installed on the network. The application was successful, the modules were specified and the work was shared amongst the ITECs. A year later the network was fully functional, consisting of seven online hosts, each with ten modules, with a coordinated index, and easy access to students.

During this year, while using the network to find materials was easy to use, some shortcomings became apparent. Installing a module and updating indexes took too much time. These needed to be automated, and needed more powerful technology for this to be practical. A further application was made to the Learning Technology Unit to rewrite the complete suite of software for more powerful micros (PCs and Archimedes), making the whole system fully automated and easier to use for authors. Regrettably, this application was not successful, and further funding has not yet been found.

The project officially closed in March 1989, and, six months later, only three of the original six ITECs were still running online hosts. No new materials since those paid for by the MSC have been added to the system.

Evaluation

In retrospect, the project was overambitious in its aims, given its limited resources: as well as the technical development, the team undertook a major task in providing training for ITEC supervisors, and also in building a sense of community between ITECs that had no formal structures connecting them. The original project submission had not recognized the scale of the work needed at the social and organizational level for the network to stand a chance of success.

Assumptions about the level of technological literacy among ITEC staff were also misfounded. Many supervisors in electronics sections never used computers to produce materials, preferring paper and pen. Most ITEC staff had not had the chance to debate the possibilities that were opened up by communications technology, and as a consequence had a limited view of what it was about. Perhaps most importantly, the project had not come from ITECs; it was based on an analysis of their problems and a radical strategy for solving them that had been made by the ITCU. Unfortunately, this lack of involvement led to some ITECs viewing the project as being idealistic and impractical, and, most significantly, they did not start out with a sense of ownership of the project.

And yet, the project did offer a process by which the urgent and changing needs of learners in ITECs could be addressed, and also provided a means by which ITECs could avoid duplicating each other's work; one would have expected that there would have been greater enthusiasm for a project which actively promoted and enabled the creation and exchange of materials that would not have otherwise been available.

It may be that part of the reason for the network not being as successful as it might have been was that what it was attempting to do was not fully understood by ITECs or funders. The project was driven by the belief that training and education in a rapidly changing modern world needs to have more variety than hitherto. As employment patterns change, more re-training is needed, usually in completely new areas. The IT industry is the best example of this, as it generates a rate of change faster than can be kept up with by most curriculum-setting bodies.

There has probably been a need for greater variety in education before now, simply because of the interests and aptitudes of the population. Up until now, however, this has been largely ignored by the education system, partly because industry has not required a varied workforce, and partly because offering wide choice in education has been difficult to organize.

Changes in technology have led to industry demanding a more flexible workforce, and limitations in education and training provision have become apparent. The various initiatives coming from the Training Agency amongst others have been attempts to respond to these demands, but have tended to focus on changing the content of education/training on offer, and the use of technology to deliver courses. This has not addressed the systemic issue of how continual changes in education/training can be managed, and how more variety can be generated and managed in education/training provision.

There are several strategies that can be and are being used to increase the variety of learning provision. Modular courses and open learning are but two of these. What is most needed, however, is a way of increasing the variety of learning materials on offer; and this means that more people need to be encouraged to write new materials, and ways of delivering these to those in need of them must be developed. The traditional structure of examining board to professional author to publisher to learner is not adequate for this task. It is too slow to respond to changes in learning need, and it offers too narrow a range of materials because of publishers' need for high volume sales.

The Training Materials Network offered a model that was a response to this problem. It encouraged teachers to become authors, and provided a means by which their materials could reach an audience beyond their own classroom. It also provided an indexing method that allowed the increased variety of materials to be tractable to users. Most importantly, it was based on synergy as the motivating force rather than profit. A teacher could contribute one module and get access to several in return, enhancing the choices they could offer in their teaching.

It is worrying that despite the apparent need for greater variety, there are trends in education that will lead to a restriction of choice, as with the National Curriculum, and that those who offer most hope in responding to the need for more variety find themselves held in low esteem, demoralized and with restrictive contracts. Teachers need to be given more time to participate in developing the curriculum and new materials; instead, they are being turned into functionaries.

This was certainly the case with ITEC staff during the life of the project. They had lengthy contact hours, little preparation time, and in many cases the future of their ITEC was under threat. None of this encouraged staff to spend time on writing materials, or even more time on installing their materials on an online host.

Nevertheless, it is felt that the basic strategy of the project was appropriate, as were the tools developed. However, because the technology was not powerful enough, these tools were too difficult and time-consuming to use.

Technology has developed rapidly since then, and a number of new software packages available now would make a similar project much more successful. If the project were to be repeated, or if someone else were to undertake a similar project, the following would be recommended:

1 find a group of teachers who are already writing good materials, and who are already swapping them with each other, or are keen to do so;
2 provide them with computer-based tools that make the job of producing these materials easier, and lead to better quality materials;
3 write software that allows these materials to be included in a database in the quickest and easiest way possible, preferably by pressing a single key;
4 make all the communications between institutions fully automatic, so that indexes can be updated without anyone having to do anything;
5 make sure that online communications are kept to an absolute minimum, to keep costs down;
6 automate communications as far as possible so that
    (a) participants' work takes place off-line
    (b) exchanges can take place overnight at off-peak rates;

7 provide a friendly user interface that will allow easy searching for materials for teachers and students alike.

It is felt that decentralized networks offer more scope in projects of this sort than any centralized system can. People need to communicate with their peers, and need to use technology over which they have a sense of control, both of which are better achieved with distributed systems. They need to be carefully designed, with participation from the users if at all possible in the design process.

Conclusion

The Training Materials Network sought to develop a technology-based strategy to enable the exchange of learning materials between ITECs, and was successful in implementing a communications network between them. Its impact was less than it could have been because of the context in which it had to operate, that of a demoralized and underfunded group of ITECs. At the outset, the project did not take sufficient cognizance of this; nor did it adequately involve the ITECs. Nevertheless, it provides a democratic and decentralized model for generating and distributing a wider range of learning materials than would otherwise be possible, by enabling teachers to write and publish materials.

At a time when curriculum reform has narrowed the range of options available for students, choice for learners can still be increased by providing a wide range of materials within each subject. This can be best achieved by collaboration between teachers in their development. The Training Materials Network enabled such collaboration, and so has relevance for all subject areas. It is hoped that the experiences had by the project will be learned from, and will provide useful information for other communications-based projects.

Chapter 8

Mapping the Offers: Databases of Special Educational Needs INSET

Oleg Liber

Until March 1990 I worked as INSET Coordinator at the ILEA Teachers' Centre for Special Education. With ILEA's demise I became coordinator of a project known as SENJIT, the Special Education Needs Joint Initiative for Training, based at the London University Institute of Education. SENJIT provides subscribing local authorities with Special Educational Needs in-service training (at the Institute and locally), publications and information. Most of the work described below was done between April 1989 and March 1990 at the Teachers' Centre.

A vast range of activities is available to teachers under the banner of special educational needs in-service training. Local Education Authorities provide their own. Institutes of Higher Education and Her Majesty's Inspectorate put on more. Disabilities may have one or more associated voluntary organizations pumping out still more; and then of course there are the private consultancies and more generalized associations (National Council for Special Education, National Association for Remedial Education) setting out their stalls. There has been no easily available comprehensive listing of this provision. Teachers have a hard time finding what they want.

If the teachers don't find the courses, the courses don't fill up. Resources are wasted; courses are cancelled. The impression is one of a market-place which bears little relevance to the sort of foresightful INSET planning now being developed by many institutions.

Any discussion of possible improvements in the situation must take into account four things:

1 a concept of the process by which in-service training needs are being met and should be met in the future;
2 a comprehensive picture of the INSET currently available in the field;
3 a comprehensive picture of which agencies are able to offer INSET;
4 the means of communication between INSET providers and planners within LEAs and institutions. This will frequently need to be at a very early stage to allow for sensible planning.

At the ILEA Teachers' Centre for Special Education we addressed these issues. What follows is an account of our work. We sought the help of Information

Technology. Sometimes we have been delighted with the outcome; on other occasions we have been disappointed.

There has in recent years been a significant shift in the process by which INSET needs are identified and attempts to meet them planned. Developments include:

- a move away from a belief in the individual's right to go on any course he/she feels like, regardless of the needs of the rest of the community/ institution, to a realization that corporate needs, and particularly corporate development plans, must be set in the balance;
- a realization that the planning of staff development in a context of corporate and individual need should take place far more frequently within institutions (colleges or schools) and less at LEA level;

and, as something of a countervailing force to those above,

- the Education Reform Act and the National Curriculum.

If the ERA had not come along, there might have been a far more steady shift to school-planned and school-delivered INSET than has been the case. But the changes in practice dictated by the Education Reform Act meant that both Institutes of Higher Education and Local Education Authorities were kept busy devising and running courses and conferences around this theme.

However, as the schools have domesticated the National Curriculum, the relationship between the institution-devised development plan and the agencies offering training from outside has again become a matter for sophisticated planning involving above all a need for those working in the institutions to know what is on offer.

The trend towards the devolution of training budgets within the move towards local financial management will hasten the schools' assumption of training responsibilities (though it should be noted that LEAs do retain the legal responsibility for INSET in their area). Further, it will make even more acute the need for consideration of the interface between external providers of training and individual institutions.

Very often teachers in the special educational needs field need specific training. The need to find the precise training package is particularly important. But the staff development tutor is faced with the maze of offers outlined above. We decided to work to provide a map of this complex field and to try various ways of making the map and further information available to teachers and their colleagues.

The Databases

Our ILEA colleagues working in the Advisory Team for SEN post-16 education had already had evidence of the demand for a booklet on courses available. We therefore felt it reasonable to make a start on our mapping of the special educational needs INSET on offer by devising a database of all the courses and conferences (all phases) notified to us by any organization. We included any non-award-bearing training event within reach of teachers in the south-east, without of course making judgements about quality. The database used was Dataease running on a 1MB RM Nimbus.

The compilation of such a database simplified the compilation of a parallel database of INSET providers: this in turn by use of the Dataease cross-referencing facility greatly speeded the entry of new data.

We thus had what amounted to the first map of SEN in-service training (short courses) in the south-east and, less comprehensively, elsewhere in the country. Furthermore, we could see exactly where the providers were and the sort of INSET they were offering.

We can therefore claim to have come some way towards providing a south-east regional answer to the questions implicit in points 2 and 3: we knew what was happening (except in the case of that provided by institutions for themselves) and we knew who was offering it. Thus far the technology served us well. Entering, listing and collating was straightforward. The material collected was made available to ILEA teachers in these forms:

- by full-page advertisements in ILEA News, the ILEA house newspaper, which went to every teacher in ILEA, and ceased production in March 1990;
- by termly booklets circulated to all institutions in ILEA and to many Further Education Colleges and Adult Education Institutes elsewhere;
- by individual contact by phone, letter or Campus 2000.

Advertisements

We know from the spate of enquiries after each advertisement that teachers read them. We know also that course providers were pleased with the publicity and extra participants attracted to their courses.

Booklets

The booklets were equally successful in attracting teachers to courses. But as they only appeared termly they dated quite quickly: course organizers do not work to termly cycles.

Telephone

We had many individual enquiries about the courses advertised, normally by telephone. We also found ourselves acting as a clearing-house for queries about long and award-bearing courses (not at present listed on the database).

Few individuals rang up to ask 'Find me a course on such and such an area' which is perhaps a little surprising. I believe that this is partly because choice of personal INSET still takes place on a window-shopping basis ('Let's see what's around'). As institutional and individual needs are integrated (through an appraisal system?) individuals will be encouraged to hunt down courses with a training need in mind.

We received, however, frequent phone enquiries from LEA managers in staff development seeking help with the design, funding or delivery of INSET. Direct online access to INSET providers might well help this group, though for a variety of reasons such developments have been a long time coming (see below).

Letter

Very few people wrote letters of enquiry, except about complex personal training problems involving long award-bearing courses or to book a place on a given course. Obviously writing a letter takes longer than making a phone call, but this cannot be the only reason teachers are less given to using this form of enquiry. I suspect that, rather like choosing a holiday, the decision to commit oneself to an advertised course is one to be made cautiously: no small ad, however well worded, will give you all information. Teachers like the speed of the telephone for deciding on the flavour or fit of a course: will it suit them?

Online

We never had an online enquiry about a course, despite regular advertisement of our numbers.

Information for the Databases

Information on courses came on paper, very frequently in the form of a batch mail-out from a teachers' centre or training institution. Less often we were informed by telephone. Information did not come on Campus 2000, though we were part of that system.

Courses in Schools or Colleges

There was of course one category of short non-award-bearing INSET which does not appear on the database. These were the institution-based INSET courses which run these days through the life of schools and colleges (often in clusters in the primary sector). At their best, these are well-planned and coherent with the Institutional Development Plans: at their worst, they are flung together at short notice with no relation to anything other than the fact that the Staff Development Tutor is trying to wear too many hats at the same time. In either case a link to INSET providers could help, whether the providers are in IHEs or LEAs.

For both types of INSET manager, at LEA or institutional level, we hoped to pioneer the development of a system which was less of a newspaper small ads system and more of an interactive network. We hoped that it would be possible using Campus 2000 to link into the offices of training managers and use technology to share ideas and activities. This did not happen. Some of the problems are with the sort of enterprise that Campus 2000 has become in the UK.

(i) It is an enthusiasts' system, rather similar to the world of the radio ham, or the truckers' short wave ('that's a 10–4 good buddy'). These worlds are normally male: how many women Campus 2000 users do you know?

(ii) It is apparently under-resourced in terms of staff to assist with creative developments to the system. We have tried hard to get satisfactory help with this.

(iii) The need to re-type input makes it a slow and therefore expensive way to move pre-written data around. Artwork is also a problem. It is therefore little used in the school or college office. A fax can do these things much quicker.

(iv) Where the system is in a school it is used in a teaching situation, normally set up by one of the aforementioned enthusiasts, and can be very successful. Whether more than one or two members of staff ever have anything to do with it must be debatable.

All of this is sad, because Campus 2000 or similar systems offer such wonderful potential for communication. A system could be envisaged in which, rather like the best sort of travel agent, the staff development tutor could not only book places on courses from the school office but, perhaps more importantly, could send out the clearest messages of what sort of staff development initiatives were needed and in what training activities the institution was involved. Other institutions could then make contact direct and share their ideas. IHEs would have a sounding-board for their plans and a ready way of finding out about institutional needs.

This is not, however, the situation, nor is it one which is likely to come to pass without further research and development, to say nothing of funding. The fact is that the strengths of online communication have not been clearly identified in the administrative field of education and training. It is not as a medium a lingua franca, like newsprint or the telephone; it is, at least in the UK, something esoteric. (Minitel in France is a very different phenomenon: available to and used by all without fuss, it is simply part of the furniture of office life. I note that the Republic of Ireland is now adopting the Minitel system. It appears that their planners, as with the French experience, have a very clear commitment to infrastructure development. The system will be offered at a low price in the first instance.)

Blame for this state of affairs should not be laid at the door of the introducers of Campus 2000 and similar systems. Our own work has convinced us that the whole business of communication within and between educational institutions has not been studied properly in the UK. Of course the literature on the cells of the structures, the classrooms and lecture halls, is extensive, and frequently immensely helpful. But the material communications systems (the bells?) that hold the cells together are hardly studied at all. Similarly the material communications systems that link the institution to the outside world appear to be both limited and profoundly hierarchical, and certainly make few appearances in the literature.

To summarize:

● nationally, the commitment to online facilities as a standard means of solving communications problem is weak;

- issues of communication between individual institutions and the outside world are little discussed.

So, it is hardly surprising that online communication is not effectively used in educational administration. We have so little evidence on what might be a good communication system and so few attempts to draw paradigms from other sectors that it is hard to say just how useful one of them could be. One might ask: is the telephone used effectively in educational administration? It is certainly used: but what constitutes effective use? Answering such questions demands study of the institutions at work, as well as a knowledge of the systems available.

Because of the success of the database we are maintaining and expanding it as the work of the Teachers' Centre is transferred to the London University Institute of Education. But we know there is much more to be done to create a responsive interactive system. Responsiveness and interaction are to be sought particularly when institutional time and other resources are at a premium. Teachers are intensely and rightly critical of training and staff development activities which they consider wasteful of their time. Communications systems could offer a way of assisting the proper identification of needs and thus help to avoid taking people away from their classes to courses they see as valueless.

We hope to see and be part of studies which will:

(a) examine institutional communications at work, focusing particularly on the needs of the staff development tutor;
(b) lead to action research within a small group of institutions within the development plan of a Local Education Authority.

It would be sad if the potential for online communication in the field of in-service training remains an untapped potential for much longer.

Chapter 9

Computing: An Ideal Occupation for Women?[1]

Peggy Newton and Eevi Beck

Introduction

Computing appears to be an ideal occupation for women. It is clean and modern and unlike engineering it evokes no images of dirty workshops or heavy lifting. It requires a careful approach and attention to detail — skills in which women excel (Linn, 1985). The work is often flexible and increasingly allows the possibility of working from home. Yet in recent years the proportion of women entering computing has dropped rapidly. Anecdotal evidence suggests that in the late 1950s and early 1960s almost half the programmers and systems analysts were women, whereas by the mid-1980s the figure had dropped to about one-fifth (Lockheed, 1985; Newton and Haslam, 1988). The trend is even more precipitous in the number of young women studying computer science at universities.[2] In 1977 women accounted for almost a quarter of university entrants in Computer Science in the UK, whereas ten years later women represented a bare 10 per cent of first-year students (Universities Statistical Record, 1988) (see figure 9.1 and table 9.1). A stark example of this phenomenon was reported by Southampton University which had 33 per cent women students on courses in 'Mathematics and Computing' and 'Computer Science' in 1978–1979 and no female students on either course by 1985–1986 (Lovegrove and Hall, 1987).

How can this trend be explained? One possibility is that the nature of computing has changed and that girls and women no longer have the intellectual abilities required for computing. However, this seems an unlikely explanation. It does not fit with the body of evidence suggesting a large overlap in the cognitive abilities between females and males (Maccoby and Jacklin, 1975). It also contradicts findings from a large survey of US schoolchildren suggesting that girls are superior to boys in several specific areas of programming (Anderson, 1987) and studies of children's cognitive abilities showing no gender differences in procedural thinking, which appears to be an important aspect of computer programming (Kiesler, Sproull and Eccles, 1985).

Another possible explanation is that women are turning away from scientific and technological subjects. However, university admission statistics do not support this interpretation. Between 1977 and 1987 there were increases in the proportion of women entering courses in physics, chemistry and engineering. In

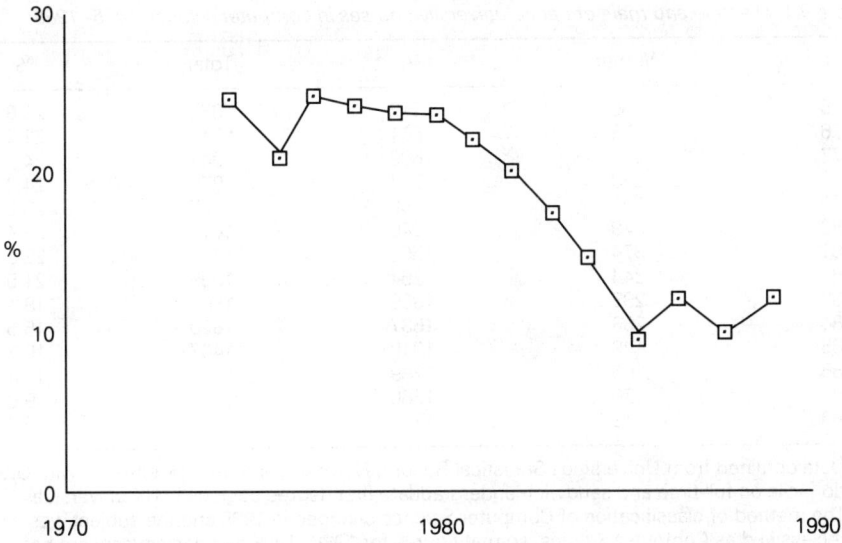

Figure 9.1   *Women as a percentage of UK undergraduates in Computer Science*

physics the proportion increased from 12 per cent to 17 per cent; in chemistry the figure rose from 21 per cent to 34 per cent; whereas in engineering there was over a threefold increase with the proportion rising from just over 3 per cent to over 11 per cent (Universities Statistical Record, 1988). Only the figure for mathematics was relatively constant, remaining at approximately 30 per cent over the ten-year period (see figure 9.2 and table 9.2).

A third possibility is that girls have been systematically discouraged from applying for courses in computing by their previous experience of computers and their perceptions of computing as a career. This strikes us as the most likely explanation and is the one which will be explored in this paper. Our focus is on the UK, since both the rate of decline and the low proportion of women in the industry are unparalleled in the United States, France and the Far East (*Business Week*, 1989; Virgo, 1989). We will argue that several trends have converged to make computing appear an unsuitable occupation for women in the UK. Although these trends are in a large sense societal, they have had a particularly potent effect on adolescent girls when they are faced with important career choices in secondary school. To understand this process it is necessary to consider computing in its cultural context and to examine changes in the image of computing.

Changes in Computing and its Image

The computing industry has changed rapidly in size, in organization and in its public image. Twenty years ago computing was an unknown field to most members of the public. Computers were the province of large organizations, and relatively few people had extensive experience of computers before entering the

Table 9.1   Female and male entrants: university courses in computer science 1975–1988[1]

Year	Women	Men	Total	%
1975	160	512	672	23.8
1976	158	561	719	22.0
1977	204	639	843	24.2
1978	233	737	970	24.0
1979	299	966	1265	23.6
1980	379	1240	1619	23.4
1981	374	1306	1680	22.3
1982	344	1254	1598	21.5
1983	295	1309	1604	18.4
1984	283	1537	1820	15.5
1985	149	1318	1467	10.2
1986	166	1289	1455	11.4
1987	170	1560	1730	9.8
1988	213	1781	1994	10.7

1 Data obtained from Universities Statistical Record. Numbers refer to new entrants with UK domicile on full-time and sandwich undergraduate first degree courses in UK universities. The method of classification of Computer Science changed in 1985 and the subject was reclassified as Computer Studies, so that figures for 1986–1988 and earlier years are not strictly comparable.

field. The popular view of computing was neutral and bureaucratic, tied up with large machines, punched cards and the notion that 'you're just a number'. This remote image contrasts sharply with today where small personal computers are featured in magazines, advertised on television and sold in high street shops. As we will argue below, the image of computing has become predominantly a male image — tied up with notions of 'boys' toys', of male power and of fascination with technology.

The Jargon Barrier

The growth of imagery associated with computers can be seen both in popular culture and in the development of a specialized computer culture. In the everyday world computers have acquired a wealth of cultural meanings, ranging from usage of terms like 'user-friendly' to notions of the antisocial world of the hacker and destructive computer games. The development of a specialized computer culture is seen clearly in the barrier of mysterious jargon: RAM, ROM, bit, byte, bus, ASCII, filestore, modem and so on. Kiesler, Sproull and Eccles (1985) argue that computing is far more than a set of skills. They suggest that it is a culture, '. . . embedded in a social system, consisting of shared values and norms, a special vocabulary and humour, status and prestige, ordering and differentiation of members from nonmembers' (p. 453). They contend that initial socialization to this culture is very important and that to become effective in using computers requires both social knowledge of the computer culture and technical knowledge of computers as machines. Although these cultural symbols of computing alienate some boys, their strong male associations with images of war and destruction are far more likely to alienate girls.

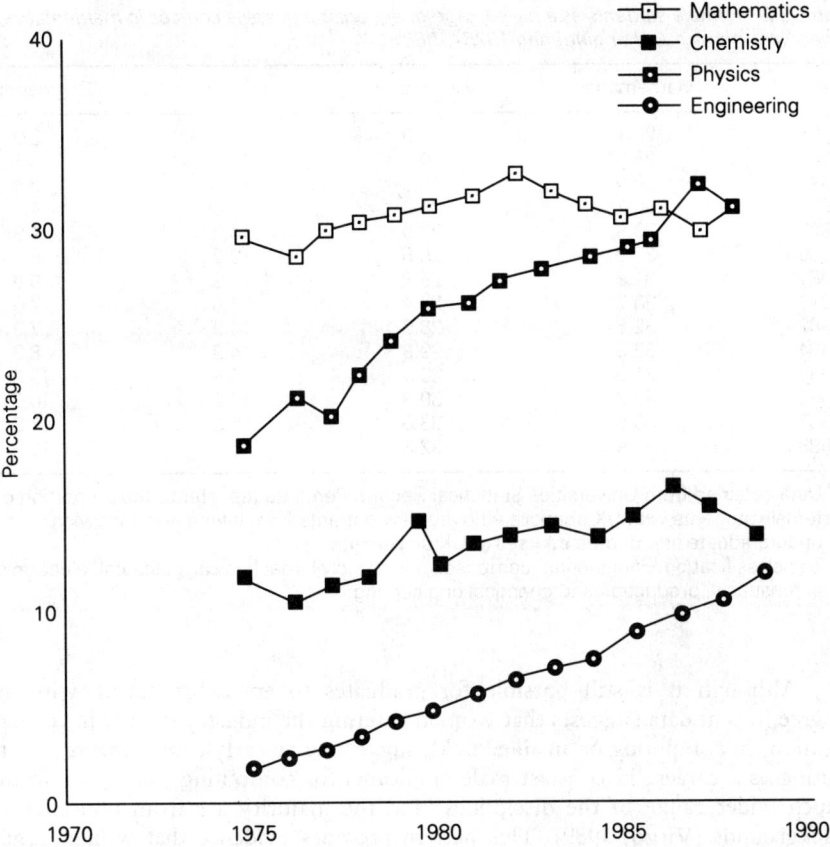

Figure 9.2   Women as a percentage of undergraduates at UK universities

Professionalization of Computing

With the growth of the computer industry, the knowledge associated with computing has been formalized. In the early days entrants required few, if any, formal qualifications. Many employers trained their own staff and relied on tests of programming aptitude to select their trainees.[3] Although some of these arrangements still pertain, there are now a large number of potential qualifications in computing, including GCSEs, 'A' levels, ONDs, HNDs, City and Guilds and degrees in Computer Science. As the field has expanded it has become increasingly professionalized with the British Computer Society being empowered to inspect educational institutions and set up formal standards. It may be argued that these changes have enhanced the status of the profession and are characteristic of most professional fields (Perkin, 1989; Johnson, 1972); however, they have served to limit the number of women and other non-traditional applicants by making entry to the field appear to be lengthy and circumscribed.

Table 9.2   Female students as a percentage of entrants: university courses in mathematics, chemistry, physics and engineering 1975–1988[1]

Year	Mathematics	Chemistry	Physics	Engineering[2]
1975	29.1	17.3	10.4	2.3
1976	28.2	20.7	10.0	3.1
1977	30.5	18.6	11.0	3.4
1978	30.7	21.0	11.6	4.2
1979	30.8	23.0	14.7	4.9
1980	31.2	25.6	13.2	5.2
1981	31.9	25.8	14.8	6.6
1982	33.7	27.4	14.6	7.6
1983	32.5	28.3	14.9	7.9
1984	32.3	29.8	14.2	8.3
1985	31.9	30.1	15.4	10.3
1986	32.2	30.3	17.2	10.7
1987	30.7	33.6	16.5	11.3
1988	31.9	32.3	15.7	12.2

1 Data obtained from Universities Statistical Record. Percentages refer to the proportion of female students with UK domicile who are new entrants for full-time and sandwich undergraduate first degree courses at UK universities.
2 The classification 'Engineering' comprises general, civil, mechanical, electrical, electronic, aeronautical, production and chemical engineering.

Although it is still possible for graduates to enter computing with any degree, recent data suggests that women entering the industry usually have qualifications in computing or an allied field, suggesting an early commitment to computing as a career. In contrast male applicants for computing jobs come from a much wider range of the disciplines, and the majority are from non-scientific backgrounds (Virgo, 1989). This pattern provides evidence that women regard computing as a 'man's world'. To enter this increasingly male-dominated field they feel the need for the record of achievement and feelings of confidence provided by formal qualifications, whereas men are likely to assume that they are naturally 'good at computers.'

How have computers become so clearly a male preserve? Some of the forces which contributed to the gendering of computing clearly reflect the wider cultural influences already discussed; however, we will argue that one of the most important events influencing young women during that time was the introduction of computers in secondary schools. To understand the basis for this statement it is necessary to look at how and why computers were introduced in schools in the UK.

Computers in Secondary Schools

Most schools acquired computers under the Micros in Schools Scheme, which began in secondary schools in 1980. Sponsored by the Department of Trade and Industry, the Scheme was extended to primary schools in 1982 with goal of a 'micro in every school' (EOC, 1983). This goal was largely achieved in secondary schools by 1984 when 98 per cent of schools reported having at least one microcomputer (BBC, 1985). Although the programme was publicized as an educational reform and was accompanied by the DES-sponsored Micro-electronics Education Project (MEP), the programme had clear commercial and industrial aims. It can be argued that the Scheme was more concerned with supporting the ailing British computer industry and in providing favourable publicity for the sponsoring Department than in producing meaningful educational change. Certainly the Scheme has been repeatedly criticized for being too rapid and for having neglected many of the educational implications of introducing computers. In their evaluation of the Scheme, the Centre for Applied Research in Education noted that 'it was widely welcomed as an enabling measure, but widely criticized as rushed, ill thought out and coercive' (CARE, 1988).

Perhaps the most serious problem with the introduction of computers, particularly in mixed schools, was one of access.[4] In 1986 the average number of computers per secondary school was nine, and there was wide variability between schools (CARE, 1988; Carter, 1987). In a survey of forty-three schools in Greater Manchester conducted in 1985, Carter (1987) found that the child: computer ratio ranged from 1:85 to 1:124. One survey found that the average time each pupil was expected to spend using a computer was 5.3 hours per term and that many pupils had no contact at all (Carter, 1987). An examination of policies for allocating the use of computers in mixed secondary schools suggests that girls are far more likely than boys to miss out on experience with computers. This can be attributed both to the physical and the social location of computers within schools.

Location of Computers

The decision to introduce computers in secondary schools first rather than primary schools had the effect of producing clear associations with particular subject areas. Computers were most likely to be located in departments of mathematics or Computer Studies, thus linking their usage with mathematics and science. This subject link was particularly unfortunate for girls, since they are less likely than boys to have positive attitudes towards science and mathematics (Kelly, 1981; APU, 1981, cited by Culley, 1986, p. 22). The emphasis on science and mathematics was also reflected clearly in the pattern of teachers receiving training courses in computing and in the educational software currently available for micros. Under the Microelectronics Education Project teachers of mathematics were the most likely to be trained, followed by science teachers, Computer Studies teachers and geography teachers (BBC, 1985). Not surprisingly, male teachers were more likely than female teachers to be in charge of computing, thus serving to reinforce the masculine image of computing and to provide both formal and informal barriers to girls studying computing. The problem was (and continues to be) exacerbated by the shortage of computers and by the attitudes of teachers responsible for them.[5]

Teachers' Attitudes

Carter (1987) found that female and male teachers differed sharply in their attitudes towards how computers should be used in schools, how computers should be allocated and how female teachers might serve as role models for female pupils. In a survey of fifty-four women and seventy-eight men in charge of computing, he found that female teachers tended to have egalitarian views, believing that computers could be used to teach any subject and that they should be available to all pupils. They also felt that their personal involvement in computing would have a positive effect on girls' attitudes towards mathematics, science and technology. Male teachers saw this effect as much more limited and as being confined primarily to attitudes towards computing. In addition, male teachers had more elitist views, holding that priority for computers should be given to pupils of high ability, particularly boys with an interest in mathematics and science. They also felt that computers were best used in the teaching of mathematics and science. These findings substantiate other research on teachers' attitudes suggesting that female teachers are more likely to hold egalitarian attitudes towards gender roles, are more likely to be aware of the needs of female pupils and are more likely to favour 'positive action' measures which will encourage girls to participate in non-traditional areas (Pratt, 1985; Kelly *et al.*, 1985).

Teachers' attitudes are also reflected in policies for computer clubs and access to computers outside of lessons. As described by Culley (in this volume), boys tend to monopolize computers in computer clubs and establish a strongly male culture which is derogatory towards girls. This problem is often exacerbated by a shortage of computers in the school, so that girls find that the only time they can use computers for their homework is during computer club time. Although Culley (1986) found a few schools who reserved some computer club time for 'girls-only', this practice appears relatively uncommon. In our own sample of girls from schools in Greater Manchester none of the girls reported 'girls-only' sessions, and informal discussions with teachers in several schools suggested that most teachers felt that such a policy would be highly undesirable. Thus many girls studying computing are faced with the problem of gaining access to machines and putting up with the uncomfortable atmosphere created by the boys. Although some of them may have computers at home, it has been repeatedly shown that parents are much more willing to buy computers for their sons than for their daughters (Culley, 1986). And even when there is a suitable home computer, girls may have to challenge their fathers or brothers to gain access to the machine. In the face of these disadvantages, it is not surprising that many girls give up on computing and label the field as 'male territory'. These attitudes are seen clearly in our own work on schoolgirls' attitudes towards a career in computing.

Perceptions of Computing as a Career

Our data is based on a sample of 143 female fifth-formers who attended an open day on computing as a career at the University of Manchester in the summer of 1988. These girls represented forty-eight schools, eleven of which were single-sex and thirty-seven mixed. All were intending to enter a degree course at a university or polytechnic. The sample cannot be seen as representative of schoolgirls and is likely to include a relatively high proportion of computer enthusiasts and girls studying science. However, it provides a useful sample of girls with the academic background necessary to apply for polytechnic and university courses in computing.[6] Every girl in the sample had studied mathematics at GCSE and 72 per cent had studied physics at GCSE; 31 per cent were studying computing. However, when the figure is corrected to include only schools where computing or Information Technology was available as an examination option, the proportion rises to 65 per cent. These statistics underline the strong scientific and technological interests of girls in this sample.

Computing as an Option

Information on the availability of computing or Information Technology as an option at GCSE could be obtained from forty out of the forty-eight schools in the sample. Twenty-eight offered computing; however, this figure obscures dramatic differences between mixed and single-sex schools with 86 per cent of mixed schools but only 27 per cent of girls' schools offering computing or Information Technology to their pupils. This difference is highly significant (Chi squared = 113.38, p < .0001). Half of the girls' schools not offering computing were independent schools and half were state schools. Without a larger sample and further information explanations for this difference must remain speculative. However, two hypotheses merit further investigation. One suggests that computing is seen as a vocational subject and not 'properly academic'; the other suggests that computing is perceived by the school and/or by parents as a 'boys' subject' and as not necessary for girls.

Paradoxically, although computing was often not available to girls in single-sex schools, girls were significantly more likely to study computing if they attended single-sex schools than if they attended mixed schools. All girls attending single-sex schools which offered computing as an examination option were studying it (N = 9). In contrast, 63 per cent of girls in mixed schools were studying computing when it was available as an option. This difference is highly significant (Chi squared = 40.3, p < .0001). Because the numbers are small and may reflect a selection bias, interpretation of this data must remain cautious. However, the pattern is similar to observations of physics in a study carried out by the HMI in the early 1970s. They found that although girls' schools were significantly less likely to offer physics as an option, girls attending single-sex schools offering physics were much more likely to study it than girls in mixed schools (DES, 1975). In both subjects, girls in mixed schools are likely to feel uncomfortable in male-dominated classrooms and may need an extra measure of commitment and determination to put up with the 'hassle' and often overt or covert discrimination they experience. In computing, girls face the added difficulty of gaining access to a machine and finding sufficient time to do justice to the subject.

We asked the girls to respond to a checklist of reasons to explain why they had studied computing. Their responses indicated that they perceived computer skills as extremely important for employment, and that they recognized their growing presence in society: 'Computers are becoming very important in society' (endorsed by 85 per cent); 'Studying computing improves job prospects' (74 per cent); and 'I want to get a job working with computers' (62 per cent). Also important was an interest in and enjoyment of computing: 'I am very interested in computers and new technology' (83 per cent); 'I enjoy using my computer at

Table 9.3 Reasons for studying computing[1]

Reason	N	%
Computers are becoming very important in society	40	85.1
I am very interested in computers and new technology	39	83.0
Studying computing improves job prospects	35	74.5
I want to get a job working with computers	29	61.7
I enjoy using my computer at home	24	51.1
I wanted to learn more about writing programs	24	51.1
I enjoyed studying computers in the third year	11	23.4
I like playing computer games	8	17.0
My parents advised me to do it	7	14.9
My teachers advised me to do it	6	12.8
Other positive reasons	6	12.8
I didn't like the other options available to me	4	8.5

1 Sample based on responses of 47 fifth-form girls studying Computer Studies at GCSE who
  attended an open day on careers in computing.

home' (51 per cent) and 'I wanted to learn more about writing programs' (51 per cent). Much less important in their reasons for studying computing were previous experience of computing at school or parents' or teachers' advice. Table 9.3 shows a complete list of reasons and responses.

Studying computing for GCSE was strongly related to intention to study computer science at university (Chi squared = 60.0, 1 df, p < .0001). This analysis strongly suggests that young women see experience with computing as necessary before they opt for it as a degree subject. It fits with previous data one of us has collected on young women becoming technicians in engineering, suggesting that previous experience with some aspect of the subject was highly valued (Newton and Brocklesby, 1982). Such prior experience is useful in any degree or career choice, but it appears to be particularly important when opting for a non-traditional and strongly male-dominated field. Young women need to be convinced that they like the subject and that they are good at it. They are also concerned about embarking on a course where they assume that the young men will have had much more previous experience with computers than themselves. However, their degree and career decisions are also influenced by their perception of computing as a career.

Computing as a Career

As part of our survey, we asked young women what factors they saw as most important in making a career choice and which ones they expected to find in computing as a career.[7] Their responses suggested that they were most concerned about a job which made full use of their abilities and which also offered opportunities for promotion and paid well. They also valued highly the opportunity to make their own decisions. (See table 9.4.) When these characteristics are compared with the ones that they expected computing to offer, there are some striking discrepancies. Whilst 'making full use of my abilities' ranked first in the list of 'most important' job characteristics, it ranked as thirteenth on the factors expected in computing. Another large discrepancy was in 'involvement with new

Table 9.4   Most important factors in career choice[1]

Factor	N	%
Makes full use of my abilities	46	61
Opportunity for promotion	37	49
Good pay	26	34
Able to make my own decisions	19	25
A career which will last all my life	16	21
Contributes to society	16	21
Working with people	15	20
Opportunity to travel	14	18
Security	12	16
A career which fits in with family commitments	9	12
High status	7	9
Working in a team	5	7
Close involvement with new developments in technology	5	7
Working on my own	0	0

1 Based on the responses of 76 fifth-form girls attending an open day on careers in computing. Respondents were asked to indicate the three most important factors in choosing a career.

Table 9.5   Factors expected in computing[1]

Factor	N	%
Close involvement with new developments in technology	55	72
Opportunity for promotion	52	68
Working in a team	45	59
Good pay	43	57
A career which fits in with family commitments	39	51
Contributes to society	38	50
Working with people	34	45
Working on my own	33	43
A career which will last all my life	32	42
Security	29	38
High status	28	37
Able to make my own decisions	28	37
Makes full use of my abilities	27	36
Opportunity to travel	25	33

1 Based on the responses of 76 fifth-form girls attending an open day on careers in computing. Respondents were asked to indicate which factors they expected to find in a career in computing.

developments in technology'. Not surprisingly this item was ranked as most characteristic of computing, but it was twelfth on the list of important factors in making a career choice. A further area of mismatch was in the opportunity to make one's own decisions. This was highly rated (no. 4) in terms of career characteristics but was seen as quite uncharacteristic of computing (no. 11). Teamwork was also an area where important career characteristics were discrepant with those in computing. 'Working in a team' was seen as highly characteristic of computing, ranking third, and yet it was considered relatively unimportant by these respondents with a rank of 12 (see tables 9.4–9.6).

Table 9.6   Comparison between rankings: Most important factors in career choice and factors expected in computing[1]

Factor	Most Important in Career	Expected in Computing
	Rank	Rank
Makes full use of my abilities	1	13
Opportunity for promotion	2	2
Good pay	3	4
Able to make my own decisions	4	11
A career which will last all my life	5	9
Contributes to society	5	6
Working with people	7	7
Opportunity to travel	8	14
Security	9	10
A career which fits in with family commitments	10	5
High status	11	11
Working in a team	12	3
Close involvement with new developments in technology	12	1
Working on my own	14	8

1 Based on responses of 76 fifth-form girls attending an open day in computing. Rankings are based on data presented in tables 9.4 and 9.5.

These findings suggest that these schoolgirls were generally pleased with the material aspects of computing, e.g. pay and promotion, but were seriously concerned about its intrinsic rewards. They did not see it as making full use of their talents and they were not attracted by its emphasis on new advancements in technology. They also had some disquiet about styles of working. They would like to be in a position to make their own decisions and yet they perceived it as an industry based on teamwork. Some of this response may be stimulated by the girls in mixed schools who had to fight for access to machines and who may have wondered how comfortable they would be in a predominantly male team. Their experience in dealing with males over computers are seen clearly in their comments about why girls don't go into computing.

Why Girls Don't Go into Computing

As a final section on the questionnaire, we asked girls in our sample, 'Over the past five years, many fewer girls and women have been going into computing. In your opinion, what sort of things put girls off computing?' We found that their most frequent response concerned the male domination of computing. They saw computing as a 'man's world' where girls and women were not welcome:

It's a man's world — more the kind of thing for boys.

A lot of boys go into computing.

(A) computer is boys' equipment.

A salient feature of this part of a 'man's world' was that boys took over; they pushed girls out of the way and they bragged about their knowledge:

Domineering boys who seem to take over and show off.

Boys who think they know a lot more about computers.

Boys who know everything.

[We get] shoved around by boys at school so rarely get access.

Boys think they know everything; [they] push girls to the side.

Another aspect of boys' claiming superior knowledge was their using it (or assuming it) to put girls down and belittle their knowledge. This clearly made some girls feel as if they didn't want to work in an environment where this would happen routinely:

[I would] not like working in an environment where men dominate and [I do] not like being put down.

If girls make mistakes, boys make fun of them.

Fear of being shown up in front of the men.

They were also uncertain about how clever a person needed to be to go into computing. Some of their comments reflected lack of knowledge about the field and the available jobs. For example, some girls believed that anyone going into computing needed to be a near genius; others thought the job was boring and menial and equated computing with word-processing. There seemed to be little room for anyone between the two extremes:

It's difficult and complicated . . . you feel you need to be a genius.

The idea of technology puts many off because it can sound so daunting and hard.

It's boring and tedious, especially word-processing.

Many girls were put off by what they saw as a separate and almost alien world. One girl described it as '. . . the mysterious aura surrounding the world of computers'; others complained of the language and terminology:

Bewildered by all the equipment, disk-drives, modems, etc.

Fancy code names and logos put girls off.

Strange language.

Another frequently voiced concern was fear of the machine or a fear of making mistakes:

Fear of machines or making mistakes.

Fear they will break the computer if they key something wrong with it.

Fear their programs will ruin the system, so they'll be shown up in front of the men.

Girls were also very critical of the way computing was presented at school and of the shortage of machines. Several complained that they were not encouraged to do computing as they were to do other subjects. One girl described how more effort went into encouraging girls to participate in the Harvest Festival than in encouraging girls to learn about computers.

Girls are not encouraged.

Girls don't have as much contact as boys.

[They] don't know much about it.

Very little information.

These comments highlight the role of the school in creating and reinforcing subject and gender stereotypes. In single-sex schools girls often do not have the opportunity to study computing and the subject may be looked down upon and devalued. In mixed schools girls have to compete with boys for the machines and are frequently forced to endure male ridicule and put-downs. There are usually relatively few machines and these are often outdated and subject to breakdowns. Knowledge about computers is often shared by relatively few teachers and their information about computing as a career is often limited.

What Can Be Done?

Schoolgirls are quite clearly rejecting computing as a career and this trend is likely to persist unless there is 'positive action' in schools, in higher education and in industry. Such positive action will involve serious changes in the image of computing, in access to computers and in attitudes towards women in computing. Although each of these issues is considered separately they are clearly interrelated.

Beyond the Glossy Brochure

Some of the failure to attract women is clearly a failure in marketing and in not presenting an image of the field which is attractive to women. As in attempts to attract women to engineering, material needs to be targeted at women. Currently much of the literature about computing emphasizes advances in new technology, images of being at the 'leading edge' — at the 'forefront of technology'. Women are rarely shown and most often appear as decorative sexual objects or as silly brainless creatures — incapable of understanding anything about computers.

Changing these images will be difficult because many of the present images are deeply embedded in computer culture. However, a first step must involve finding new images of women working with computers. They should show the human side of computing and demonstrate the variety of applications of computers. Women already in computing who can serve as role models must be found. These women should be carefully chosen for their communication skills and for the image which they present to young women.

Access to Computers

One of the biggest barriers to women's participation in computing is simply one of access to computers. In mixed schools girls need to be guaranteed access to computers and this probably has to be done formally through 'girls-only' sessions for pupils studying computing and 'girls-only' sessions for computer clubs. As noted above, such sessions are rare and require committed teachers to establish them and maintain them. Research on teachers' attitudes towards equal opportunities suggests that such measures are likely to be strongly resisted by many teachers and pupils (Pratt, 1985; Kelly *et al.*, 1985). However, until computers are much more widely available in schools, there need to be formal arrangements which provide girls with entitlement to computers and ensure that they can use them without being hassled by boys.

Computer Studies and Information Technology are frequently seen as unnecessary for the further study of computing. However, our research suggests that these subjects are far more important for girls than for boys. It is here that girls gain confidence in using computers and discover that they have the ability and the interest to proceed. This confidence factor is crucial if they are to enter higher education on an equal footing with their male counterparts.

Attitudes towards Women

It may be argued that the highly gendered environment of the mixed secondary school is a microcosm of the wider world of industry where women are often not welcome. The computing industry often defends its sexism by arguing that it is a young industry and traditional gender attitudes are not entrenched. However, information on the position of women in the industry provides little cause for complacency. A survey by *Computer Economics* in 1986 found that women represented 95 per cent of data preparation staff, 12 per cent of programmers and 2 per cent of data processing managers. At higher management levels women are even more poorly represented. One study of data processing management found 2.4 per cent of board directors were women and only 4.6 per cent of women classify themselves as department managers (cited in Lawrence, 1989). Although women are becoming better represented at senior management levels in business and finance, particularly in the United States, the high-technology world of computing is widely acknowledged to be a very difficult industry for women who want advancement. Furthermore several studies have shown that although women and men enter the industry at comparable levels, women earn 25 per cent less than men with 'similar experience' ten years after university (*Business Week*, 1989).

Towards the Future

Both the academic world and industry need to look very seriously at their current practice. As the field has grown and acquired status and prestige it has become more exclusively male. The bold, hard 'high-tech' image persists, but much of computing is about communication, about the interface between people and computers, about organizing information, and about devising new ways to work. If these images are projected, more women may consider computing as a career. But for any real change to occur, there is a need for computing to take women far more seriously and to demonstrate a real commitment to providing lifelong careers for women. It must be more flexible in how it selects people for jobs and courses, and it should review and validate its selection criteria, especially its strict age barriers. As part of this exercise it needs to consider a variety of styles of working, as well as the much-vaunted team approach. The women it wishes to attract want far more than surface glamour; they want pay, they want promotion and they want challenge — a career which will make full use of their abilities.

Notes

1   This paper is a much expanded version of a chapter in *Women at Work*, edited by Jenny Firth-Cozens and Michael West and published in 1990 by Open University Press.
2   There is a similar trend in polytechnics (Connor and Pearson, 1986). However, published information for the polytechnics is based on new graduates, rather than on new entrants. Although we have focused on university statistics, my remarks are also intended to apply to the polytechnic sector.
3   Computer aptitude tests have been poorly validated and have been criticized for their male bias. Most employers continue to use them as an additional selection device even when applicants have relevant qualifications in computing, thus providing an additional barrier for female candidates.
4   We have focused on mixed schools in this discussion, since they are the more common form of secondary schooling in the UK and represent a potent environment for gender stereotyping.
5   Although this situation is improving in some schools with the introduction of CAC (computers across the curriculum), these changes are often slow and may be hampered by lack of appropriate resources and training for teachers. In addition, pupils are likely to see the computing which is taught as an examination subject as 'real computing' and not value the computing they have learned in other subjects.
6   Invitations to attend the open day were sent to all secondary schools in Greater Manchester and a large number of schools in Cheshire and Lancashire with 274 schools receiving invitations. However, interest in the day varied widely between schools, so that the sample of girls attending is not representative. Casual inspection suggests that both independent girls' schools and church-affiliated schools

were overrepresented in the sample and that mixed comprehensive schools were underrepresented. Schools also differed in their strategies for selecting participants for the open day. Some schools asked for volunteers, whereas others appear to have selected girls who were studying science subjects and or computing.

7 Respondents were asked to rate each of the fourteen items in table 9.4 on a seven-point scale, ranging from 'Very important' to 'unimportant'. They were also asked to select the three items which were 'most important' and to list those items which they expected to find in computing. Because not all respondents answered all parts of the questionnaire, this analysis is based on the replies of 76 subjects. The comparisons reported are based on the analysis of respondents' choice of the three most important factors in their career choice and the factors which they expected to find in computing.

References

ANDERSON, R.E. (1987) 'Females surpass males in computer problem solving: findings from the Minnesota Computer Literacy assessment', *Journal of Educational Computing Research*, 31(1), pp. 39–51.

ASSESSMENT OF PERFORMANCE UNIT (1981) *Mathematical Development*, Primary Survey Report No. 2, HMSO.

BBC EDUCATIONAL BROADCASTING SERVICES RESEARCH UNIT (1985) *Microcomputers in Secondary Schools* (unpublished report summarized in DES Press Notice 14/85, January).

BUSINESS WEEK (1989) 'The women who are scaling high tech's new heights', 28 August, US publication, pp. 86–9.

CARE (1988) *DTI Micros in Schools Support 1981–1984: An Independent Evaluation. Executive Summary and Recommendations*, Norwich, UEA, CARE.

CARTER, K. (1987) unpublished data, Huddersfield Polytechnic.

COMPUTER ECONOMICS (1986) survey cited by COWIE (1988).

CONNOR, H. and PEARSON, R. (1986) *Information Technology Manpower in the 1990s*. Brighton, Institute of Manpower Studies.

COWIE, A. (1988) 'Screen prejudice', *Guardian*, 25 February.

CULLEY, L. (1986) *Gender Differences and Computing in Secondary Schools*, Department of Education, Loughborough University of Technology.

DEPARTMENT OF EDUCATION AND SCIENCE (1975) *Curricular Differences for Boys and Girls. Education Survey 21*, London, HMSO.

ELSE, L. (1985) 'Dp jobs survey; women lose out in pay and status', *Computing*, 13 June, p. 22. Cited by Culley (1986).

EOC/LONDON BOROUGH OF CROYDON (1983) *Information Technology in Schools: Guidelines for Good Practice for Teachers of IT*.

JOHNSON, T.J. (1972) *Professions and Power*, London, Macmillan.

KELLY, A. (1981) *The Missing Half: Girls and Science Education*, Manchester University Press.

KELLY, A., BALDRY, A., BOLTON, E., EDWARDS, S., EMERY, J., LEVIN, C., SMITH, S. and WILLIS, M. (1985) 'Traditionalists and trendies: teachers' attitudes to educational issues', *British Educational Research Journal*, 11(2), pp. 91–104.

KIESLER, S., SPROULL, L. and ECCLES, J.S. (1985) 'Pool halls, chips and war games: women in the culture of computing', *Psychology of Women Quarterly*, 9(4), pp. 451–62.

LAWRENCE, J. (1989) 'Missing the underused Ms', *Guardian*, 31 August.

LINN, M.C. (1985) 'Gender equity in computer learning environments', *Computers and the Social Sciences*, 1(1), pp. 19–27.

LOCKHEED, M. (Ed.) (1985) 'Introduction: Women, Girls and Computers', *Sex Roles*, 13(3/4) (Special Issue) (and whole issue).

LOVEGROVE, G. and HALL, W. (1987) 'Where have all the girls gone?', *University Computing*, 9, pp. 207–10.

MACCOBY, E. and JACKLIN, C. (1975) *The Psychology of Sex Roles*, Stanford, Stanford University Press.

NEWTON, P. and BROCKLESBY, J. (1982) *Getting on in Engineering. Becoming a Woman Technician*. Final Report to the EITB and EOC SSRC Panel on Women and Underachievement. Huddersfield Polytechnic.

NEWTON, P. and HASLAM, S. (1988) 'Girls and computers in secondary school: a system failure?', paper presented at the British Psychological Society Annual Conference, University of Leeds, April.

PERKIN, H. (1989) *The Rise of Professional Society: England since 1880*, Routledge.

PRATT, J. (1985) 'The attitudes of teachers', in WHYTE, J., DEEM, R., KANT, L. and CRUICKSHANK, M. (Eds) *Girl Friendly Schooling*, London, Methuen.

UNIVERSITIES STATISTICAL RECORD (1988) personal communication.

VIRGO, P. (Ed.) (1989) *The Report of the 'Women into Information Technology' Campaign Feasibility Study*, ICL (available from IT Strategy Services, 2 Eastbourne Avenue, London).

Chapter 10

Gender Equity and Computing in Secondary Schools: Issues and Strategies for Teachers

Lorraine Culley

Introduction

It is a matter of grave concern that our culture is defining computers as pre-eminently male machines. Despite the fact that in everyday life computers are becoming ubiquitous, the use of the computer in education seems to be following the traditional lines of gender bias in society. The present situation raises distinctly familiar questions of equity in terms of access to and use of technology. While girls and boys might show a similar appreciation of the significance computers might have for their personal futures, boys tend to be more positively disposed than girls towards computers, are more likely than girls to take optional computer courses in school, to report more frequent home use of computers, and tend to dominate the limited computer resources that are available in school. (Hoyles, 1988, p. 1)

In 1985 almost three times as many boys as girls were entered for GCE 'O' level Computer Studies and nearly five times as many boys as girls were candidates for 'A' level Computer Science. Applications from women to enter Computer Science departments of British universities are also very low. The proportion of female applicants fell from 28.2 per cent in 1978 to 13.2 per cent in 1986 (Hoyles, 1988). Although many women work with computers, they are heavily concentrated in the low-status and low-paid jobs (Simons 1981; Else, 1985).

This chapter discusses some of the findings of a research project which examined gender differences in computing in secondary schools.[1] The research identified a complex array of influences on girls' participation in school computing, and several impediments to greater equality between girls and boys in computer use. These impediments were found both in the structural organization of school computing and in pedagogic practices. However, as Hoyles (1988) has argued, gender differences in attitude to and competence with computers are neither inevitable nor immutable. This chapter outlines a set of strategies which schools and teachers could adopt to raise the level of girls' participation in computing activities.

Table 10.1 Male and female teachers as a percentage of teachers of Computer Studies (645 teachers) by school type in 238 schools

School Type	percentage of female teachers	percentage of male teachers
Mixed-sex	19	81
Girls-only	60	40
Boys-only	18	82

Gender and the Organization of School Computing

A study of school computing carried out by a group of teachers in Croydon (EOC, 1983) concluded that although many girls had a reasonably favourable attitude to computers, in some schools the computer was perceived as a 'machine for men and boys' from which many girls had become disaffected. The Croydon report suggested that the greater reluctance of girls to choose Computer Studies options and to engage in other kinds of school computing to the same extent as boys, may be a result of a perceived link between computing and mathematics. Although girls perform well in mathematics (Walkerdine *et al.*, 1989) they are less confident in their ability than boys. An APU survey (APU, 1981) found that there was a lack of mathematical self-confidence among girls as early as 11 years of age. Girls are more likely to attribute their success to effort and luck and their failure to lack of ability, while boys are more likely to attribute success to ability and failure to lack of effort.[2]

If there is a perceived link between computing and mathematics, this may affect girls' confidence in approaching computing. This is not the only factor which might affect girls' participation in computing at school, but it may be of some significance. In my research I found several features of school computing which engendered a link between computing and mathematics and enhanced the image of computing as a masculine domain.

In most British schools, the prime movers for computing came from the cohort of mathematics or science teachers. Initially, computer expertise was largely limited to a few such individuals who became responsible for coordinating computing activities. Most of the maths and science teachers who were in the first wave of computing in schools were male. Although there is now another cohort of users in schools, the computing specialists have often maintained effective control over resources. In the schools I studied, Computer Studies as an examination option was taught mainly by teachers who either were currently also teaching mathematics or were former maths teachers. The majority of these teachers were also male. In the mixed-sex schools, only two out of a total of fourteen teachers of Computer Studies were female. In both of the girls' schools, the option was taught by a female member of staff. Evidence from the postal questionnaire shows a slightly higher percentage of women teaching Computer Studies, but men still predominate. Of a total of 645 teachers of Computer Studies, 146 were female (23 per cent). Girls were more likely to be taught by women teachers in girls-only schools, as is shown in table 10.1.

Staff other than those teaching Computer Studies are involved in teaching with and about computers in most schools. Six of the schools in the study ran

Table 10.2 Responsibility for computing by department in 238 schools

Department responsible	Number of schools	Percentage
Computer Studies	94	39
Mathematics	89	37
Science	19	8
Other	36	15

compulsory courses in Computer Awareness or Computer Literacy for some of their pupils. The presentation of these courses varied from school to school, but in most cases they had been devised by one or two individuals with a specialist interest in computing, usually Computer Studies, maths or science teachers. In three schools, staff from other departments were involved in the actual teaching of the awareness course. Although there were more women teaching on Computer Awareness courses than on the more specialist Computer Studies courses, the majority of teachers were male. In several schools, the mathematical background of the teachers was very evident in the curriculum of the awareness courses.

The more general use of computers across the curriculum was limited. Several schools used computers as a learning aid in remedial education and most schools taught word-processing skills as part of typing or Business Studies courses. Overall, however, the biggest users of computers were the maths and science departments. The results of the postal questionnaire showed a similar picture. In answer to questions about which departments used computers, while almost every department was represented, the most likely users were science and mathematics departments. Over 70 per cent of teachers using computers in their teaching were male. This figure reflects the higher percentage of male maths and science teachers, but even in areas where women teachers are well represented, such as geography, history and music, it was still the case that the male members of departments were more likely to involve computers in their teaching. According to a BBC survey, almost two-thirds of schools sampled had a member of staff with responsibility for 'computing across the curriculum' and these were overwhelmingly male. A similar sex bias appeared in the case of staff training in computer use.[3]

In the schools visited, the identification of computers with mathematics was further heightened by the allocation of departmental responsibility for school computing. Six schools had established separate departments of Computer Education or Computer Studies. In two schools, computing was under the responsibility of the mathematics department. Even where a specific department of computing had been established, however, the staff in the department were often engaged in teaching maths for a proportion of their timetable. Maths and computing were thus inevitably linked in the eyes of pupils. In the schools replying to the postal questionnaire, departmental responsibility was mainly allocated to Computer Studies departments, maths departments and science departments as shown in table 10.2.

In the schools visited, the location of computers also tended to emphasize a link between computing and mathematics or science. All the schools had a room or rooms to house computers. In four schools these were located in the science block or area of the school. In two schools the computers were located in the maths area and in two schools they were located in what could be described as a 'neutral' area.

In all the schools Computer Studies was a very popular option. In the mixed-sex schools, boys were much more likely to opt for the subject than girls, though in the girls' schools there was considerable demand for Computer Studies courses. The evident popularity of computing may be a significant factor affecting female take-up. Several teachers suggested that the competition for places may put girls off choosing the option. Case studies of six schools in Australia also concluded that competition for resources made access to computers more difficult for girls (Crawford *et al.*, 1989). In my research, several schools used mathematical ability as one of the criteria in the selection of pupils for Computer Studies options. The image of computing as a mathematical subject and as a difficult subject is enhanced by such a selection mechanism. This is particularly likely to affect the popularity of the subject with girls. In the case of science subjects, it has been shown that one of the strongest factors influencing subject choice, especially for girls, is the perceived difficulty of the subject (Omerod *et al.*, 1979). Conversations with girls in the schools revealed that Computer Studies was regarded as a 'difficult' subject and that those girls taking it were regarded as 'brainy' and as 'swots'.

Two schools in the study reported that allocation of places on Computer Studies courses was on a 'first come, first served' basis. In reality, this often meant that those pupils who displayed the greatest enthusiasm and persistence would be at an advantage. In the mixed schools, these 'enthusiasts' were more likely to be male.

Girls, Boys, and Home Computers

A perceived link between computing and maths/science is only one aspect of a complex set of factors involved in the different level of participation of male and female pupils in computing activities. The differential access to home computers is also of some significance. My research showed a considerable degree of gender difference in home computer use. Of the 974 fourth and fifth year pupils surveyed, 56 per cent of boys and 22 per cent of girls reported that they had a computer at home. A significant gender difference was maintained amongst pupils taking Computer Studies exam courses, where 65 per cent of boys and 28 per cent of girls had a home computer. This inevitably places girls at a disadvantage.

The research revealed that home computers were much more likely to have been bought for boys than girls and were used much more by boys and fathers than girls and mothers. Both mothers and fathers were reported as being keen for their children to learn about computers at school. Most home computers were used solely for playing games. A survey in the US has also shown that 70 per cent of the main users of home computers were males. Males were reported as spending significantly more time playing games and programming than females, but only slightly more time using the computers for other applications (Lockheed, 1985).

Until very recently, home computers have been heavily marketed as 'toys for boys'. Several commentators have argued that the type of software aimed at the home market largely consists of games which are likely to be much more attractive to males than females. The themes of many games concern male sports, various forms of destruction, land battles, space wars and physical adventures. The style of much games software is aggressive, competitive and violent (Clarke, 1986; Hoyles, 1988). Computer games have provided a significant impetus for many boys to become more acquainted with computers and with programming in particular. Games form a key part of an important social network outside schools from which girls are excluded. Crawford *et al.* (1989) found that girls resisted engagement with the 'male toy' at home. Girls 'generally saw computer games as an extension of arcade machines and part of the "macho male domain" where "nice girls don't go". They generally spoke of their brothers' games as boring, sexist or offensively violent' (p. 29). The inequality in home computer use clearly has implications for computer use in school.

In the schools I studied, computers were made available to pupils at lunchtime and out of school hours, but few girls took this opportunity to use the computers. Girls were only 10 per cent of those pupils who used computers outside lesson time. In most schools, computer rooms were 'male territory' and girls were often only grudgingly accommodated.[4]

Gender in the Computer Classroom

One consequence of the difference in home computer use is that many girls are less familiar with computers than boys and less confident in handling them in school, at least initially. In the schools I visited, many boys assumed a lack of interest, knowledge and competence on the part of girls. Fitzgerald *et al.* (1985) also found that boys regarded themselves as more competent and confident in using computers than girls. Crawford *et al.* (1989) found that because of their lack of experience of computers at home, girls were more likely to perceive themselves as lacking expertise and this contributed to their relative passivity in the computing classroom.

My research included observations of both Computer Awareness classes with roughly equal numbers of girls and boys, and Computer Studies classes where girls were in a minority. The observations showed that boys were able to secure for themselves a disproportionate share of physical resources and teacher attention.

Computer Awareness courses usually began with a discussion session during which the teacher reviewed previous work, explained a new procedure or program, outlined applications and so on. There then followed a practical session during which pupils would operate the computers, loading and running programs. In these lessons the behaviour of boys and girls and their respective interaction with the teacher differed markedly in several respects. In almost all the lessons observed, boys overwhelmingly dominated the class discussions, answering considerably more of the questions which the teacher addressed to the class as a whole. The boys asked considerably more questions of the teacher and made significantly more comments on the content of the lesson. In many of the classes, even where they made up 50 per cent or more of the population, girls answered less than 10 per cent of questions and remained very much on the periphery of discussions. Girls were also marginal to the class in a physical sense, often seated in groups at the back or side of the classroom. Boys tended to sit either at the computers they had earlier commandeered or at the front of the class.

In the practical part of lessons boys would typically acquire the newest computers, those with disk-drives and colour monitors. Pupils usually worked in single-sex groups. The female groups tended to share the facilities they were using quite well, and adopted a more cooperative approach to the working out of problems and entering data. The male groups tended to generate more arguments about 'turns', more competition and more concern about individual and group performance. This generated more noise and more attention from the teacher. Mixed-sex working groups were relatively rare and only entered into when unavoidable. In these groups, almost without exception, boys would dominate the keyboard while girls looked on. On the few occasions when teachers insisted that a boy give over control of the computer to a girl there was considerable resentment expressed. Male groups tended to demand the teachers' attention more than female groups and did this by waving hands and by calling out. Consequently more attention was given to the boys' needs.

In the more specialist Computer Studies option classes, girls were very much in a minority. The pattern of interaction between pupils and teacher was very similar to that in the awareness classes, although as the pupils were older there was a more 'restrained' atmosphere. The girls tended to be very reticent, often making no contribution whatever to class discussions. In general boys were more confident and more outspoken and asked more questions of teachers. The girls almost always sat together in a small group, often in a physically marginal position in the classroom. The male pupils simply behaved as though the girls did not exist. Few examples of ridicule or hostile comments were observed but, when questioned, several girls revealed that they had been subjected to this kind of behaviour by boys. For example:

> When we go on the computer and make a mistake the lads just take the piss out of us. They laugh and talk among themselves. They think we are no good at it. They are dead keen. They always want to go on the computers and so we get left to the end and then there's only five minutes left to do your program.

> The lads always get to go on the computer first . . . they cause trouble otherwise. The computers keep them quiet.

> Boys think they are definitely superior to girls at computing . . . they don't like the girls to answer questions. It would be better if there were more girls. Boys look at you funny as if to say how dare you answer that question . . . what do you know about it?

Few teachers made any effort to counteract the tendency of boys to dominate the classroom, although some did recognize this as a problem.

Most of the Computer Studies teachers regarded boys as more interested in computing than girls. Teachers appeared to measure 'interest' in terms of certain kinds of activity. Computer 'enthusiasts' were largely defined as pupils who were keen to spend a large part of their free time with computers, either 'tinkering' or playing games. Such pupils were more often male than female. Boys and girls achieved similar examination results but girls were seen as successful largely because of their diligent and methodical approach to the subject, while boys were regarded as having more 'flair' for computing than girls. This is illustrated by the following comment from one Computer Studies teacher.

> I have yet to see, over all the years I have been teaching computing, a girl who is a computer expert. There have been girls who have got good examination results but they have probably got just as good exam results in other subjects. They have produced the work for the course well and they have got the mark and the grades, but put them in front of a computer and they don't really want to know. There are lads there who have got appalling exam marks but they can make the machine do anything they want it to do. They just haven't bothered to turn it out in the right form for the exam because that's not interesting. They just want to get on the machine, where the girls will do the work that's required and do it well, but they are not actually interested really . . . not in the same way as the boys. The computer doesn't seem to offer them anything which holds their interest. It could be the fanatical hobbyist approach that the lads have — they just take them up and find it something enjoyable to work with, whereas the girls don't.

Although some boys 'fail' they are nonetheless seen as enthusiastic and powerful computer users. Girls may achieve well in coursework and exams, yet this success is not always seen as evidence of 'real' interest or 'real' expertise.

Some teachers were willing to accept that the experiences of girls in school may have contributed to the reluctance of many to become more involved in computing. For example:

> All the time I have been teaching computing I have become worried that the girls showed very little inclination to tinker away on the machine, but that's not to say that I didn't have good exam results from girls. I did, had equally good results — they did very well. So it's not lack of ability in the subject that they feel . . . they simply would do the minimum that they need to hand in. After a while I asked the question why don't they want to tinker, why won't they come into the computer room, which is open at lunchtimes, and use the computers at other times, and I thought that one way to find out, to cross off one reason — if I have a girls-only session will they use it? And in fact its been successful. . . . The boys would run to the computer room straight after lessons and be there — sometimes you haven't even finished your lesson and they are waiting to get in. They are keener in that way, but once you say to the girls 'OK you don't have to run and shove and push', then they'll come and use it, and it has been very popular, certainly all this term.

Other teachers, however, did not regard their own attitudes or practices as especially influential and were more likely to look for explanations of girls' approach to computers as something inherent in girls or in computing. As one teacher commented:

The computers themselves just don't seem to attract the girls and I just don't see any way of improving that. I mean computers are computers and they are not suddenly going to start doing something interesting to girls.

When asked about gender difference in subject choice, most teachers sought to explain this by reference to 'sex-role stereotyping', operating principally through agencies such as the family and the media. Teachers did not regard school experiences as particularly influential.[5]

Career Aspirations

The importance of career aspirations for the subject choices pupils make in school is difficult to assess, though Pratt *et al.* (1984) suggest that they are a significant influence. My research revealed a marked gender division in the career aspirations of fourth and fifth year pupils. Very few girls were considering a career in computing, whereas this was a popular choice with boys. A high proportion of girls were hoping to work with children or as a secretary. Of those girls taking Computer Studies options, work with computers ranked fourth after secretarial work, work with children and work in a bank. Among boys taking Computer Studies options, work with computers ranked first. Work in computing also ranked very highly in the choices of boys who were not taking Computer Studies, taking second place after a career in the armed forces. This is in marked contrast with the non-Computer Studies girls, none of whom aspired to a career in computing. Girls were not unaware of the widespread application of new technology in many fields of employment, but most did not regard a course in Computer Studies as important to the kinds of work they saw themselves doing.[6] A survey of pupil attitudes to computers in thirty-two Australian schools also showed that males perceived computers as having a larger role in their future. Males, more than females, claimed that when they were 30, they were likely to be using computers quite a lot in their jobs, in the home and for entertainment (Hattie and Fitzgerald, 1988).

The research described here has shown that there are clear differences in the access of girls and boys to computers, both at home and at school. Yet it would be wrong to conclude from this that 'girls are not interested in computers'. Many girls are keen to use computers and find them interesting, though they do not always exhibit enthusiasm in the same way as boys. It is certainly the case that girls are more polarized in their attitudes towards computers. A survey of attitudes to computers in Australian schools found that as many girls as boys enjoyed using computers but many more girls than boys ardently disliked them. The survey also found that when girls use computers, they learn as much and often learn faster than boys (Hattie and Fitzgerald, 1988).

In the two girls' schools I visited there was a great deal of enthusiasm for computing. The majority of girls' schools in the postal survey also reported that computing was very popular with girls and that the biggest obstacle to girls' participation was lack of equipment rather than lack of interest. The gender difference in participation in computing in mixed-sex schools, cannot, therefore, be the result of some inherent trait in girls or due to some intrinsic feature of computers.

It must be seen as a consequence of the way in which computing is constructed as a gendered activity in the mixed-sex school.

Creating gender equity in school computing will require more than simply ensuring equal access to computing facilities. Schools need to focus on the structures and processes which constrain girls' participation. Active intervention is needed, to examine the content and the context of the curriculum to ensure that girls' interests are not excluded and to ensure that teaching methodologies are those which are likely to produce the active participation of all pupils. The remainder of this chapter discusses strategies which schools could adopt to encourage girls to participate more fully in computing activities.

Intervention Strategies

Gender equity must be a central feature of the development and review of a school policy on computer education. Computers have been introduced into many schools on an *ad hoc* basis and many schools do not have any clearly defined objectives for their use. There have been a range of competing developments in both policy and practice in schools computing, sometimes operating within the same institution.[7] It is important that staff from humanities and social science departments are involved in the development of policy, which should include objectives for staff as well as pupils. Schools need to develop indicators to monitor gender differences in participation and performance in computing activities and to evaluate interventions. A comprehensive policy for gender equity is likely to involve structural/organizational interventions as well as a review of curriculum issues. The following suggestions are not intended as a blueprint for action, but single-strategy solutions are unlikely to be successful.

Structural/Organizational Interventions

Schools need to break the historical link between computing and maths/science. The school computer room should be located in 'neutral' space and regarded as part of a school's information management service in the same way as the school library. The overall coordination of school computer use could be the responsibility of a non-maths/science department or the joint responsibility of different kinds of department. Staff from non-maths/science departments should be encouraged to participate in computer awareness courses. Teachers of all subjects should be encouraged to explore the ways in which computers may aid their teaching, and given opportunities to develop competence and confidence in handling computers. Hoyles (1988) and Lockheed (1985) argue that curriculum-focused courses in which the power and utility of the computer in learning a range of subjects are displayed, may provide a better route to the greater participation of girls than computer literacy courses. Information Technology would thus be seen by pupils as applicable to a wide range of disciplines and would be utilized by women as well as men.[8] This obviously requires extensive staff development and it is crucial that gender issues are raised as a central part of all in-service work.[9]

If schools wish to encourage more girls to take optional courses in computing, they may need to review the operation of options schemes. Options schemes are unlikely to be a major factor in subject choice, but they can act as an additional disincentive to girls to choose non-traditional courses (Pratt *et al.*, 1984). Some schools I visited operated a restrictive options scheme in which it was not easy to choose computer studies in combination with many of the subjects which are most popular with girls, such as typing or community care.[10]

There is a growing interest in the establishment of single-sex classes in coeducational schools, as a policy mechanism to improve the achievement levels and participation rates of girls in certain subject areas. The majority of experiments of this kind have been in mathematics education. The evidence for a class-type effect on girls' *achievement* is inconclusive (Rowe, 1988). Some studies have demonstrated significant gains in girls' *confidence* in maths in single-sex classes (Smith, 1986; Rowe, 1988) and this may affect female participation in higher-level maths options. At the present time, however, the effectiveness of single-sex grouping as an appropriate strategy has yet to be established (Rowe, 1988). Willis and Kenway (1986) have pointed out several inherent dangers in the strategy. For example, teachers might regard girls' classes as lower-interest/ability classes and have lower expectations of them. They argue that 'separating girls from boys (boys from girls) will not, in itself, change the perceptions of the teachers and administrators in the schools, any more than it will automatically change the attitudes of the students themselves' (p. 145). Willis and Kenway make the point that while the strategy has superficial appeal, it could divert resources and attention away from the more important issue of curriculum reform. If schools are to consider single-sex classes in computing, they must ensure that a change in the sex structure of classes is not seen as a substitute for a thorough examination of curriculum content, teaching methodologies and assessment practices.

There is a much stronger argument for ensuring that girls can have access to free-time use of computers in a girls-only setting, where they could develop skills and 'tinker' in a supportive environment. Girls could be given access on certain days of the week and/or there could be a girls' computer club. It must be recognized, however, that girls may need active encouragement to participate and that it may take time to secure girls' involvement. It is important that girls-only sessions are supervised by teachers who are competent in computing and sensitive to gender issues.

Curriculum Interventions

A gender-inclusive curriculum is of equal value to girls and boys; is equally connected to the experiences and interests girls and boys typically acquire outside the formal classroom; does not take the male perspective to be the human perspective; and uses inclusive language and pedagogy. (Clark, 1989, p. 3)

A commitment to gender equity in computing must involve an examination of subject content, subject context and teaching and learning styles. It is also important for teachers to examine what it is they value in the computing classroom and to look at ways in which certain forms of assessment may disadvantage girls. Teachers must recognize that their attitudes and practices are an integral part of the process by which computing is constructed as a gendered activity.

Teachers designing Computer Literacy or Computer Studies courses must ensure that mathematical examples do not dominate the course and that a wide range of applications are presented. The experiences and achievements of women and men should be included. The computing curriculum is one place where gender divisions in school and in employment could be made visible to pupils and discussed. As Clark (1989) has argued, pupils are active in the social construction of gender and must be actively involved in the identification of gendered patterns of experience and in the process of change. Gender equity requires the explicit study of the construction of gender by both boys and girls. For example, pupils could be given information about women's and men's participation in the computing industry and changing labour market opportunities. It is important that such issues be approached from an equity perspective, however, if stereotypes are to be challenged rather than reinforced.

The software that teachers use should be carefully selected and examined for the way it constructs males and females. Teachers could collaborate to develop checklists for use in software evaluation to ensure that it reflects their educational objectives in a non-sexist way. For example, how are males and females presented? Is the language sexually inclusive? Is the software motivating for all pupils? Do examples build equally on the experiences and interests of girls and boys? Does the software provide the opportunity for group work and cooperative learning and is it likely to develop the confidence of pupils?

Teachers need to develop an understanding of classroom dynamics, and examine the ways in which boys may dominate the computing classroom. Teachers could collaborate to develop classroom management strategies which aim to involve girls more centrally. Again, pupils could be involved in discussion of patterns of gender interaction.

Teachers must begin to examine the effects of different styles of learning and teaching, which may have a relevance to the participation and performance of girls. For example, research in the UK (Hoyles, 1988), in the USA (Hawkins, 1984) and in Australia (Hattie and Fitzgerald, 1988) suggests that girls prefer to work collaboratively rather than individually. Sutherland and Hoyles (1988) have demonstrated gender differences in styles of programming and modes of working. They argue that teachers do not always recognize the value of approaches which are more typical of girls than boys. Who achieves more, is at least partly dependent on how we assess and organize the activity (p. 62). In many ways, this issue represents the most fundamental challenge to current practices in school computing and more research in this area is urgently needed.

Summary

This chapter has identified several features of school computing which contribute to the construction of computer use as a gendered activity. It has been argued that a comprehensive review of the content and context of the curriculum is necessary if girls and boys are to be given equal opportunities to benefit from education with and about computers. The chapter has suggested that schools develop a computing policy which includes a programme of active intervention on gender issues for both pupils and staff. The final part of the chapter has outlined several strategies which schools should consider in their effort to ensure that both boys and girls experience working with computers as enriching and empowering.

Notes

1   The research was carried out in eight secondary schools in three LEAs. Six schools were coeducational comprehensives. Two were girls' schools, one of which was a comprehensive and the other an independent school. The research included a detailed examination of the organization and functioning of computing activities within each school, observations of computer classrooms, and interviews with teachers and pupils. A questionnaire was administered to 974 fourth and fifth year pupils in the schools visited. In addition to the school-based research, further information was obtained from a postal questionnaire returned by 238 schools in ten LEAs. Further details of the methodology of the study can be found in Culley (1986).

2   Lack of self-confidence in any school subject is not, of course, an inherent trait. It is important that we see this as a consequence of schooling and attempt to discover the mechanisms through which girls become less confident of their success or more anxious about their performance.

3   Microcomputers in Secondary Schools, BBC Educational Broadcasting Services Research Unit (unpublished).

4   Several teachers reported that many of the free-time users of computers were pupils who had access to a computer at home.

5   Clark (1989) discusses the ways in which a simplistic view of sex-role socialization can produce serious problems for gender equity practices in schools.

6   In most schools, pupils were given little information on careers before options were decided upon. Most careers teachers did not regard it as part of their job to attempt to counteract existing gender-typed career patterns (Culley, 1988).

7   The issues here are complex and controversial. They concern the priority schools place on learning *about* computers and learning *through* computers. Within these categories there are further difficult decisions, e.g., the relative emphasis on programming, the extent to which computer awareness should be embedded in the curriculum, etc. See Bigum *et al.* (1987) for an interesting discussion of the nature of educational reform in the context of the introduction of new technology.

8   Although there are serious limitations to the strategy of 'role modelling' (see Byrne, 1989; Clark, 1989), it is important that girls see women as competent and confident in handling the technology.

9   Such changes may not, of course, be easy to accomplish. There may be logistical problems of relocating facilities; funds for staff development may be inadequate; there may be resistances from teachers who have not accepted that computing has anything to offer their specialism and from Computer Studies teachers who may have a great deal of personal investment in the control of resources.

10   The utility of courses in Computer Studies is being questioned by many schools. The programming element of these courses tends to be dominated by BASIC which has little relevance to most industrial or commercial computing or to higher education courses in Computer Science. Computer applications could also be effectively taught in conjunction with extant curricula. A reduction in numbers taking Computer Studies would free resources for other uses.

References

ASSESSMENT OF PERFORMANCE UNIT (1981) *Mathematical Development*, Primary Survey Report No. 2, HMSO.

BIGUM, C. *et al.* (1987) *Coming To Terms with Computers in Schools*, Deakin Institute for Studies in Education, Australia.

BYRNE, E. (1989) *Role Modelling and Mentorship as Policy Mechanisms: The Need For New Directions*, Department of Education, University of Queensland, Australia.

CLARK, M. (1989) *The Great Divide*, Commonwealth Department of Employment, Education and Training, Canberra, Australia.

CLARKE, V. (1986) 'Why are girls under represented? Suggestions from the literature', *Australian Educational Computing*, Vol. 1, No. 1.

CRAWFORD, K., GROUNDWATER-SMITH, S. and MILLAN, M. (1989) *Gender and the Evolution of Computer Literacy*, School of Teaching and Curriculum Studies, University of Sydney, Australia.

CULLEY, L. (1986) *Gender Differences and Computing in Secondary Schools*, Department of Education, Loughborough University of Technology.

CULLEY, L.A. (1988) 'Option choice and careers guidance: gender and computing in secondary schools', *British Journal of Guidance and Counselling*, Vol. 16, No. 1.

ELSE, L. (1985) 'Dp jobs survey: women lose out in pay and status', *Computing*, 13 June.

EQUAL OPPORTUNITIES COMMISSION (1983) *Information Technology in Schools*, Manchester, EOC.

FITZGERALD, D., HATTIE, J. and HUGHES, P. (1985) *Computer Applications in Australian Classrooms*, Commonwealth Department of Education, Australia.

HATTIE, J. and FITZGERALD, D. (1988) 'Sex differences in attitudes, achievement and use of computers', *Australian Journal of Education*, Vol. 31, No. 1, pp. 3–26.

HAWKINS, J. (1984) *Computers and Girls: Rethinking the Issues*, Bank Street Technical Report, No. 24.

HOYLES, C. (Ed.) (1988) *Girls and Computers*, Bedford Way Papers No. 34, Institute of Education, University of London.

LOCKHEED, M.E. (1985) 'Women, girls and computers: a first look at the evidence', *Sex Roles*, Vol. 13, No. 3/4, pp. 115–122.

OMEROD, M.B. *et al.* (1979) 'Girls and physics education', *Physics Education*, 14.

PRATT, J., BLOOMFIELD, J. and SEALE, C. (1984) *Option Choice; A Question of Equal Opportunity*, Slough, NFER-Nelson.

ROWE, K.L. (1988) 'Single-sex and mixed-sex classes: the effects of class type on student achievement, confidence and participation in mathematics', *Australian Journal of Education*, Vol. 32, No. 2, pp. 180–202.

SIMONS, G.L. (1981) *Women in Computers*, National Computing Centre, London.

SMITH, S. (1986) *Separate Tables*, Manchester, Equal Opportunities Commission.

SUTHERLAND, R. and HOYLES, C. (1988) 'Gender Perspectives on LOGO Programming in the Mathematics Curriculum', in HOYLES, C. (Ed.) *Girls and Computers*, Bedford Way Papers 34, Institute of Education, University of London.

WALKERDINE, V. *et al.* (1989) *Counting Girls Out*, London, Virago.

WILLIS, S. and KENWAY, J. (1986) 'On overcoming sexism in schooling: to marginalize or mainstream', *Australian Journal of Education*, Vol. 30, No. 2.

Chapter 11

Computers, Dominant Boys and Invisible Girls: Or, 'Hannah, it's not a toaster, it's a computer!'

John Beynon

Introduction

Computers into education (hereafter referred to as IT/Education) is subject to many paradoxes. For some they benefit and energize classrooms, whilst to sceptics they constitute a threat to education itself (e.g. Meighan and Reid, 1982; Baker, 1983, 1985; Apple, 1986; Karger, 1988). For others, IT/Education has promised much but, to date, the results have been disappointing (e.g. Suhor and Jester, 1984). Again, in spite of the considerable literature on educational computing, social scientists (in particular, ethnographers) in both the UK and the USA have, surprisingly, kept their distance (Beynon and Mackay, 1989) and, indeed, there have been comparatively few 'naturalistic' (defined liberally) studies of pupil-computer interaction in classrooms. In spite of technology's huge potential to transform curriculum and pedagogy, the central irony is that the study of its actual classroom implementation is grossly under-developed. There are, however, recent promising signs that studying computers from the pupil/teacher (as opposed to the hardware/software) end is, at last, being perceived as important. It is to further this that I have argued elsewhere (Beynon, 1989a; 1991) the urgent need for ethnographic studies of computers into education. The ultimate aim would be an ethnography of IT/Education which would incorporate both micro-substantive and micro-formal theories (Hammersley, 1980) 'grounded' in data gathered across a range of both primary and secondary classrooms in the UK and covering both introduction and implementation. The fact remains that little is known about how teachers are employing micros; the constraints under which they operate; the impact upon teaching, learning and subject subcultures; and, most importantly, how pupils are using and reacting to them. The intended and unintended outcomes of the 'technologized' classroom deserves close scrutiny, as do the social history of the microcomputer's design and the assumptions concerning teaching and learning processes software encapsulates. Is, for example, the charge justified that micros have the potential to 'deskill' both teachers and pupils (in that much software, teachers report, has little of enduring educational significance).

This paper is based on an ethnographic case study, the data for which was gathered by non-participant observation and informal interviewing, of computer usage in Mr Micro's classroom in Green Acre Primary School near Cardiff in South Wales in the year 1987–1988. My intention was to explore how pupils actually used computers and the kinds of tasks and task-related talk they occasioned. As I recorded, both in a journal and on audio tape, how pupils worked in groups on the microcomputers, gender-differentiated usage emerged as a major recurring theme. I now focus on this by, firstly, reviewing some of the pertinent literature on girls and computing, before, in the second main section, addressing the Green Acre data. I end with a summary of the principal issues to emerge out of the data.

Literature: Girls Into Computing

One writer, Olson (1988), tackles head-on the computer's role in the stratification of the curriculum and summarizes work which indicates variations in computer use between the commerce and business streams (mostly girls) and the academic streams (mostly boys), in that the latter are more likely to be learning statusful technological skills, the former pseudo and general skills. He comments that 'girls, particularly working-class girls are, then, once again streamed out of technical and professional careers'. He quotes Walkerdine's (1988) work on how the 'undercutting' of girls in mathematics is achieved by a combination of teachers, parents, pupils and streaming. Olson, like Apple, argues that whilst the computer holds out the opportunity to increase both access to and the control of information with both speed and efficiency, it is, likewise, a potential multiplier of the inequalities that stratify classes, genders, and First and Third Worlds. Included in this process are games and program formats which, directly and indirectly, contribute to the subordination of women. He writes:

> Although computer ads. usually show the family as a whole using the computer in educational ways, the games tend to be disproportionately popular among teenage males. Such 'popular forms of education' feature games which are sexist, racist, militaristic and competitive in form, emphasizing the joys of technical domination and mastering which are associated with successful masculinity.

Even so, differences in class culture, he argues, mean that computers in the hands of working-class boys tend to be used as a 'personal video arcade', whereas in contrast middle-class boys are far more likely to be exposed to more technically skilled and demanding formats such as graphics and advanced word-processing activities.

The obstacles encountered by girls and women teachers are referred to in two recent UK projects. In their Microcomputers in Primary Schools Project, Hall and Rhodes (1988) report that:

- the child computer 'experts' they encountered in classes did not include any girls. Teachers should avoid reinforcing the emergence of such 'superior' male pupils by involving all pupils in using micros;

- more male teachers attend courses and make use of microcomputers, but female teachers should be given the opportunity to become more involved and so redress what is an unbalanced role model being presented to children;
- there is a need to monitor whether girls are receiving the same range of opportunities to use micros as boys.

Similarly, the CARE-based study (Somekh, 1988) reports that:

There is clearly still a need to ensure that girls are encouraged to use micros and shown positive models of women teachers using them effectively. There is no evidence that girls are hesitant in using micros in the early years of the Primary School, but they often begin to be hesitant towards the end of the Junior School.

This problem is compounded by the fact that many pupils find their experience of computing discontinued when they arrive in the secondary school, and this usually proves to be a greater long-term handicap to girls than to boys.

The CARE study emphasizes the crucial need for women teachers to get involved:

... there is general agreement that girls show as much enthusiasm for computers as boys when their teachers are aware of the potential problem and the school has an effective policy for girls' use of computers. Women Primary teachers are gaining in confidence, but there remains a pressing problem in many Secondary Schools where it is, almost exclusively, male teachers who are concerned with computers.

The study also mentions that in one secondary school girls were grossly under-represented in the computer options, whereas in another they were equal in number to the boys, and attributes the presence of an innovative female Business Studies teacher as being the crucial intervening factor. In similar vein Evans and Hall (1988) assert that in spite of a number of gestures towards equal opportunities in education girls are still being disadvantaged in the UK, especially in relation to computing and electronics. Indeed, the situation is worsening as measured in terms of the percentage of girls out of the total number of university students studying Computer Science. They point to the problems emanating from computing's macho image, with twice as many boys as girls having access to a microcomputer in the home and, even in primary schools, machines largely controlled by men and used by boys. In view of this they call for positive discrimination towards girls to be tackled at three levels simultaneously, namely schools and colleges; Local Education Authorities; and at the level of central government and related agencies.

The depressed participation of girls in mathematics, science and technology in UK secondary schools has been noted by numerous recent writers (for example, DES, 1980; Doherty, 1987; Johnson and Bell, 1987; Johnson and Murphy, 1986; Kahle, 1985; and Kelly, 1981). There have been a number of attempts to tackle this. Humphrey (1987), a teacher, reports on a project in a primary school to encourage girls by removing the micro 'physically and ideologically' (note the latter) from the mathematics department; using more 'girl-friendly' software; and insisting on more women staff being involved. Similarly, Brown (1988) argues that the situation must be tackled at root by 'developing experiences which contribute to girls' technological development in primary education'. The battle is largely lost if left to the secondary stage. However, File (1988) reports on the Insight Into Computing Course at a College of Technology which successfully attracts girls. On a wider, more science-based front, two notable projects which have helped promote the interests of girls are Girls Into Science and Technology (GIST), and Women Into Science and Engineering (WISE). The former has, I would suggest, been especially influential (Whyte *et al.*, 1985) in that the research team collaborated with teachers in both raising awareness and attempting to do something about equity of access in science and technology in the ten study sites, in which they followed a total cohort of some 3000 pupils from the time they entered secondary school until they made their option choices three years on. The interventionist strategies employed were varied, from classroom observation and the administration of pre- and post- attitude and aptitude tests to more up-front measures specifically designed to attack a sex-stereotyped science/technology, such as visits by women scientists and discussions covering attitudes, sex roles and women at work. These strategies were mediated through teachers and attempted to counter the 'edging out' of girls in science and craft lessons. The book raises the question of what a feminist science/technology in schools might look like, clearly a major project for the future, as is the teaching about technology in a non-technological way to non-technologists.

There seem to me to be two particularly important studies which address girls and computing in schools, namely the report by Willis on recent research in Australia, and that by Culley in the UK.

The research by the Commonwealth Schools Commission (1984) remains one of the most exhaustive projects to date and makes the case that girls require far greater access to technology if a whole generation is not to lose out. But access, as Sue Willis (1987) makes clear, is no easy matter and can mean a number of diverse things operating at different levels. It can, for example, entail:

- ensuring the equal availability of computer facilities and experiences (that is, both learning about and through computers) to all (however, it is not just a question of resources since the quality of experience children obtain from computers, whether at home or in school, is still likely to be differentiated along class and gender lines — witness the Green Acre data presented later in this chapter);
- encouraging girls to make increased use of computing;
- changing the structure of a computing environment and curriculum which has probably been defined and implemented by white middle-class males and, thereby, encodes interests which may exclude girls, many working-class students and minority groups;
- defining equity (research in the UK, the USA and Australia has indicated that in mathematics, the physical sciences and engineering increased participation by girls is not guaranteed by merely providing access in terms of resources, even if these are accompanied by inducements to participate — again, witness the Green Acre data).

Willis bases a true regard for equity on two principles so as to ensure that

- the educational uses to which computing is put does not further disadvantage girls and others;
- all students have equal access to critical understanding of the social, environmental, industrial and economic effects of new technology.

Indeed, she points to a very big goal indeed, namely 'social equity':

> This is in order that they can learn to think critically about the possible uses and effects of the technology, and come to understand that there are decisions to be made which will shape the uses to which it is put, and that these discussions have implications for social equity. As a result, there should be at least the possibility that they will participate in the political processes which determine the uses to which the technology is put.

In her review of the Australian evidence Willis points out that equality of access was in question in a number of schools. Furthermore the lack of interest by girls in using computers was widely regarded by teachers as simply a reflection of boys' and girls' different interests, about which, it was assumed, little could be done. On the other hand, the access issue in some schools was being taken seriously and was leading to positive action. Neither was it just a matter of access of girls *within* an institution to computers, but of schools themselves to adequate computing facilities that would allow them to fulfil an equity policy, given that those in wealthy areas were clearly more likely to be better equipped than those in poorer communities. In one (a parochial girls' school) it was found that pupils were particularly disadvantaged because of the depressed support from parents who did not believe that a large investment in computers was justified for daughters. Fortunately, this was an exception and, indeed, such negative attitudes were not held by parents towards other girls' schools in the study. Most teachers, too, agreed that there should be equal access to computing and 'no evidence was found in the schools visited of any formal or informal intent, by teachers or administrators, to exclude students from access to computing resources on the basis of such variables as gender or race'. However, a number of teachers noted that in situations in which students were supposed to share equipment it was not, in fact, equally available: in competition for keyboards the boys usually won, as the following teacher comments testify:

> The boys pressure the girls not to take part in the Computer Club . . .
> the stronger, more aggressive male usually dominates . . . the girls tend
> in the main to drop into the background and let boys have the keyboard.

Single-sex groups, 'girls-only' sessions, and peer tutoring were amongst the strategies employed to counter this, but with only limited success. In out-of-class usage boys again dominated computers and teachers pointed to the fact that girls usually had restricted access to home computers, normally the property of brothers and fathers. Furthermore, in some schools priority of access to computing facilities was accorded to Computer Studies, which effectively excluded many girls since it was strongly associated with science and mathematics. Indeed, the location of computers in either subject area erected strong practical and psychological barriers for girls. This contributes to the now considerable literature on the negative psychological overtones for girls of the relationship between computers and mathematics/science: many are alienated from what they have come to regard, both consciously and unconsciously, as 'men's machines'. However, Willis is able to record that a number of schools were attempting to break the association: in one, for example, computers were administered and repaired by women and had been relocated into the 'neutral' area of the library.

Other schools, Willis reports, were re-examining the role of the 'girls' ghetto', namely word-processing, and had taken seriously the criticism that the technology curriculum is leading girls towards becoming 'IT slaves' whilst boys are being directed towards becoming 'the managers'. Furthermore, girls' presence in large numbers in word-processing classes is seen as doubly disadvantaging in that it excludes them from higher-status computer skills at a time when the amount of office work available to women is in decline. Moreover, the long-term impact of word-processors is likely to widen the gap between typists and secretaries/personal assistants as much routine office work is downgraded (Lyon, 1988). Willis comments:

> . . . less able students and many girls are channelled into courses that prepare them as low-level workers for the new information industries. . . .
> To allow girls to believe that they prepare themselves for the 'good life' in the Information Society by learning Word Processing is to falsify facts . . . understanding of the uses and effects of the technology are fairly superficial in many schools.

A further problem is the still widespread belief by teachers and parents that girls 'naturally' have less aptitude for computing and this somehow 'justifies' the differentiation of computing experiences made available in schools. Equally disturbing is the fact that many teachers reported themselves feeling quite powerless to reverse the anti-computing attitudes girls brought with them to school. An important implication of the study is that there may be real differences in the ways boys and girls, granted equal access, use computers, as the following teacher comments suggest:

> . . . girls are noticeably less willing to experiment with computers and to learn by trial and error. . . .

> . . . girls prefer to engage in tasks where they are working towards an outcome, whereas for boys using the computer is an end in itself.

> . . . it is almost as if computer games are inherently male and graphics inherently female.

It is already clear that the way computers are being introduced into schools in the UK, the USA, Canada and Australia may well be excluding girls from what Willis aptly terms 'a whole range of futures'. It is an understatement to say that the clear relationships between gender differentiation and both the visible and hidden curriculum need urgent research scrutiny and action.

In the UK, as is evident from her chapter in this volume, Lorraine Culley's research (1986; 1988) is highly significant in that not only does it look at ways in which computing has become a masculine activity in secondary schools, but argues that:

> . . . in girls-only schools there is no shortage of enthusiasm for computing; that Computer Studies is a popular option; and that Computer Clubs thrive. Since outside social influences are unlikely to be radically different for girls attending single-sex schools, the processes involved in the organization of teaching with and about computers in a co-educational setting must be significant.

She readily acknowledges that the practices of schools and teachers are not the sole factors involved in gender stereotyping, which clearly carries the weight of wider social forces. Computing in secondary schools is essentially a masculine domain and thus helps re-create existing social and gender relations, attitudes and assumptions. It is massively associated with male staff, and with mathematics and science departments; it fits in neatly with the gender differentiation of subject/option choices; and, as a result, it plays relatively little part in girls' hopes for the future, whereas it is central to those of many boys. Since home computing is dominated by fathers and sons, girls are undoubtedly less familiar and confident with computers and boys assume this is just part of 'being a girl'. Amongst her many suggestions to counter gender-based bias in computing are:

- a breaking of the link between mathematics and Computer Studies and a continual monitoring, from a gender standpoint, of option organization and choices;
- the elimination of mathematical and technological bias from Computer Awareness courses;
- the involvement of more female teachers in computers across the curriculum;
- an examination of the subtle processes of gender differentiation and a countering of boys' domination through the introduction of alternative teaching strategies;
- single-sex classes in Computing/Computer Studies, with gender itself on the agenda of Information Technology and INSET courses.

A most interesting parallel interventional programme in the USA is the Women's Action Alliance which has been working with junior high and middle schools to reverse girls' 'computer avoidance' before it becomes fixed. Their recommendations resulted in an Equity Project which, it is claimed, doubled girls' computer use. Amongst the many strategies employed were those which aimed:

- to publicize and alert colleagues to the problem and issues;
- to target girls, attack their preconceptions, and change the management of access;
- to design computer activities specifically around girls' interests;
- to stress the social, peer collaboration aspects of computer activities;

- to stress, on a number of fronts, both the usefulness and fun of computing;
- to extend measures seen to be effective in narrowing the computer gender gap.

The final text to which I intend to refer on the gendered aspects of computing in classrooms is the collection of papers edited by Hoyles (1988). Although the common theme is the teaching and learning of mathematics through computer activities, the papers nevertheless succeed in raising a host of wider issues with reference to girls' usage. Moreover, Hoyles's introduction is a succinct, but highly useful, summary of recent work in the area, not all of it readily available to readers who are not researchers.

Hoyles in her introduction highlights a point addressed by Culley in this volume, namely that applications by girls to study Computer Science at university are now down by 50 per cent since 1978 (from 28.2 per cent to 13.2 per cent), as are acceptances. Computers are largely still 'locked' (both physically and ideologically) inside mathematics departments, and the huge aversion felt by many girls towards mathematics is transferred to Computer Studies. Hoyles, a Professor of Mathematical Education, comments on the irony of this since the professional use of computers has relatively little to do with mathematics. Moreover, the culture of computing (and, of course, of technology generally) in our society has been shaped as a 'male domain': most buyers are men and users are predominantly men and boys (Culley, 1986). The imagery employed to promote computers time and again depicts men as the experts and managers, women as supportive and decorative (Ware and Stuck, 1985). Simons (1981) shows that women occupy the lower strata of computing jobs and, therein, are often the victims of sexism (Lloyd and Newall, 1985). It is hardly surprising that girls develop, early on, negative perceptions of computers and of their own involvement with them (Siann and MacLeod, 1986; Chen, 1986; Moore, 1986). Conversely, boys learn to value computers and see computing as important for their personal features (Gardner, 1985; Wilder, 1985; Hughes *et al.*, 1985). Boys are far more likely to enter into formal schooling culturally and practically positioned to accept and be motivated by computers. They are at an advantage early in their school careers and the evidence is that they use them more extensively and to more purpose than girls (Hess, 1985; Fife-Shaw, 1986). They monopolize machines, dominate both game-playing and programming and, in the process, further alienate girls (Moore, 1986; Culley, 1986). The evidence to date is that girls in coeducational contexts do less well than in girls-only contexts (Gardner, 1985) at computer-led tasks, although the paper by Hughes *et al.* (1988) contradicts this. Furthermore, the learning styles of boys and girls would appear to be culturally shaped in a way that results in boys being more likely to be stimulated by and to react to 'computer challenges', whereas girls are more likely to lose interest if their efforts are not quickly successful or acknowledged (Carmichael, 1985).

The paper by Burke *et al.* is an account of the introduction into mathematics classrooms of SMILE, a pupil-centred, resource-based learning program which allowed girls to organize resources to suit their own particular styles of learning. It not only encourages pupils to exercise autonomy in their learning, but works against traditional gender roles exacerbated, much evidence suggests, by computer access and usage. The objective is to create a computing environment specifically supportive to girls by using female role models and highly positive images of them using computers. Teachers and pupils collaborated in a pupil-centred curriculum which fostered a highly encouraging, non-conflictual and non-competitive ethos which granted credence to a variety of ways of working. Similarly, Sutherland and Hoyles's paper addresses gender differences in modes of working and cognitive styles of LOGO mathematics. Girls were found to be less likely to fight for control than boys. Moreover, boys did not typically verbally support their partner's contributions, but were more likely to engage in a competitive speech style. They comment, for example, that boys 'seemed concerned to establish their autonomy and impose their problem representation and solutions ... their interactions were often simply suggestions for actions which were not negotiable as they had already been worked out in advance'. They note a difference in interactional style in that girls emphasized the importance of receiving help from their peers, whereas boys saw group work as distracting from their individual achievements. Moreover, they argue that 'boys who preferred individual work focussed on the individual challenge involved and the opportunity for being able to puzzle things out for themselves without arguments from peers. Girls who liked individual work in contrast emphasised how they could progress at their own pace'. Sutherland and Hoyles's work involved close attention being paid to social and contextual issues such as modes of working and cognitive style, and they maintain that there were distinct gender differences in the ways in which boys and girls interacted with the computer; the nature of collaboration and pair discussion; and attitudes to modes of working. They refer in particular to the work of Carmichael (1985) which indicated that girls more often choose loosely-defined goals and boys more well-defined goals when programming in Turtle Graphics. Indeed, girls appeared more likely to stay with ideas with which they were familiar and favour a more subdued approach to programming. This 'soft mastery' is one, Sutherland and Hoyles argue, which LOGO favours and inculcates in its users. They point out that the exclusion, often, of programming from the computer curriculum usually available to girls reinforces sex stereotyping and is hugely disadvantageous: it is essential if true computer competence is ever to be attained.

The issue of gender-differentiated programming styles is taken up in the Hoyles volume by Noss, who calls for research to explore 'the specific ways in which girls and boys differ in what they take away with them from their computer experiences, but [also] into the interaction between the computer, learning styles, and the development of mathematical conceptions in general'. Noss's case is that in dealing with LOGO we are dealing with an 'essentially cultural phenomenon', one which may not only aid mathematical understanding but prove especially rich and beneficial for girls. Reference is made to Papert's (1980) assertion that computers could result in young people developing computational concepts earlier than the numerical, thus reversing a universal of cognitive development. The suggestion that some of cognition's most important developments occur not by learning new facts but by managing existing ones is also seen as highly significant for teachers. Noss points to the need to 'consider the ways in which boys and girls interact with the culture generated by the LOGO environment; that is, to think of the computer as influencing not only the setting within the classroom, but also the culture within which children do and learn — that is, as an interaction between existing cognitive and affective styles and preferences, and new possibilities opened up by the computer'. The latter point is taken up in the paper by Burns and Smart, which focuses on the manner in which sixth-form girls related to computers and the way in which technology can enhance the learning of mathematics through the use of the Newton Microworld (in which they could explore Newton's laws for themselves). The objective was to create a supportive environment for computer usage by girls in which computers were regarded as tools with which to work both individually and cooperatively to sort out ideas. It is clear that group pressures influence individual learning pathways and the whole area of working partnerships is in urgent need of further documentation. In another paper, Hughes *et al.* point out that 'there have been virtually no systematic comparisons of what actually happens when children learn with computers in single-sex and mixed-sex groups'. Indeed, gendered effects have been noted with children as young as 6 using LOGO and it is often asserted that girls perform best when in single-sex groups and removed from the inhibiting influence of boys. What is interesting about the Hughes paper is that it concludes that 'the girls who worked in single-sex groups were at a serious disadvantage compared both with boys and with girls who worked with boys . . . girls need boys more than boys need girls'. This conclusion follows on from previous studies by Hughes which suggested that girls benefit less from the LOGO experience than do boys.

Each of these studies tells us something about the gendered nature of pupil-computer interactions and, in the process, underlines the paucity of research on group dynamics and the micro-social and cultural pressures at work. From an early age boys are more likely to be using computers at home (Hughes *et al.*, 1987); building manipulative competences; and establishing their sense of 'being good at computers', what might be termed their 'technological esteem' and which, it would appear, few girls acquire. Importantly, the Hoyles volume makes it clear that equity policies alone will not necessarily result in fuller female participation. Rather, attention must be paid to the wider cultural factors affecting attitudes to technology generally and, in particular, computers. Girls need to come into contact with not only 'technologized' female role models, but male teachers who are aware of the subtle forms gender differentiation can take, especially within the particular male arena of IT/Education, and have thought about how they might intervene and do something about it.

The overwhelming message emerging from the literature reviewed above is that for girls computers are a big turn-off. But why? What are the mechanisms, both visible and invisible, formal and informal, operating in schools which contribute to this? Surprisingly the studies quoted above give little or no idea of the interpersonal *interactional* processes experienced by girls in schools which render computing both a difficult and an inappropriate territory for them to enter. It is asserted that boys amd male teachers either consciously or unconsciously exclude them. Far more needs to be known about how schooling contributes to this actual and attitudinal 'decomputing' of girls (and, undoubtedly, of many boys too) and the actual processes in play both inside and outside the school. Only then will it be possible to tackle these in any systematic and principled manner.

To illustrate the way in which educational ethnography can focus on such processual details of classroom life I now turn to data gathered in Green Acre, an open-plan primary school. The pupils were 9 to 10 years of age (Standard Three) and the data extracts have been selected for their representativeness from some thirty hours of journal and tape-recorded material. Mr Micro was an able, energetic and innovative teacher in whose classroom computers were integrated into the curriculum and extensively employed. Pairs or mixed groups of four pupils worked throughout the day on two BBC micros. Green Acre served a predominantly affluent, middle-class catchment area and there was considerable support from the parents for Mr Micro's computer activities.

Data: Mr Micro's Computer Classroom

I want first to say something about Mr Micro's philosophy of computing and his perception of himself as a 'Lone Ranger' pioneer, and of his battle to win additional resources and implement his ideas as, he set out to encourage in his pupils a critical view of computers:

> A lot of these kids accept because it is on the computer that it must be right. The computer can't lie, and all that! I remind them that both the hardware and the software have been made by people and can only be operated by people. They haven't a life of their own!

He placed education very firmly in front of the technology and for him computing was only part of the wider value inherent in the activity:

> I have great faith in the talk that goes on around the micro. There's a lot of collaboration in problem solving, a lot of give-and-take. You just cannot measure what has taken place by the output alone . . . it is the process that counts. The actual product is very often of quite secondary significance.

Mr Micro was an active leader of in-service sessions in neighbouring schools and his philosophy was twofold:

> First, educational technology is not about circuits or clever micro-electronics — it's about kids using and extending their learning by means of computers. Second, unless you are very careful technology will interfere with education. I also ask them not to accept software, not to be blinded by the advertiser's blurb. 'Does it aid your curriculum and does it work?' — those are the questions that have to be asked.

He was, moreover, a 'Papertian', an advocate of the possibilities of LOGO, which he described as

> . . . learning by doing. It forces kids to do their own thing but within clear-cut parameters. There's nothing cold or mathematical about LOGO — it's far more to do with kids and kids working together to solve problems.

However, Mr Micro resented the position in which he (as a highly committed and innovative 'leader' of computers-into-classrooms in the locality) found himself:

> I have very few opportunities to find out what is happening in other schools. I am stuck in a backwater as far as developing educational computing is concerned. That is why I enter all the computing competitions. It's good to see the school in competition with the more affluent south-east authorities. I enter competitions to keep in touch with where it is all happening. I could do so much if only I had more equipment and more support. At the moment I'm the lone Lone Ranger around here!

His view of himself as an under-resourced teacher 'ploughing a lonely furrow' in Green Acre surfaced repeatedly in my interviews. He was clearly frustrated by the apparent lack of support from his colleagues.

> Apart from Fred no one else around here is either aware of the possibilities or even gives them a second thought. At least he is thinking of using the micro for Welsh teaching and is talking about the potential it has for language teaching in general. Apart from that I'm on my own around here!

Mr Micro's resource problem was one I commented upon repeatedly in my field notes as the following example illustrates:

> Time and again there is a queue to use the computers. Kids jostle each other — 'Hurry up, we're on next', etc. There is enthusiasm, but little equipment!

He expressed his frustration being a 'Lone Ranger' from another angle:

> These kids have a basic exposure to computing and then they lose out when they pass on [to the next teacher]. As it is I'm just a year in their lives. Yet when they are with me each has an average of 15–20 minutes a day on a machine, which is an hour and a half per week, at least. That's maybe 50 or more hours during the course of the year, probably more. Believe you me they learn a lot in that time.

Mr Micro presented himself, with ample justification, as a pioneering teacher not just in the context of his school, but in the authority. But he also worried about 'running clear' of his colleagues and commented:

> I sometimes think I ought to slow down and give more time and effort to encouraging the staff here in Green Acre — although, believe me, in the past I've tried! But most of them continue to show little interest, including the head!

Mr Micro was strongly of the opinion that his strenuous efforts to promote computers within Green Acre had been met with precious little enthusiasm. He detailed the issues which most concerned him. Foremost amongst these was the absence of a wholehearted show of support from the head:

> Firstly, it concerns me that my personal computer policy is not yet a school one since the head is not prepared to give me his full backing. Fundamentally he is all too pleased to capitalize on the favourable publicity, but deep down he dismisses computers as just another gimmick, here today and gone tomorrow! But when we got into desk-top and produced the *Green Acre News* he took it straight to the governors and said, 'Look at all this high-tech stuff we're up to in Green Acre!', and he really impressed them. There's no doubt that the publicity helped put Green Acre on the map around here. Secondly, it concerns me that I've given the school seven long years and it has taken me all that time to get things really well organized. But now it's getting boring and my only hope is an Advisory Teacher post, preferably in the near future! Otherwise I might give the whole thing up, opt for an easier life, and go back to conventional teaching. Thirdly, I welcome the involvement of parents to expand computing in the school. I believe the pressure would be a positive one, but the head feels threatened — he believes he should make all the decisions concerning the curriculum. I think he knows the parents would come out on my side and he'd lose face for not going for additional resources. Finally, I've had a disagreement with him recently — he didn't approve of me going to lecture to the BEd students in Severn Side College. It was time out of school as far as he was concerned.

In my time in Green Acre Mr Micro attempted to exert pressure for greater resources and a higher profile for computing throughout the school by harnessing and utilizing parental pressure: parents, seeing in technology assured career opportunities, were naturally keen to see more computers in use. He was concerned, too, by the fact that pupils had, once they left him, little to do with computers until they went to the secondary school and

> . . . then it's all Computer Studies and such like. At the moment I feel I'm just wasting my time here. I really feel it is time for me to move on.

However, his hopes were dashed at a staff meeting in which the head refused to resource an expansion of computers. I recorded the situation thus:

> Yesterday they held a staff meeting in which responding to parental pressure concerning the expansion of computer activities was high on the agenda. They discussed at some length a request from Mr Micro to put on a demonstration at a PTA meeting of what typically went on. The head had, however, decided against this on the grounds that it might lead to parents questioning why their children did not have ready access to the computer. Mr Micro felt that his plans for expansion had been finally rejected and feels he now has no future in Green Acre.

At the end of the year his enthusiasm was rewarded and he became an Advisory Teacher based in the authority's Technology Centre with a brief to expand microcomputing in the area's primary schools.

The above account of Mr Micro's assertive championing of computers in Green Acre and his eventual frustration and departure may, at first, appear quite irrelevant in a paper which examines pupil-machine interaction and gender-differentiated usage in a primary school classroom. However, it is here to make a point. Computers in Green Acre were equated immediately and unequivocally with Mr Micro by both staff, parents and, of course, pupils. Indeed, the name by which he is known here is not my invention: it was what he was called by the pupils in his class, so closely was he associated as a person with the technology he deployed in his teaching. Mr Micro's introduction of computer activities into Green Acre was, at first, a quest based on interest and, more latterly (and understandably, given his personal investment and undoubted expertise), based on careerist motives and eagerness to be promoted into a role in which his experience might be more profitably employed. Computing in Green Acre was narrowly focused on Mr Micro as an innovative, energetic and ambitious teacher: in this sense it was essentially *male* and was not diffused in any way by the involvement of other staff, let alone female colleagues.

Another reason for relating Mr Micro's journey out of Green Acre is because it provides an insightful cameo of the manner in which microcomputers were introduced into UK schools in the early to mid 1980s. In an earlier paper (Beynon and Mackay, 1989) I showed how, under the then Secretary of State (Kenneth Baker), microcomputers were 'off-loaded' onto schools with little time for teachers to train or think about the implications. As a result it was the Lone Ranger enthusiasts — usually male and usually with a background in mathematics — who took up the job of implementation. Most colleagues, especially those in the humanities, were happy not to be involved, and so these teacher enthusiasts (like Mr Micro) often 'ran ahead' of the staff. At a time of severe cuts in funding they purposely moved into or stumbled upon one of the few new ladders of promotion and it is these former teachers who are to be found as Advisory Teachers, Advisors or in charge of local authority Technology and Design Development Centres. Mr Micro's career trajectory was in part shaped by the way in which government policy was implemented, in part by his own enthusiasm and drive which first ensured he became an 'expert' (to be called upon for INSET work, Baker Days and BEd teaching) and then took him out of the classroom.

Before examining the data on pupil-computer interactions it is worth briefly detailing how he ensured that computer activities did not intrude or interrupt the everyday life of his classroom. The ways in which teachers cope and the coping strategies they employ to manage diverse situations, from discipline through to curriculum and personal dilemmas, has been a major research focus in the recent past (e.g. Beynon, 1985). Mr Micro incorporated computers into his pedagogy by employing three broad sets of coping strategies which can be summarized under the following headings:

- the control of computer activities;
- the monitoring of computer activities;
- the boosting of pupils' computer confidence.

Computer Control

Mr Micro controlled all computer activities carefully by framing the tasks and inspecting the outcomes. He imposed on pupils a system of disk organization and storage, and the products of all computer activities had first to be checked and approved by him prior to their printing or retention. To summarize, Mr Micro insisted on the centrality of the teacher and the necessity for him/her to be fully aware of what pupils were doing and for what purpose.

Computer Monitoring

Mr Micro controlled groups working at the micros by a combination of long-distance inspections supplemented by frequent and regular interventions. He stressed that the computer was infallible and only its users made mistakes: like a pen it only did what its user ordained. As he made clear to pupils he could check what had been done, but this was accomplished in a friendly and supportive manner.

Computer Confidence Boosting

Mr Micro repeatedly told pupils not to have any fear of computers or computing: he emphasized the need for considered and systematic working and for pupils to collaborate and help each other. He emphasized, too, the need for 'computer stamina' or 'sticking at it until you work it out for yourself . . . you mustn't let the software or the machine beat you!'

I now move to the study of pupil usage of computers in Mr Micro's LOGO-oriented classroom. The data consists of observational field notes, transcribed tape recordings and interviews.

Pupil Usage of Computers

Mr Micro was well aware of the danger of possible gender bias when micro-computers are introduced into classrooms. However, this was viewed in terms of women 'shying away' from the technology:

> I'm well aware of the gender issue. It's rife when dealing with computers. A lot of women teachers shy away, as do girls. Conversely, some men and boys actively embrace computers.

His assumption was that equal access existed in his classroom and that that, in itself, was enough. He felt that boys were not privileged but that there were certainly problems in secondary schools in the development and promotion of computer environments often as an adjunct of mathematics. Moreover, although (some) boys may (sometimes) dominate (some) girls, this was not because of his micro work or characteristic of it: the opposite, in fact, in that his micro usage was based on groups mixed in terms of both sex and ability. The micro was, in that sense, a means of attacking sex stereotyping in the classroom and had the potential to bring boys and girls together in genuine working relationships. I put it to him that I had observed girls being dominated and generally bossed around by boys. He acknowledged this but argued that it 'only happens seriously on occasions'.

> Yes, I'm aware of that. I notice it myself and I've tried to discuss it with them. A lot of teachers have commented on it in the [INSET] courses. Many are now opting for all-boy and all-girl groups. Personally I want to try and stick to mixed pairs and groups. In my experience it only happens seriously on occasions, and only with some boys, certainly not all. In fact, Rebecca there is the opposite. She bosses the boys and lays down the law in no uncertain manner!

He denied any suggestion of unintentional sexism in his pupils' interactions with computers and redefined it in terms of ability differences and intra-group conflict, more to do with working in groups than gender per se:

> I do not agree that boys dominate girls. Of course, some boys dominate girls, but adversely there are some girls in the class who'd never let a boy dominate them. Quite the reverse in fact. Conflict *within* groups is more of a problem. Bright kids can handle such conflicts but those of lesser ability are far more likely not to be able to handle conflict.

I now examine the evidence under four headings:

- Girls' complaints re male 'computer bullies';
- Dominating boys and invisible girls;
- Dominating girls;
- Gender differences in pupils' views of computers.

Girls' Complaints

Early in my field notes I noted:

> This afternoon a group of girls complained bitterly to me about boys claiming to 'know all about it' and 'pressing all the keys' and 'keeping us off the keyboards'.

A conspicuous culprit was Stephen, who along with six or so other boys I designated a 'computer bully'. A few examples will suffice:

> I watch Stephen who hogs the machine and prevents Samantha getting a look in. She complains to me later about the boys pushing girls off the computers and 'pressing the keys to prove they're boys and good at computing'.

On another occasion Hannah complained bitterly to me about Stephen's domination of the keyboard:

> If you work with Stephen you get really bored because he has to do everything himself. No one else can take part!

I also noted:

> A girl said to Stephen, 'Can we use someone else's suggestion now Stephen?' Stephen dominates the group and the girls explain: 'He's always on the computers ... he never lets anyone else get a look-in ...'

One pupil, Hannah, redefined the problem of aggressive 'excluding' micro conduct in terms not only of boys, but also both of dominant girls (an aspect I shall pick up later) as well as group size when she reported:

> Scott and Mark are enjoying themselves and rattling on but Jessica and me, we're bored! Normally I like doing things on the computer and I enjoy playing computer games at home. But four of you on a computer in school is too may and some of the boys and some girls like Alex and Samantha just want to boss you around.

Dominant Boys/Invisible Girls

Girls repeatedly divulged to me that (some) boys 'slagged off' girls (Susan) when it came to computers. Susan provided insight as to how this interference was actually carried out:

> Some of the boys tell the girls they're no good on computers. They come up behind you and interfere and push all the keys and change things and say you've done it all wrong'.

Andrew was one of the principal culprits when it came to using micro activities to assert himself over peers, especially girls. I recorded that 'Andrew unleashed onto a computer changes into a bully' and provide the following vignette as an example of what I observed one afternoon as he worked with Emma:

> On the evidence of my observations this afternoon it seems to me boys work better together, as do girls, but that there is often [not always] conflict in mixed-sex groups. I watched Andrew boss Emma, for example: 'It's not Repeat!' He leant over and grabbed Emma's hand. She keys in his orders, but argues 'I didn't draw a circle when I was there'. He says, 'Stop arguing, just get on with it!' She follows his instructions. Later he says, 'Now print. This probably won't work, but I have to try it out before I make up my mind about what I want, how I want to do it'.
>   In the lead-up to this he has repeatedly grabbed Emma's arm and taken over on the keys, his fingers moving expertly and quickly. A tiny head emerges as a result of Andrew's instruction and so he goes off to

get Mr Micro. Meanwhile Emma tries to sort it out on her own. He returns: 'Emma what are you doing?'. 'I'm working it out for myself!' 'No you're not!', and so on.

Girls have a hard time when working with Andrew. He's dominant, he shouts, and he does things quickly and pays no heed to anyone else but himself. Andrew unleashed onto a computer changes into a bully! In spite of Emma's frequent protestations of 'Andrew, don't touch anything', he forcibly took over.

A frequently observed trend was for girls to be relegated to functionaries, to be 'LOGO scribes' and keyboard operators, mere 'carrier outers' of (mostly) boys' orders. As in the case of Andrew above, the boys assumed the decision-making and order-giving role as if it was theirs by right. I noted that:

> In the ten groups I have observed in which this division of labour occurred, boys were keyboard operators for 70 per cent of the time, whereas they were recorders/scribes for only 20 per cent of the time. Conversely, girls were keyboard operators for 30 per cent of the time, scribes for 80 per cent. Moreover, the role of scribe was often a backseat job and, since girls often sat together, this meant that boys dominated the area immediately in front of the keyboard, whereas girls literally 'sat back', thus:

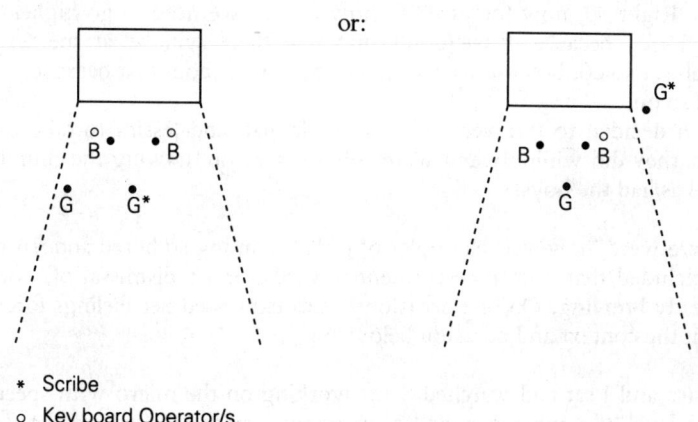

```
*  Scribe
o  Key board Operator/s.
```

It must be stated clearly that I recorded numerous incidents when boys excluded and marginalized girls from micro participation by dominating both the decision-making and the keyboard so that girls were reduced to passive onlookers and non-participants. One example of the many entries in my field notes will suffice to illustrate what I described as a 'common occurrence':

> Scott, Stephen, Jessica and Hannah make up the group, but the boys monopolize the keyboard and make all the decisions. They talk to each other and ignore the girls, who sit quietly behind them.

I decided to intervene on behalf of the girls who, although silent onlookers, had clearly been taking everything in. Pupils, it appears, do not always have to be active participants in order to be 'working and learning':

> In a group I observed this morning the boys, as typists, completely controlled the interaction. [The pattern was thus as in the first diagram above]. The girls sat separately and watched whilst the two boys, Mark and Stuart, chatted incessantly about what and why they were doing this and that:

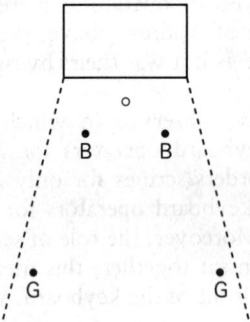

> 'Right 90, now forward 50, now 60 . . . we need to go higher . . . why? . . . because if we don't that line there will be at the wrong level . . . so 60, because we don't need to worry about that because. . . .', and so on.
>
> I decided to intervene and asked Hannah and Jessica to take over. This they did willingly and were able to carry on drawing the church as well as had the boys.

There were, however, examples of girls becoming so bored and frustrated at being excluded that a deep resentment towards, and a dismissal of, computing was already brewing. On one occasion Jessica expressed her feelings forcibly and I recount the context and occasion below:

> Jessica and I sat and watched Scott working on the micro with speed, a high level of competence, and obvious enjoyment. I asked her about her feelings concerning the task in hand [to explore angles] and she said: 'I'm really bored. I just sit back and he [Scott] takes over and enjoys himself. It's supposed to teach us about angles, but I'd rather learn about them in some other way. I don't know what the person who put the program together had in mind — to learn about angles, I suppose. But I don't understand a lot of it. Most lessons I just watch Stephen or Scott dominating things and talking away. I don't understand most of what they say.'

However, there was an even darker side to the gender-related character of micro-based group activity which recurred, and this was the tendency for girls who participated and contributed to have their contributions either rebutted or ignored:

Mark: LT5? No, I don't think so!
Bethan: Yes, it's LT5.
Mark: No, I'm not doing that!
Bethan: It will! Do it and you'll see.
Mark: No, I'll do it another way.

Ironically, in connection with the Bethan-Mark duo, I noted that Bethan was only allowed to take over in a crisis, 'leaning over and punching the keys when Mark was stuck'.

Girls Fight Back: Dominant Girls

My observations indicated that boys did not always have things all their own way. For example, I described Stephen and Hannah as being 'locked in an acrimonious tussle which is often both comic and abusive, although the social and cognitive benefits of their uncompromising competition are possibly considerable'. An example of what I recorded concerning their group follows:

Stephen barks out: 'Hannah, put LT45!'
Hannah: 'I will if you want me to, but it'll be wrong. It should be LT40.'
    Although Stephen appears to be in control, in their quiet, undemonstrative way Hannah and Jessica are in the driving seat. They let Stephen and Mark make mistakes then pick up the pieces:
    Hannah: 'Clear the screen, Stephen, 'cos you're not getting anywhere! Try. . . .' [She gives a number of instructions.]

I commented that, firstly, dominant pupils, whether male or female, squeeze out less determined or interested peers in the group who end up taking on an observer's role. Two girls, for example, complained to me about the battle between Matthew and Emma. Secondly, whilst 'dominant pupils' might be the best way of describing what I observed, the fact remained that there were far more dominant boys and very few, in comparison, assertive girls. Only in a small number of instances did I observe groups in which a girl or girls controlled proceedings and, thereby, placed quiet boys in the same backseat position as the quiet girls previously detailed. Moreover, in order to 'push in' or 'take over' a girl needed support, either from friends or Mr Micro. I noted that:

In Dragon's Garden this afternoon Bethan pushed in and insisted that she and her friends took their turn on the keyboard. A group of boys reluctantly gave way only after Mr Micro had been asked to intervene.

Occasionally I noted one group of girls hustle another off a computer and it must be stressed that this was exceptional and nearly always instigated by the determined Bethan or Hannah. At such times boys often withdrew their participation altogether, as is illustrated by this extract, when the two most assertive girls joined forces:

For the first half of the session they sat thus:

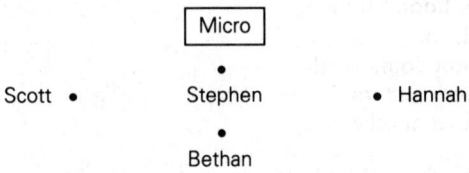

In the second half, however, Bethan took over: 'Get out of the way, Stephen', she said, 'it's our turn now!'

Thereafter she and Hannah took over control of the computer, ignoring Stephen's protests. In the end he left and wandered off, soon followed by Scott. For the second part of the afternoon the pattern of participation was thus:

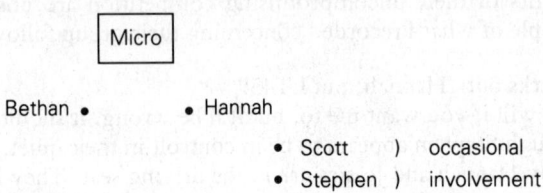

An interesting footnote to the gender-related aspects of micro usage in this classroom was the role of Gethin, a large, computer-confident boy popular throughout the class, who sometimes acted as a kind of 'surrogate teacher' in helping pupils when they got really stuck. Because of his exalted role he was sometimes enlisted by some girls to help hurry other pupils off the computer, or to get them out of a fix, as below:

I have noticed that girls are often cast in the role of typists to key-in orders formulated and given by the boys. If they make a mistake they are insulted. Examples include the following rebukes:

'Hannah, it's not a toaster, it's a computer!'

'Emma, why are you so hopeless?'

'Can't you do anything right, Jessica? You've just made *another* mistake!'

Sometimes, however, the girls hit back:

'Stephen, why don't you just have a snooze instead of bossing us around all the time?'

Stella is joined by two friends and in their company she becomes more combative and assertive towards Mark, who has spent the afternoon dominating proceedings and excluding her from full participation on the micro.

Finally, in observing the interaction and operation of groups I noted that some girls (notably Bethan) were often superior communicators and instructors when they were allowed to participate on an equal footing. An example follows:

> Girls seem to me to be better teachers of boys than vice versa. I watch Bethan and Mark work together. She has a far superior understanding of what is required and how to go about achieving it. Bethan tells him to 'draw an O on the screen with your fingers and then work out whether the Turtle should go left or right by turning around in your chair. What you must *not* do is press Escape: if you press that you lose it!' As they work, the snowman they are drawing disappears off the screen, but Bethan takes over and helps Mark construct a smaller version. 'You've got to make the left turn bigger in order to make the circle smaller. Got it?'

Pupils' Views on Computers/Computing

In my conversations with pupils it was manifestly the case that girls were more critical and analytical and less accepting of the possible benefits of micro technology. This is not to say that there were not girls who enthusiastically welcomed computer work: during my fieldwork two were sent by their parents to a residential computing course for primary school children organized by the Local Education Authority. They were, thereafter, strong advocates of computing and one commented that 'computers are good because they help you apply knowledge; problem solve; learn by typing out your ideas; and are a fun means to learn'! Similarly, some boys (but a far smaller minority) were dismissive of computers. What surprised me was that there was such a definite gender-related difference in boys' and girls' views of computing, a difference which is worth exploring further.

Pupils varied widely in how they viewed computers and in their assessments of their value and relevance to them. One determining factor in this was the level of academic attainment (on the bases of Mr Micro's records and verbal accounts to me of their performance levels): high achievers were far more likely to be supportive of computing, whereas low achievers were markedly less so. High achievers emphasized the learning potential of computers, whereas low attainers — if they were supportive of computing — saw it as primarily adding some additional variety to the school day and little else. I was surprised, too, by the fact that many of these primary school pupils were already making sophisticated distinctions concerning the capabilities of computers, albeit founded on very limited (mainly LOGO 'screen turtling') experience.

It can be said that computer advocacy was based on the following tenets:

- that computers were synonymous with an ill-defined, nebulous but 'exciting' future;
- that computer competence was necessary for future employment;
- that computers were fun and exciting, especially Dragon's Garden and other game-like formats;

- that computers were intellectually challenging especially if, like the 'high fliers', you were beginning to explore, albeit in embryonic form, simple programming skills;
- the wish to respond to and please parents, from whom there was considerable pressure to 'get into computers' and from whom Mr Micro himself derived most of his support and encouragement;
- the belief that in some undefined way computers helped you think and work things out, especially in mathematics, and might even one day replace teachers (or, at least, part of the teacher's function).

Conversely, it was the girls who articulated the great majority of criticisms of computing. In Mr Micro's class if you were a boy you were most likely to be a computer advocate, even if you were a low achiever. If you were a girl, you were far more likely to be a computer critic or rejector, even if you were a high achiever. What points did girls raise? Hannah, for example, was both a high achiever and good at computing, yet she had this to say concerning the amount of computing undertaken in Mr Micro's class and the nature of 'real work':

We can't do much real work like History or using books with Mr Micro. It's all using computers — too much computers! I'd like to do some real work but my parents say you can't do everything you want in school and they like the fact we do so much computing. They're glad I'm in Mr Micro's class and say I should be pleased too. I like him as a teacher but I just think we do far too much computing.

Another high-achieving, computer-competent girl, Bethan, focused on what should not be done on a computer:

Bethan feels she could do all her maths on computer and some writing (for example punctuation, spelling and cloze work), but not the 'thinking and planning which you can do with a pen'. She believes, too, that 'a lot of things like information in books and working things out' cannot best be done on a computer: 'Lots of things can be done with computers, but I don't think they will ever replace the teacher'.

This was reiterated by another girl:

A computer can never be a proper teacher because it can't teach. There may be things you don't understand that you get right, but the computer can't tell you about them. You need the teacher to help you and to tell you things like that.

Rebecca, meanwhile, questioned Mr Micro's insistence that all creative writing be word-processed, an issue taken up, too, by Sharon, who also referred to parental pressure:

'Using pens is better than hitting keys all the time', grumbles Sharon. 'But my parents say you've got to know about computers today or you'll not get an important job. I'm always afraid of doing things wrong, or breaking a disk, or printing-out wrong. I'm dead scared when I load my disk always.'

The data I have quoted, gathered in only one classroom, nevertheless raises a number of tentative pointers to future ethnographic research into children's usage of the microcomputer and also some open questions. I shall term these 'issues arising' and be no more specific than that, and address them under four headings, namely: interactional; the social context of IT/Education implementation and operation; microcomputing as a male domain; and, finally, equity.

Issues Arising

Interactional

- The ways in which girls attempted to cope with their lack of keyboard access and power, whether through collective action or by enlisting the support of Gethin, the surrogate teacher, are worthy of note. Girls who were aggressive risked becoming unpopular with boys and girls alike and so, for some, a passive response was the safest, most rational, and easiest one. Teachers must ask themselves how a classroom climate of genuine peer partnership re micro usage might best be fostered given the resources they have available?

- Group work demands teachers pay far more attention to the typical structures of male and female pupil talk and interactional styles. Here was repeated evidence of boys adopting a 'bullying' discourse which excluded most girls from participation. What are the implications for software design and usage of such gender-based, habitual interactional traits, and how might schools best address them?

- 'Culture' can be described as the system of shared meanings within a group or groups. What Hoyles (1985) has called the 'culture of class-room computing' must *not*, therefore, be taken to refer just to the technology, but to the classroom relationships it supports or, indeed, prevents or obstructs.

- Finally, a wider and more contentious point as far as UK schools are concerned: how might IT/Education be used to extend educational choice and equality of opportunity (what Michael Apple (1986) would describe as part of social literacy) and thus foster the creation of knowledge and wisdom (as opposed to mere information) in pupils and teachers alike? How might this be best made to work on the interpersonal, micro level of computer groupwork?

The Social Context of IT/Education Implementation and Operation

- The Green Acre data showed a busy and perceptive teacher whose care-fully considered policy of mixed group equality of access to computers was, nevertheless, defeated at source as boys excluded most girls from full participation. He was largely unaware that even within the context of apparent equality of access girls were still, in fact, being disadvantaged.

- The emphasis to date in IT/Education research has been upon issues relating to technology and cognition rather than upon the social context of its introduction and use.[1] Indeed, the data above is indicative of the manner in which computers have been introduced into UK schools — that is, in a hurry before teachers have the opportunity to fully think through, prepare and monitor their operation. Although both an able and energetic teacher, Mr Micro could not, given his role as a class teacher, adequately monitor all that was happening as small groups worked apart from the main body of the class on the micros.

- Boys exerted both physical (domination of the keyboard) and verbal (exclusion from decision-making) powers over girls. Pupils need to be helped to work together in collaborative, non-sexist and non-racist ways. Indeed, there is a strong argument for single-sex groups in which case the power of intra-group domination from dominant boys and girls will still not be solved. The whole composition, operation and inner dynamics of groups and partnerships must be more carefully researched.

Microcomputing as a Male Domain

- The Green Acre data portrays some of the pressures daily experienced by girls as they interrelated both with boys and computers. The evidence, although limited, is disturbing in that boys were clearly already appropriating computers as a male domain in which to display their 'superiority' over girls who were verbally bullied and even, at times, 'slagged off' (Lees, 1983). Computers had become another resource for them to construct and express a stereotypical masculine identity of being 'expert', 'knowledgeable' and 'in control' (Hearn, 1987).

- Elsewhere (Beynon, 1985; 1989b) I have charted the construction of a particular masculine identity in a secondary school and the processes at work which occasioned and confirmed this. It may be that computing, like much sport, has aspects which offer boys both actual and symbolic opportunities to dominate within institutions (Askew, 1988). These need to be identified and countered if education is to be democratized and produce adults who can relate and work together in spite of gender, class, race or age differences.

- Indeed, given the evidence gathered in Green Acre it could be claimed that the microcomputer in the primary school as an object of study may well be only incidentally about microcomputing per se, but mainly about the 'off the ball' incidents it occasions.

Equity

- Schools are not, obviously, solely responsible for gendering: the ways in which Green Acre male pupils behaved towards girls was building on images and expectations they brought with them into Mr Micro's classroom.[2] However, schools and individual teachers do have considerable powers of intervention and pupil-acculturation (Rutter et al., 1979). In what ways might the primary school computing experience be used to sensitize pupils (in harness with other curriculum strategies) to improved gender relations and reformed notions of masculinity and femininity?

- The computer interactions observed in Green Acre displayed a high degree of sexist behaviour, a topic which is now firmly on the UK educational agenda (Askew and Ross, 1988; Cockburn, 1987; Weiner, 1985; Stanworth, 1983). What is perhaps surprising is that girls were so definitely 'turning off' computers (through not having the opportunity to 'turn on'?) at such an early point in their school careers (cf. Hughes *et al.* (1987), who found analogous sex-stereotyping in children's attitudes towards computers in the primary school).

- It is clear that if girls are not to be 'edged out' of technology then intervention must start early in the primary school (perhaps in the reception class? — see Paley, 1984) and not be delayed until later when attitudes have already hardened (Collis, 1987).

- To be successful, access to computing should be part of a wider Equity Policy in each primary and secondary school. Indeed, teachers must be far more alert to possible gender imbalance in microcomputer access and usage, not just as something in itself but as part of the wider issue of equal opportunities in the primary classroom across all areas of the curriculum and resource deployment. They should also, as part of this, attempt to make visible and examine the multi-faceted processes of the hidden curriculum and its role in gender differentiation.

Acknowledgment

Parts of this chapter featured in a paper delivered to the IT/Education Symposium at the BERA Conference held in the University of East Anglia, September, 1988.

Notes

1 An exemption to this is the study of IT/Education in Barnaby Comprehensive (reported in Bliss *et al.*, 1986, and Chandra *et al.*, 1988). The study is limited in scale and is ruined for me by a too-ready recourse to Frame Factor Theory and to White and Lippitt (1968) on leader behaviour and member reaction. However, it is notable for stressing the social context of the school in which computers are introduced and used, and one hopes now for more extensive ethnographic data on this theme to be forthcoming, both in the UK and from studies currently starting in the USA and Canada (for example, at the University of Western Ontario, directed by Professor Ivor Goodson).

2 Any Equity Policy, certainly in relation to IT/Education, will have to tackle (some) boys' already distorted images of girls. I have recently observed 6-year-olds learning how to use micros under the direction of a female teacher in an infants' school in the Rhondda, north of Cardiff. I recorded the following conversation with Gwyn, who was supposed to be 'partnering' another boy but who was, as the teacher had warned, overwhelmingly dominant. I learned that he played on a computer at home and I asked him whether he thought that girls were 'as good on computers as boys'. The recording is as follows:

Gwyn: My computer's too hard for any girl, my computer is. Girls would never do my computer.

Me: Why?

Gwyn: Girls can't play He-Man 'cos you've got to run fast and jump over beams and holes and if girls did that they'd fall in!

Me: But that's just a game!

Gwyn: No, girls can't do anything on my computer. You've got to be tough to play with a computer.

At 6 Gwyn, it would appear, has already categorized girls as being second-rate. Indeed, the nature and impact of computer games on young minds needs urgent research attention. Turkle (1984) and Olson (1988) independently argue that computer games are frequently sexist, racist, militaristic and competitive in format, emphasizing the joys of technical domination and mastery associated with our culture's view of 'successful masculinity'. Albury (1985), meanwhile, explores masculinity and its linkages with technology and technological choice with reference to Spielberg's film, *E.T.*, whilst Fiske and Watts (1985) on video games comment that 'what the playing subject is doing, in grasping the controls, is gaining the power to control not just the machine, but his own meanings, and these meanings we intimately connected with masculinity and its relationship to power and subordination.' All point to a dearth of work on the gendering function of computer games, video arcade games and video films.

References

ALBURY, D. (1985) '*E.T.*: technology and masculinity', in RADICAL SCIENCE COLLECTIVE (Ed.), *Making Waves: The Politics of Communication*, London, Free Association Press.

APPLE, M. (1986) *Teachers and Texts: A Political Economy of Class and Gender Relations in Education*, London, Routledge and Kegan Paul.

ASKEW, S. (1988) 'Aggressive behaviour in boys: to what extent is it institutionalised?', in TATTUM, D.P. and LANE, D.A. (Eds) *Bullying in Schools*, Stoke-on-Trent, Trentham Books.

ASKEW, S. and ROSS, C. (1988) *Boys Don't Cry: Boys and Sexism in Education*, Milton Keynes, Open University Press.

BAKER, C. (1983) 'The microcomputer and the curriculum', *Journal of Curriculum Studies*, 15, 2, pp. 207–14.

BAKER, C. (1985) 'The microcomputer and the curriculum: a critique', *Journal of Curriculum Studies*, 17, 4, pp. 449–51.

BEYNON, J. (1985) *Initial Encounters in the Secondary School: Sussing, Typing and Coping*, Falmer Press.

BEYNON, J. (1989a) 'Towards a new paradigm of IT/Education'. Available from: Communication Studies, The Polytechnic of Wales, Treforest, Mid Glamorgan, CF37 1DL.

BEYNON, J. (1989b) 'A school for men', in WALKER, S. and BARTON, L. *Politics and the Processes of Schooling*, Milton Keynes, Open University Press.

BEYNON, J. (1991) 'Just a few machines bleeping away in a corner: a review of naturalistic studies of computers into education in the UK', in BLOMEYER, R.L. and MARTIN, C.D. (Eds), *Case Studies in Computer Aided Learning*, Falmer Press.

BEYNON, J. and MACKAY, H. (1989) 'Information Technology into education: towards a critical perspective', *Journal of Education Policy*, Falmer Press.

BLISS, J., CHANDRA, P. and COX, M. (1986) 'The introduction of computers into a school', *Computer Education*, Vol. 10, No. 1.

BROWN, C.A. (1988) 'Girls, boys and technology: getting to the root of the problem', *Social Science Review*, December.

BURKE, J. *et al.* (1988) 'My mum uses a computer, too', in HOYLES, C. (Ed.) *Girls and Computers*, Bedford Way Papers 34, Institute of Education, University of London.

BURNS, S. and SMART, T. (1988) 'Sixth-form girls using computers to explore Newtonian Mathematics', in HOYLES, C. (Ed.) *Girls and Computers*, Bedford Way Paper 34, Institute of Education, University of London.

CARMICHAEL, H.W. *et al.* (1985) *Computers, Children and Classrooms*, Ontario, Canada.

CHANDRA, P., BLISS, J. and COX, M. (1988) 'Introducing computers into a school: management issues, *Computer Education*, Vol. 12, No. 1.

CHEN, M. (1986) 'Gender and computers', *Journal of Educational Computing*, Vol. 2, No. 3.

COCKBURN, C. (1987) *Two Track Training*, Basingstoke, Macmillan.

COLLIS, B.A. (1987) 'Gender differences in adolescents' attitudes towards computers', *Journal of Education Policy*, No. 1, September/October, Falmer Press.

COMMONWEALTH SCHOOLS COMMISSION PROJECT (1984) on IT/Education, c/o C.S.C., Box 34, Woden, A.C.T. 2606, Australia.

CULLEY, L. (1986) *Gender Differences and Computing in Secondary Schools*, Department of Education, Loughborough University of Technology.

CULLEY, L. (1988) 'Girls, boys and computers', *Educational Studies*, Vol. 14, No. 1.

DEPARTMENT OF EDUCATION AND SCIENCE (1980) *H.M.I. — Matters for Discussion, 13*, London, HMSO.

DOHERTY, M. (1987) 'Science education for girls: a case study', *S.S.R.*, 246, 69, 28–33.

EVANS, A. and HALL, W. (1988) 'Computer education and gender inequality', in National Union of Teachers' *Education Review*, Vol. 2, No. 1, Spring.

FIFE-SHAW, *et al.* (1986) 'Patterns of teenage computer usage', *Journal of C.A.L.*, Vol. 2.

FILE, P.E., TOOLMAN, J. and DUGARD, P.I. (1988) 'Insight and attitudes to computing', paper to Women Into Computing Conference, Lancaster University.

FISKE, J. and WATTS, J. (1985) 'Video games: inverted pleasures', *Australian Journal of Cultural Studies*, Vol. 3, No. 1.

GARDNER, J.A. *et al.* (1985) 'Attitudes to Computer Studies', *Computers and Education*, Vol. 10, No. 2.

GLASER, B. and STRAUSS, A. (1967) *The Discovery of Grounded Theory*, London, Weidenfeld and Nicholson.

HALL, J. and RHODES, V. (1988) 'Microcomputers in primary schools: some observations and recommendations for good practice', available from The Educational Computing Unit, Centre For Educational Studies, King's College, London.

HAMMERSLEY, M. (1980) 'Classroom ethnography', *Educational Analysis*, 2, 2.

HEARN, J. (1987) *The Gender of Oppression: Men, Masculinity and the Critique of Marxism*, Brighton, Wheatsheaf Books/Harvester Press.

HESS, R.D. (1985) 'Gender differences', *Sex Roles*, Vol. 13, Nos. 3/4.

HOYLES, C. (1985) *Culture and Computers in the Mathematics Classroom: An Inaugural Lecture*, University of London, Institute of Education.

HOYLES, C. (Ed.) (1988) *Girls and Computers*, Bedford Way Papers 34, Institute of Education, University of London.

HUGHES, M., MACLEOD, H., POTTS, C. and ROGERS, J. (1985) 'Are computers only for boys?', *New Society*, 11.

HUGHES, M., BRACKENRIDGE, A. and MACLEOD, H. (1987) 'Children's ideas about computers', in RUTKOWSKA, J.C. and CROOK, C. (Eds) *Computers, Cognition and Development*, Chichester, Wiley.

HUGHES, M., BRACKENRIDGE, A., BIBBY, A. and GREENHAUGH, P. (1988) 'Girls, boys and Turtles: gender effects in young children learning with LOGO', in HOYLES,

C. (Ed.) *Girls and Computers*, Bedford Way Papers 34, Institute of Education, University of London.

HUMPHREY, M. (1985–1987) Referred to in the Final Report of the UK/USA Microelectronics Project. London, N.U.T. Publications.

JOHNSON, S. and BELL, J.F. (1987) 'Gender differences in science option choices', *S.S.R.*, 247, 69, 268–76.

JOHNSON, S. and MURPHY, P. (1986) 'Girls and physics', in *Assessment of Performance Unit Findings*, Occasional Paper No. 4, London, DES/APU.

KAHLE, J.B. (Ed.) (1985) *Women in Science*, Falmer Press.

KARGER, H.J. (1988) 'Children and microcomputers: a critical analysis', *Education Today*, Vol. 38, No. 2.

KELLY, A. (Ed.) (1981) 'Choosing or channelling?', in *The Missing Half: Girls and Science Education*, Manchester University Press.

LEES, S. (1983) 'How boys slag off girls', *New Society*, 13 October.

LLOYD, A. and NEWALL, L. (1985) 'Women and computers', in FAULKNER, N. and ARNOLD, E. (Eds) *Smothered by Inventions*, Pluto Press.

LYON, D. (1988) *The Information Society: Issues and Illusions*, Cambridge, Polity Press.

MEIGHAN, R. and REID, W. (1982) 'How will the New Technology change the curriculum?', *Journal of Curriculum Studies*, Vol. 14, No. 4.

MOORE, B. (1986) *Equity in Education*, Ministry of Education, Ontario, Canada.

NOSS, R. (1988) 'Geometrical thinking and LOGO: do girls have more to gain?', in HOYLES, C. (Ed.) *Girls and Computers*, Bedford Way Papers 34, Institute of Education, University of London.

OLSON, C.P. (1988) 'Who computes?', in LIVINGSTONE, D.W. (Ed.) *Critical Pedagogy and Cultural Power*, Massachusetts, Bergin and Garvey.

PALEY, V.G. (1984) *Boys and Girls: Superheroes in the Doll's Corner*, Chicago, University of Chicago Press.

PAPERT, S. (1980) *Mindstorms — Children, Computers and Powerful Ideas*, Brighton, Harvester Press.

RUTTER, M., MAUGHAN, B., MORTIMORE, P. and OUSTON, J. (1979) *Fifteen Thousand Hours*. Open Books.

SANDERS, J.S. and STONE, A. (1986) *The Neuter Computer: Computers for Girls and Boys*, New York, Neal Schuman.

SIANN, G. and MACLEOD, H. (1986) 'Computers and children of primary school age', *British Journal of Educational Technology*, Vol. 2, No. 17, May.

SIMONS, G.L. (1981) *Women in Computing*, Manchester, National Computing Centre.

SOMEKH, B. (1988) 'Micro reflections', paper delivered to BERA Symposium on I.T./Education, University of East Anglia, September.

STANWORTH, M. (1983) *Gender and Schooling: A Study of Sexual Divisions in the Classroom*, London, Hutchinson.

SUTHERLAND, R. and HOYLES, C. (1988) 'Gender perspectives on LOGO programming in the mathematics curriculum', in HOYLES, C. (Ed.) *Girls and Computers*, Bedford Way Papers 34, Institute of Education, University of London.

SUHOR, C. and JESTER, V. (1984) 'ERIC/RCS report: computer caveats', *English Education*, 16, 181–5, Urbana, Illinois.

TURKLE, S. (1984) *The Second Self*, New York, Granada.

WALKERDINE, V. (1988) 'Girls and Mathematics Project', University of London Institute of Education, W.C.1.

WARE, M.C. and STUCK, M.F. (1985) 'Sex role messages', *Sex Roles*, Vol. 13, Nos. 3/4.

WEINER, G. (Ed.) (1985) *Just a Bunch of Girls*, Milton Keynes, Open University Press.

WHITE, R. and LIPPITT, R. (1968) 'Leader behavior and member reaction', in CARTWRIGHT, D. and ZANDER, A. (Eds) *Group Dynamics*, London, Tavistock.

WHYTE, J., DEEM, R., KANT, L. and CRUICKSHANK, M. (Eds) (1985) *Girl Friendly Schooling*, London, Methuen.

WILDER, G. *et al.* (1985) 'Gender and computers', *Sex Roles*, Vol. 13, Nos. 3/4.

WILLIS, S. (1987) 'Access to the program by girls and disadvantaged groups', in BIGUM, C., *et al. Coming to Terms with Computers in Schools: Report to Commonwealth Schools Commission*, Deakin Institute for Studies in Education, Australia, September.

WOMEN'S ACTION ALLIANCE EQUITY PROGRAM REPORT [1987] c/o 370 Lexington Avenue, New York, 10017.

Chapter 12

Micros in Action: Three Classroom Case Studies

Mary Shooter, Patricia Lovering and Sheila Bellamy

Introduction

We are grateful to Peter Bartlett and Phillip Bassett and three students of the Cardiff Institute of Higher Education (CIHE) for permission to use extracts from projects submitted as part of coursework for their in-service diploma in educational computing. The diploma equips teachers, mostly in primary schools, to take responsibility for I.T. education and to observe and evaluate aspects of computer use in their own classrooms. These extracts are included not so much for what they say (although this is, in itself, valuable), but for the possibilities such case studies hold for teachers. They emphasize the fact that to understand the use of computers in classrooms demands a research paradigm that, firstly, incorporates a broad set of educational concerns; and, secondly, observes computers at their point of implementation. This includes apparently irrelevant activities that take place 'around' and even 'off' the computer but which are, nevertheless, part of the pupil's learning experience. Teachers often find their attention drawn, for example, away from pupil-computer interaction to the talk amongst pupils it occasions, even though that talk may not be strictly related to the tasks-at-hand. To understand what is happening entails employing an educational rather than a technological framework. A good starting point would be use of Wilkinson's (1991) ideational, interpersonal and textual to contextualize and make sense of pupils' 'computer talk', or McMahon and O'Neil (1990) on the role of dialogue in learning. Indeed, we believe that recourse to such educational literatures in evaluating the deployment of computers is both an essential part of teachers' technological literacy and necessary for the 'educationalizing' of educational computing. This is an issue taken further in the final paper (by Beynon) in this volume.

In the first extract Shooter examines the role dialogue plays in using LOGO. This is followed by a detailed study (by Lovering) of the function the computer can play in improving a pupil's spelling. The final extract is from a study by Bellamy of a program's role in supporting second language learning.

Case Study 1: Pupils' LOGO Talk: Mary Shooter

After the initial pre-computer work the computer was brought into the classroom and kept in a classroom bay for half a term. During that time it was shared by another class, so it was only available to the children in the mornings. Each group was timetabled to have one half-hour session (the sessions did not always last this long) of the computer each week (a group being a pair of children). Some of the children, including Matthew and Tom, were so excited by the program that they stayed in during playtimes and lunchtimes to work on LOGO.

Five classroom sessions and one final lunchtime session were taped when Matthew and Tom were working on the computer, and it is these sessions that are commented on here.

Session 1

The group had to discover the number for a quarter turn. Tom took the lead in this session — he took charge of the keyboard and throughout the session it was he who took the initiative. He was careful, however, to bring in Matthew and sought his acceptance before commencing a command:

Tom: Right, what shall we try?
Matthew: Umh.
Tom: What about 10? Shall we try 10?
Matthew: Yeah, let's try it.
Tom: I'll put in FD 200. Then do it. Oh!
Matthew: You forgot the space.
Tom: Oh yeah — FD space 200. That's it.
Matthew: Done it.
Tom: Now I'll do 10. RT space 10.
Matthew: That's not enough — try 200.
Tom: No, that'll be too much. Look we've only turned that much (puts hand on screen) and that's 10. We've got to go round that much. It's nearer 100.
Matthew: Do 120 then.
Tom: OK, let's try it.
Matthew: Yeah, that'll be right.
Tom: No, it's too much, I'll turn back LT space 120 and we'll try 100 — OK?
Matthew: Alright.
Tom: It looks near, but it's not quite right.
Matthew: No, it's right.

They continued until they tried 90. Then they tried going round four times to check it. They were delighted to have worked it out and 'proved it'.

In this session Matthew is definitely the quieter of the two boys, while Tom is very much in control. It is Tom who shows the greatest use of cognitive speech, especially where he tries to work out how far to go round. We can see him working out how far 200 goes if 10 goes so far. Matthew generally uses more interactive speech, giving Tom support and a useful piece of information — 'You forgot the space'.

Session 2

In this session the boys were trying out their procedures for shapes — some they had already tried working out, some they worked out while at the computer. During this session Matthew took over the keyboard and it may be this that makes him more assertive, or he may just be more relaxed and familiar with the program.

Matthew: Right, you read out what we worked out for the square.
Tom: OK — FD space 200 RT space 90. FD space 200 RT space 90. Then the same again.
Matthew: FD space 200 RT space 90 and again. There it is — our square.

The oral work continued in the same vein as the boys transferred their procedures to the computer. There was no cognitive speech involved; they had done their working out before coming to the computer. Now notice the change when they try a new procedure. (Meanwhile the teacher has shown them how to use the command repeat).

Matthew: OK — let's do a hexagon.
Tom: Put in repeat.
Matthew: Done that — now what number?
Tom: Well, we did 4 for a space what do you think?
Matthew: 10?
Tom: No, how many sides has a hexagon?
Matthew: Umh, 6.
Tom: Right, so put in 6. Now we've got to work out the turn — hang on. (Gets a piece of paper and pencil.)
Matthew: What're you doing?
Tom: Look, 360 is a whole turn, so . . . if I do this (writes sum down) it's . . . 6 into 36 is 6 . . . . it's 60.
Matthew: 60 what?
Tom: I'll tell you in a minute — put in the bracket . . . then FD space 100.
Matthew: Let's try 500.
Tom: No, that won't work. It's too big — it goes everywhere.
Matthew: (Types in 100) Now what? RT isn't it?
Tom: Yeah, then 60.
Matthew: Why?
Tom: Cos it's the turn. Look, I worked it out — (shows him the paper).

In this extract there is some hard thinking going on, and this is obvious in the language being used. Tom is playing the teacher, taking Matthew through the number of sides to working out the 'turn'. The language is mainly cognitive but Tom is also showing excellent Level 2 social skills in the way he leads Matthew to the answer.

Session 3

During this session the children were asked to draw a circle without any preliminary work off the computer. Tom is on the keyboard.

Tom: How're we going to do it then?
Matthew: Well, it needs lots of little lines like this (draws on paper).
Tom: Yeah, so we need to go a little way. What do you think — 10? 5?
Matthew: Try 5.
Tom: (Puts in command FD 5). No — it's too small. I'll put in 5 more (FD 5). That's it! Now how much turn? It's got to be small.
Matthew: 1?
Tom: That's too small.
Matthew: 2? (Tom shakes his head) 5?
Tom: We'll try 5 (RT 5). Now we've got to do it lots more. You do the numbers, I'll do the letters.

This excerpt shows Matthew's first cognitive contribution without a specific lead from Tom: 'Well, it needs lots of little lines ...'. Throughout the rest of the conversation Tom gives him specific leads — Tom's questions suggest that he may have already decided on the best course himself.

Session 4

In this session Matthew and Tom are trying to draw a house — they have just reached the apex of the roof and are not sure where to go next.

Tom: We could just rub out that line if we put in PE and you could take it back.
Matthew: (Mumbled response — not identifiable.)
Tom: I think it's that (pointing to roof line) ... cos it isn't central.
Matthew: (Another mumbled response.)
Tom: No, it's the central bit of the line ... isn't central there.
Matthew: Bring it back a bit.
Tom: Instead of bringing it back all the way we'll rub out a bit.
Matthew: That's PE.
Tom: OK — Now how much back?
Matthew: 20.
Tom: Yeah, let's try it ... what do you think — is it central? ...
Matthew and Tom: Yeah ...
Tom: How much turn do we need? 180?
Matthew: 195?

Tom:	Left, no right turn 195. Is that enough?
Matthew:	Bit more I think.

In this excerpt there is much more collaborative, cognitive thinking. Matthew is not only playing a supportive role, as in the other sessions, but an active one too. Tom, too, is taking less of a lead and for the first time is following up Matthew's suggestions rather than just using them as prompts to his own thinking.

Session 5

In this session Matthew and Tom experimented with variable shape procedures. Tom starts on the keyboard:

Tom:	To square colon L return. Repeat.
Matthew:	4.
Tom:	Bracket forward space colon L right 90 bracket end.
Matthew and Tom:	(Read the screen.) Square defined.
Tom:	Right, let's see if it works. Repeat 36 bracket square right 10 bracket (reads the screen). No it doesn't know how to do it. Keep . . . 36, that's 36 squares. We'll keep 36 bracket square umh L right 10 bracket. (Reads screen.) Doesn't know L.
Matthew:	Put a colon in.
Tom:	Repeat 36 bracket square colon L right 10 bracket. No . . .
Matthew:	Do it this way. Repeat space 36 bracket square L right 10.
Tom:	(Reads screen.) L has no value.
Matthew:	Want me to do it?
Tom:	Do you know what to do? (Change places — Matthew takes over keyboard.)
Tom:	I've got it! I know it! I've got it!
Matthew:	Repeat 36 bracket square . . .
Tom:	Now the number instead of L.
Matthew:	That's it! It has to be a number! 100?
Tom:	Yeah.
Matthew:	Right, repeat 36 bracket square 100 right 10 bracket OK?
Tom:	Yeah.
Matthew:	Return — yeah look!

In this session we see a real collaborative effort. Both boys are thinking hard and both are making suggestions and contributions. They have a good idea for a pattern but they keep making the same mistake, until finally, through trial and error, they remember what to do.

Session 6

This session was a voluntary session at lunchtime when Matthew and Tom were working on a puzzle for the other children. They had drawn a five-hole golf course on the sheet and were now trying to work out the quickest way of going round the course. They were getting very stuck.

Matthew: We'll let them start and don't count those moves.

Tom: Right that's fair — now they should get to hole 2 in 3 shots.

Matthew: How far do you think that is? (Points at sheet on screen.)

Tom: 100?

Matthew: 100 (types in command). No — too far.

Tom: Go back 10.

Matthew: Not enough — I'll do another 10.

Tom: No, less than that — try 5.

Matthew: OK 5.

Similar exchanges went on as the boys laboured round the course until they came up with a solution.

Tom: Hey, we're doing this the wrong way round!

Matthew: No we're not. We started at one and then we go on.

Tom: No, I don't mean . . . I mean we should start with the commands . . .

Matthew: . . . and then make the golf course . . . Yeah, we make the lines on the screen . . .

Tom: And write down our commands.

Matthew: And then make the golf course.

Tom: Yeah (clap hands with Matthew).

Matthew and Tom could hardly conceal their delight with their solution from the other children. They went ahead (in other lunchtime sessions) to simplify their commands, then copied the Turtle track onto the acetate sheets and added the golf tees, holes and other decorative features. Their classmates are still trying to complete the course in par! Their language reflects their collaborative thinking and their ability to pick up on each other's ideas. It is interesting to see how they even finish each other's sentences.

General Observations

It was clear to the class teacher as she observed her children working at the computer that their oral language was an important part of their work. She noticed that the children who seemed to talk the most to each other as they worked seemed to be the children who worked most effectively at LOGO. She noticed too that those children who became most involved and did the most talking were those children who carried on talking in the playground 'We should have done 145', 'No that would have been too much — let's try 120 . . .'.

These are casual, incidental observations, however, of all the children involved. More detailed conclusions (or perhaps observations would be a less finite word) can be drawn from the recordings of Tom and Matthew as they worked on the computer. There certainly seems to be a pattern in the oral language, which changed as they proceeded through the sessions.

During the first two sessions the greater part of the language is interactive. It is almost as if the two children, although already familiar with each other as friends, are getting to know each other in a new context. They treat each other very politely and the teacher observed that their approach to the computer in those early sessions was polite and almost respectful. They worked steadily and carefully and considered each move before they approached the keyboard. In the tape recordings their voices are very calm and controlled, and the pace of the conversation is fairly slow. In these early sessions, too, Tom is the dominant member of the pair. He takes the lead at the computer and Matthew simply supports and agrees. At this point the class teacher was concerned that Tom would dominate throughout the sessions and that Matthew would have no opportunity to develop. In the second session the teacher suggested that Matthew should have a turn on the keyboard and this did seem to affect his contribution. However, Tom was still the dominant member.

Gradually, however, as they continued to work together, a change came over the relationship. Matthew became more confident and as his confidence developed he began to make cognitive as well as interactive contributions. As his contributions changed, Tom took less of a lead and began to respond more positively to Matthew's suggestions.

By the sixth session the partnership seemed to have achieved a perfect balance with both children making an equal contribution and each showing respect and consideration of the other's suggestions. The work in this session seems a truly collaborative effort, their verbalization has greater pace and there is a sense of excitement in their interaction. They approached the keyboard with an air of excitement and some haste, unworried at the thought of making errors.

Future Research

Following on the development of the working relationship of the two boys, it would be interesting to see how each pupil would operate with a new partner. Matched with similar children, would they show similar characteristics or, having developed collaborative skills in this study, would they operate in different ways? Further observations of these two pupils could provide some interesting indicators of how children should be grouped for such activities.

The method of grouping children is also an avenue which would be interesting to pursue in a further study. Would similar combinations of children show the same pattern of development of oral language and of computer work as the two boys in this study? Would all pairings of children be as ready and as relaxed in their verbalization, or would some children be much more silent as they worked? And, if so, would their effectiveness be marred by their inability to verbalize.

The questions that arise from this brief study are numerous and serve to remind us, as teachers, how much we have to learn from our pupils.

Implications for Future Classroom Work

The class teacher felt that the recordings underlined the importance of talk in the learning situation, and this served simply to confirm her belief in this important link. The children seemed most actively and enthusiastically involved, however, when their oral language was more cognitive and this seemed to develop after they had had time to accustom themselves to working together and in more open-ended, problem-solving tasks. It seems that the children needed a few sessions to accustom themselves to working together at a new task before they were ready to move into more completely cognitive exchanges.

In this study we were fortunate to have two pupils who were so ready to verbalize, though the knowledge that the tape recorder was there and that their teacher had asked them to 'talk about' what they were doing and 'explain' their work must have provided a stimulus to talk (though it must be said that with some children the presence of the tape recorder would be inhibiting). In the everyday classroom situation the class teacher needs to consider how to promote oral language at the computer: she may use a tape recorder, or simply encourage the children to 'talk about what you are doing', or she may need to intervene and promote discussion with carefully worded open-ended questions.

The study, then, suggests the following points for consideration by the teacher:

1 The pairing or grouping of pupils needs to be carefully considered:
   (a) Are they matched in ability?
   (b) Is one pupil dominant?
2 The cognitive tasks set at the start of the project need to be at a fairly basic level so that the children have the opportunity to get used to working together.
3 The children may need encouragement to verbalize and this encouragement may take different forms.
4 The work of the children must be monitored to ensure that points (1), (2) and (3) are fulfilled.

Finally, and most importantly, this study emphasizes the crucial role that talk plays in children's learning.

Case Study 2: An Eye For Spelling: Patricia Lovering

Session 1

Geraint had only used the computer once before in school with the special needs group. He appeared very enthusiastic to use it now to try and improve his spellings. As an introduction we took the sound 'ai' and chose the package's nine second viewing time. He keenly observed the words being built up around the pattern and had no problems reading them.

Transcript 1 (Using an Eye for Spelling)

Teacher: Look carefully at the word. Now try and type it in.
Geraint: Says 'fail' but types in 'fali'. (See print-out 1 below)
Teacher: What's wrong with that?
Geraint: I dunno.
Teacher: Have you got all the letters, are they in the right order?
Geraint: Yes, there were four, I've put four.
Teacher: Look again at the word. Can you see what you've done?
Geraint: (Quite a long time passed before he answered) Oh I can see what I've done, the 'i' is in the wrong place.

'Tail' and 'Nail' were then typed in correctly but very slowly. He had difficulty finding his way around the keyboard and this frustrated him and he became agitated as it was taking him so long. He then attempted the word 'mail' (See print-out).

Geraint: Oh why is that wrong? That's what it said.
Teacher: What was the pattern we saw at the beginning? What did all the words have in them?
Geraint: They all had 'ai' I haven't put 'ai' in this.

He looks again and types it in correctly as well as 'snail' and 'sail'. When it came to 'trail' he put double 'i' first, then corrected it. When he came to 'tailor' he was saying 'ai' to himself all the time but made a mistake with the ending.

Teacher: Good boy, you've got the 'ai' sound but why do you think its still wrong?
Geraint: I can't see, the word says 'tailor'. (Looks again at the word) Oh it's 'or' at the end not 'er'.

'Sailor' is then typed correctly.

Word	Response
fail	
	fali
	fail
tail	
	tail
nail	
	nail
mail	
	male
	mail
rail	
	rail
snail	
	snail
sail	
	sail
trail	
	traiil
	trail
tailor	
	tailer
	tailor
sailor	
	sailor

At this stage I printed out the results and we looked at them so he could see his mistakes. He was very keen to have a copy to show his friends.

Session 2

This time we used the second program Starspell. Geraint appeared alert and keen to get going. The timing in this confused him from the start. The words seemed to disappear before he had time to remember them and he was annoyed with himself. He also could not find where the letters were on the keyboard fast enough again. After the first attempt we decided to have another go, suggesting he really concentrated on the screen all the time. The responses are shown below.

Word	*Response*
wait	
	walk
	wait
aim	
	aim
sail	
	sail
nail	
	nail
rain	
	rain
paint	
	panait
	pant
	paint
painting	
	paintnig
	paining
	painting

He was pleased with himself until he came to 'paint'. His response here shows his weakness with sequencing. He could not see what was wrong with his first response, insisting that it was right. I showed him the word again but still his second attempt was wrong, but on studying it he then put in the missing 'i'. With 'painting' he kept saying 'ai' to himself and got that part right but the ending mixed up. His second attempt he missed out the 't' but finally got it right on his third attempt. The target time for the exercise was three minutes and he took six minutes, so he was disappointed.

I felt a lot of his frustration was due to his lack of keyboard skills so I decided to let him become more familiar with the keyboard layout before we next attempted the spelling programs. Improving his confidence in himself was one of my aims and until he was competent on the keyboard he would soon become frustrated as had been shown in the first two sessions.

Session 3

This session we used the digraph 'ea' on an Eye For Spelling.

Transcript

Teacher: Let's look at the pattern and see how the words are built up.
Geraint: They've all got 'ea' in them, haven't they?

(He watches the program building up each word in turn. His concentration is very good and he does not take his eyes off the screen)

Teacher: Now let's see if you can type the words yourself. What has each one got in?
Geraint: 'ea'. All I've to do is remember that. (Smiles).

He came to the word 'each' but typed 'eagh'.

Teacher: Read the word you've typed in.
Geraint: I've put a 'g', it should be a 'c'.

He came to 'east', typed in 'eat', saw it was wrong and corrected himself. This was the first time he had done this. 'Easy' he typed correctly and 'ease' although he read 'else' for this. This showed perhaps his visual perception was quite good. 'Eagle' was typed correctly but he had a few problems with 'easier'. First he put 'easterer', said that was wrong and then put 'eaier'. When asked what was wrong he straight away said the 's' was missing. 'Easiest' was correctly typed straight away. I felt during this session that he was happier with using the computer. He typed quicker and did not become frustrated. He also seemed to be checking his work, showing close visual inspection was taking place.

Word	Response
each	
	eagh
	each
east	
	east
easy	
	easy
ease	
	ease
eagle	
	eagle
easier	
	eaier
	easier
easiest	
	easiest

Session 4

Another vowel digraph Geraint has problems with is 'ou' so I decided to try three combinations with this letter group in. The first was 'ould' and the print-out below shows Geraint's responses. The only mistake was in the word 'smoulder' and he saw straight away that he has missed out the 'l'.

Word	Response
could	
	could
would	
	would
should	
	should
boulder	
	boulder
smoulder	
	smouder
	smoulder
shoulder	
	shoulder
mould	
	mould

In the same session we took 'ough'. He found problems with reading some of these thinking they all had the 'f' sound at the end. Once he could read 'all' we started the program. During the build up his eyes never left the screen and his concentration was very good. His fingers were itching to get started and he was saying 'ough' to himself all the time. He started with 'cough' but immediately spelt it as he always has, 'coff'. When the computer said he was wrong he knew straight away, before I had to prompt him, that he had forgotten to use the 'ough' letter string. No more mistakes were made until he came to 'although', putting two 'll's' at the beginning, but correcting himself in his second attempt. (See print-out below). He appeared much more confident now.

Word	Response
cough	
	coff
	cough
tough	
	tough
rough	
	rough
enough	
	enough
though	
	though
although	
	allthough
	although
plough	
	plough
through	
	through

Session 5

This session we decided to use the second program Starspell with the 'ough' letter string. The first time Geraint had used this he became agitated as the time for visual display of the word is much shorter than on an Eye For Spelling. I did shorten the viewing time in the last session to six seconds and he had no difficulty, so it will be interesting to see his reaction to this program with a similar viewing time now.

Word	*Response*
plough	
	plough
dough	
	dough
though	
	though
rough	
	rough
tough	
	tough
cough	
	cof cough
thought	
	though
	thought

One word he could not read was 'dough', so we spent time talking about this before he began. Again he was saying the letter string to himself all the time. He seems to have gone away from trying to remember it by the individual sounds. Thought he typed incorrectly and said he thought it said 'though'. The target time for the program was four minutes but he completed it in two minutes so was extremely pleased. When asked which of the two programs he liked best he said: 'The other one because it gives me more time and shows the build up of the words'. This was interesting as the visual display time was almost identical now, but he did not think so. He was more familiar with the other program so I think this influenced his choice at this time.

During the same session I decided to try the same letter pattern on an Eye For Spelling but taking the harder letter group of 9–11 words.

Transcript

Geraint: Some of these words are the same as before.
Teacher: Good boy, are they all the same?

Geraint: No, there's one at the bottom I haven't had before, the one that has 'ful' at the end.
Teacher: What's the pattern in them all?
Geraint: (Straight away, with no hesitation) 'ough'.

From the print-out you can see the mistakes were made on the last three words. He did not know the rule of dropping an 'l' when adding 'full' so this accounted for the mistake here. With 'through' he was thinking of 'thought', part of the previous word. After he had typed in the last word 'thoughout' he looked at it and immediately said, 'I've missed the r', before I had time to ask him. Self-checking was in evidence here.

Word	Response
rough	
	rough
cough	
	cough
bough	
	bough
bought	
	bought
fought	
	fought
thought	
	thought
thoughtful	
	thoughtfull
	thoughtful
through	
	thought
	through
throughout	
	thoughout
	throughout

Session 6

His first response to these next words was, 'They're much too hard for me!' After seeing the build-up he appeared more confident. He had watched closely and attentively, noting the letter string of 'tion' and seemed to be dividing the words into syllables. Looking below at his responses shows some of his dyslexic tendencies. In 'occupation' he transposed the letter 'u'; in 'destination' he omitted the 'in'; and his first attempt at 'recreation' bore little resemblance to the word. With 'multiplication' he needed four attempts but one thing now had changed. He did not mind attempting them again and showed no signs of frustration.

In 'operation' he put the 'a' and 't' the wrong way round, but self-corrected it straight away.

Word	Response
plantation	
	plantation
operation	
	operation
association	
	association
destination	
	destation
	destination
irrigation	
	irrigation
occupation	
	occpuation
	occputation
	occupation
recreation	
	recepation
	recration
	recreation
information	
	information
multiplication	
	mutipcation
	mutipliation
	mutiplreation
	multiplication

Session 7

For this session I allowed Geraint to load the program and choose the options, such as length of viewing and whether to see the actual build up of the words before beginning the typing. He said he would have a go straight away, but then changed his mind and said he had better see the build up as he thought that it helped him to remember the words. He chose to see them for six seconds and did quite well as you can see from the print-out below. Only two words were incorrectly spelt the first time. The letter string was remembered correctly, problems being with the first two syllables in 'temperature'. With 'agriculture' his first attempt showed no resemblance to the word, but in his second attempt the only mistake was 'll'. The words here were longer than any previously attempted and this could have been the reason for these faults. He printed out the results for himself. He then attempted the same letter string on the other program. Again he loaded and set the conditions and had no problems in beating the time set. He seems now completely at ease using the two programs.

Word	Response
adventure	
	adventure
temperature	
	tampiature
	temperature
moisture	
	moisture
agriculture	
	agtiperture
	agricullture
	agriculture
future	
	future
nature	
	nature

Using Starspell he had the following responses achieved in one minute when the target time set by the computer was four minutes. He showed evidence of breaking the words into syllables and said 'ture' to himself. This seems to be the way he has worked out for remembering the words. In further examples we did, this was the method he used and he had very few mistakes.

Starspell	
Word	Response
capture	
	capture
picture	
	picture
nature	
	nature
future	
	future
mixture	
	mixture
moisture	
	moisture

Conclusions

Throughout the time using the computer Geraint did seem to change in his attitude both to using it and in how he remembered the words. His keyboard skills have increased considerably and he uses the letter strings for remembering rather than by individual letters. At first he was frustrated at his slowness and annoyed when he got any word wrong. Now he is familiar with both the programs but still prefers an Eye For Spelling as he likes to see the words building up. He finds it easier to remember them. Starspell he disliked in the beginning but now he does like the game element in beating the computer. Even when we used the prefix 'ex', with words such as 'exciting', 'exercise', 'explain' and 'extremely' he tackled them with confidence and comparative ease.

His spelling age on the Schonell R1 has gone up to 8.7 now, but I feel the follow up work contributed to this rather than solely the use of the computer. I do not feel the computer can be used in isolation. Using sheets from a Hand For Spelling by the same author as the Eye For Spelling, reinforced the letter string and also linked into handwriting. Other sheets used the words experienced on the computer in context and gave a more meaningful learning situation. The spelling programs on the computer I feel have helped Geraint develop a way of looking at words which, if continued, may help him to overcome some of his problems. He now seems to check himself far more than he did in the beginning and shows enjoyment rather than frustration, and some signs of perseverence. Active self-testing is perhaps the most effective method of learning material such as spelling.

A recent Schonell test has shown evidence of building up, listening for syllables, and some of the letter strings we had used on the computer such as 'ful', 'ea', 'oa' and 'ould'. A small step in the right direction has been taken.

Future Implementations

I would like to see the programs used in all of the junior classes not only for the pupils who have problems with spelling. I feel all pupils could benefit from the structured approach. Geraint has shown it is quite easy to use and I'm sure many could develop successful strategies for learning to spell by using the two programs. Individual programs can be easily devised and the print-out option would be extremely useful in the busy classroom situation. Good spelling depends so largely on visual reference. The computer can be exploited in the cause for learning to spell.

For Geraint I would like to see him continue with the programs but also develop a dictionary to help him with his writing. He finds typing on the computer much easier than writing. Writing is a laborious task to him. He has a good imagination but very little is written down in his books. His interest in the computer could be now channelled into using it as a word processor with the help of the dictionary editor. If we could build up a file for him, perhaps on the lines of the ACE spelling dictionary, this could free him to express himself as I feel he is capable. He has been hindered by his lack of spelling skills. Now he has had some success in spelling, some enjoyment, and made some progress. By preparing a file, using the vowel sounds, initial letter sounds and syllables, rather than alphabetical order for this 'dictionary', we may be able to show him the way to enjoy writing.

Case Study 3: Concept Keyboard and L₂ Learning: Sheila Bellamy

The program 'Moving in' was written for the BBC computer by Simon Hayles of Mushroom Software in co-operation with MESU Special Needs Software

Centre. It is a simulation of an empty, five roomed house with the front wall removed. By entering word by word from one of the Concept Keyboard overlays provided, or by typing in the phrases on the computer keyboard, furniture and people can be put in, moved, changed into other objects, or removed. There is also the option of changing the weather, or day into night. The people can also be made to perform a few tasks like going to bed or playing the piano. If attached to a printer it is possible to have a copy of the successful instructions entered by the children and also to obtain a printout of the house complete with the child's choice of furniture.

It was decided to use the Concept Keyboard for all the class as it gave a guide to the phrases required to operate the program. The Concept Keyboard overlay consisted partly of pictures of the objects to be moved and also of works to enable them to be moved. The general idea of the program was introduced to the whole class as part of the class project on homes but the mechanics of using it on the computer were explained to the children a group at a time. They were then left to use it, in pairs, as part of their daily assignments with perhaps a little intervention on the part of the teacher on the choice of pairing. Since the whole class was using the same program it was not obvious to the children concerned in the study that they were being monitored. Monitoring took place over a period of four weeks.

The computer was positioned in the classroom in its usual place but with the addition of a microphone and tape recorder. Infant classrooms are busy places and it is rather difficult to record children's voices because of the background noise. Use of the computer, however, has an advantage over many other activities because it requires the children to remain in one place and to face the screen and, therefore, the voice is always directed towards the screen. On this occasion the microphone was taped to the trolley between the monitor and the printer with the lead emerging from the back of the trolley and being attached to a tape recorder on a window sill nearby. The children saw the microphone but after a few days it was ignored and it became possible to switch the tape recorder on and off at random without them being aware of it.

The children chosen for the project first used the program on a day when the teacher's aide was available and were given help naming the rooms and the articles of furniture. On the next occasion they used it with another project member only; and, finally, with an English first language member of their class group. Recordings were taken of as many of these occasions as were possible.

The children first discussed with the teacher's aide the picture of the house and its surroundings, the names of the rooms and the objects to be put in the rooms. All three of the children were capable of 'labelling' the articles. The word 'attic' appeared to be new to them but it only caused confusion once, when Mojahed wanted to call it a 'playroom'. This was on his second session, and since most children had been using the attic to position the children, the piano and other toys, it was quite a logical error. When it came to typing in the command words all three children had some problems, one of the reasons being that two of the children could not read very well and the second reason was that the commands called for exact wording and any deviations were not acceptable by the program. Several times the children gave the command:

'put a Jim in . . .'

The English speaking children made the mistake only once if at all. Amirul soon learned to make the correction when it was pointed out to him. For example:

Am: Make a Jim play the piano.
Adult: Can you remember what we said earlier?
Am: Oh yes, make Jim play the piano.

When Mojahed and Ahmed were working together their lack of reading skills became very evident and Mojahed tried to recognise the word he needed by its initial letter. In fact, they became rather frustrated and were pleased to install anything in the house regardless of their first intent as the following will illustrate:

Moj: Put a clock in the living room — where's l–l–l?
Ah: Yes, where's l–l?
Moj: Put a clock in the l–l.
Ah: Shall we guess?
Moj: No, don't press that! Yes, that's the right one. Look, I did it, I put the clock in the bathroom.
Ah: Where?
Moj: There, there, that red one — I put the clock in the bathroom.

Mojahed and Ahmed soon lost interest when working together as they became frustrated with their lack of success. With neither of them having much reading ability they were unable to help one another and Mojahed in his frustration was heard to say:

'Come on Ahmed you're not doing anything'
and, in fact, Ahmed eventually wandered away to join a group playing
with some Lego.

It must be noted that despite the difficulties they were having, at no time did Ahmed and Mojahed resort to the use of Arabic. This may have been influenced by the fact that English was the medium for operating the program. This aspect is very important and deserves further study. Mojahed then struggled on in an attempt to master the program on his own, giving a running commentary on his actions. He was very heavy handed with the concept keyboard and sometimes words he had selected were printed out twice, thereby invalidating the command. Another of Mojahed's problems was the fact that a room containing a bath, etc., and a toilet is usually referred to in colloquial English as a bathroom, and not a toilet. He kept giving the command:

'put the toilet in the toilet'

and was disappointed when the computer was unable to do it. This was partly a failure of the program, but English speaking children were able to adjust more easily.

A few days later Ahmed was able to have another turn with the help of the ESL teacher. This resulted in him having more success and his interest and attention span increased a hundredfold. Since he regularly works with this teacher on a one-to-one basis he was soon having meaningful dialogue with her about the program:

Ah: We need a piano.
T: Where shall we put it?
Ah: I think in the attic.
Ah: Did it do that?
Ah: There's the man isn't he?
Ah: If we press that, do he come?

He was also explaining the mechanics of the computer to her:

Ah: No! That's not a number that's a rub out.
T: What do you mean?
Ah: If you do something wrong you have to press that.

Later on in this session it was only possible to decipher the ESL teacher's voice on the recording as Ahmed had reduced his voice to a whisper. At the same time it was noted that the background noise had decreased as the rest of the class gathered around another group evaluating what they had been doing. He may have dropped his voice so as not to disturb the discussion on the other side of the classroom or perhaps it was a simple case of not wanting to be overheard.

    When Mojahed had a turn with his friend, Sam, he also had more confidence and showed that he too knew how to delete his mistakes:

Moj: No, you can't put nothing in there — it's filled up.
Sam: Change it then
Moj: That's the rub out. (indicating the concept keyboard)
Sam: Use the delete. (indicating the qwerty keyboard).
Moj: Yes, there's two rubbers.

Later on, however, he completely misunderstood what Sam was asking him to do, although it must be acknowledged that Sam's instructions were not exactly clear, but children often use the term 'press' when they mean 'enter'.

Sam: Press 'Jim play the piano' and it will go 'doo de doo de doo'.
Moj: Ok. Where's press?
Sam: There's Jim.
Moj: I know, but where is press?

When Amirul used the program with Shaun they got on very well, each one helping the other with their mistakes. It was Amirul who noticed that they had accidentally repeated the word 'a' in an instruction and was quick to rectify it; and it was Shaun who drew Amirul's attention to a vital missing word:

Am: Put a chair in attic.
Sh: No, no, put a chair in THE attic.
Am: Yes, yes, put a chair in THE attic.

They also commented on one another's decisions and Amirul was heard to make the comment, "Why didn't you think first?" After Shaun had tried to put two pianos in one room. Together, these two boys also used the facility to move and remove objects while the others had only been able to cope with putting things in the house. They also experimented with changing the weather, and turning 'day' into 'night'.

The results gathered from these recordings were interesting and enlightening. They also suggested further investigations. With regard to common skill levels, each of the children were able to label objects even if they could not always read them. Also, all the children monitored and directed their actions by giving a running commentary on what they were doing. There were obvious limitations in the program in relation to its use in the present investigation. Unfortunately, the program only prints out the correct entries as they are accepted and executed. It would have been very useful to have been able to obtain a printed record of all the entries made by the children. Their mistakes and their ability to learn from them, along with their achievements would then have been available for analysis. The program did limit the scope for conversation between users a little as there was only a limited choice of words on the concept keyboard. Over half of the recording time was taken up with running commentaries of entries of:

'put the . . . . . . in the . . . . . .'

Also much of the discussion was about the correct way to make an entry, and not about the house and its contents. The introduction of a teacher into the group led to a more interesting dialogue as she posed leading questions as to their actions and decisions.

From the oral analysis Ahmed was found to have a better command of the English language than had been previously thought. His sentences were a little jumbled but he was capable of making himself understood. There was always a delay before he responded to a question or direction, yet he always gave a reply, showing there had been understanding. It would be interesting to know how well he converses in his first language of Arabic. It was felt that his need lay in composing simple sentences. Mojahed functioned as well as was expected of him from his general conversation in the classroom. His problems came from his limited reading and writing skills — exactly the same as with English first language speakers in the class with the same literacy standards. When his work with Ahmed and with Sam was compared it was obvious that to gain the most benefit from this program he needed to work with someone of a greater ability than his own. He was much happier working with Sam, who was able to help him with his reading when he needed it. Amirul was rather nervous and shy when he first used the program with the teacher's aide and Mojahed did most of the talking, yet when Amirul spoke it was usually correct and to the point. He was also quick to learn from mistakes. He enjoyed using the program with Shaun and they soon became more adventurous in its use and explored more of the facilities available to them. These two boys appeared to discuss their next move more than the others. This may have been because they had a better rate of success with their entries due to their higher standard of literacy. At times it was a little difficult to understand Amirul's speech on the tape, but Shaun did not appear to have any problems understanding him. Amirul's main need is work on pronunciation.

Tough (1977) states that once a child has learned to use one language correctly to communicate its needs, to report, reason and predict, then those skills are easily transferred to a second language. It was felt that Mojahed and Amirul were in the process of transference while perhaps Ahmed was still in the process of learning these skills in his first language.

The first positive conclusion to be drawn from this study is that there is very little difficulty in recording children's conversation when they are using a computer. The computer can act as a stimulus for conversation, however the choice of program in this case may not have been the best as it limited the conversations to what was written on the concept keyboard. It gave the children a starting point from which to start a conversation, but perhaps a collaborative piece of creative writing on a word processor would serve the purpose better.

Secondly, whilst children are able to learn from one another while using the computer, their taped conversations are only partly successful for assessing young English Second Language children. Great care must be taken in pairing the children to work together and it is essential that if there is to be a productive dialogue there should be some degree of teacher participation for part of the recording.

Thirdly, this work has opened up a line of investigation centred on the verbal interactions of children working together on a classroom computer. The results have an important bearing on the assessment of language difficulties, and language/confidence development in children with English as a Second Language. Further research is indicated where perhaps children who only speak English could be used and the results compared with this study. Also, what would be the result if older children, of both First and Second English Language speakers, were studied?

Bibliography

McMahon, H. and O'Neill, B. (1990) 'Capturing dialogue in learning,' Occasional Paper, IT in Education Research Programme, Swindon, ESRC.
Tough, J. (1977) *Listening to Children Talking*, London, Ward Lock Education.
Wilkinson, A. (1991) 'Evaluating group discussion', *Educational Review*, Vol. 43, No. 2, pp. 131–141.

Epilogue

Technological Literacy: Where Do We All Go From Here?

John Beynon

Introduction

It was with pleasure that Hughie Mackay and I accepted the invitation by Falmer Press to edit a volume to demonstrate our belief that a new paradigm, drawing upon cultural and educational studies, to 'read Technology' was long overdo (Beynon, 1991). What started off as a single volume has, over the past two years, developed into three, of which this is the third. In the first (Mackay, Young and Beynon, 1991) we set ourselves the task of enabling readers to understand technology by gathering together a coherent collection of perspectives drawn from the sociology of technology and cultural studies. We aimed to provide a 'toolkit' for teachers to analyse technology from economistic, social political, feminist and cultural standpoints. In the second volume (Beynon and Mackay, 1992) we compiled a collection under the theme of technological literacy which raised issues about the role of technology in education and in the National Curriculum. Once again the approach was cultural, educational and critical. This third volume has focused more specifically upon computers in classrooms and has attempted to raise a range of educational questions, both directly and indirectly, concerning their deployment in teaching and learning. The key question as far as we are concerned is 'What is it that teachers (and, through them, their pupils) need to to know (and, thereby, be able to do) to be regarded as technologically literate?'.

In giving the three volumes a progressively focusing structure, starting with the abstract and theoretical and moving towards the pragmatic and implementational, Hughie Mackay and I had the following objectives in mind:

- teachers need to be 'empowered' as far as technology is concerned by being accessed to readings and ideas which they would not normally encounter;
- teachers need to appreciate the non-neutral character of technology and acquire a sophisticated and comprehensive technological literacy to guide and inform their work within the National Curriculum;
- teachers need to be given confidence to re-affirm the value of their skills and knowledge and not be steamrollered into premature and inappropriate practices;

- teachers need to acquire a conceptual framework and discourse in which both to talk about computers and evaluate their classroom uses;
- teachers need to theorise technology and avoid becoming trapped into coping with ill-considered and unwise implementation.

We are especially insistent on the last of these because too often we have seen the purchase and deployment of both hardware and software run ahead of any clearly researched and articulated justification for its educational use. In such circumstances, machinery itself is presented as justification enough, with no sense of it being a small part of something infinitely more complex and greater than the acquisition of narrow skills. The glitzy promotional packaging of promises viewed in the cold light of actual outcomes equals disillusionment. We have found that equation repeated time and again in talking to teachers who have too readily succumbed to an IT in education that has proved, at the end of the day, to be more technology than education.

In calling for an expanded definition of technological literacy we have committed ourselves from the outset both to encouraging teachers to assert themselves and to 'educationalise' technology, and to providing them with the tools to do this.

Section one: Language, Thought and Computing

The commonsense view of language is that it is a neutral medium for the transmission of informaton. Against this can be set the Whorfian (1956) view that language is far from neutral and that in both its syntax and semantics it selects, amplifies and reduces aspects of experience. Technologists have taken the neutrality of language too much for granted and have treated it as a mere agency through which inputs and outputs are unproblematically transmitted. This 'conduit' view of language (that is, that it conveys objective, decontextualised knowledge) carries with it a simplified view of learning which has been incorporated into microcomputing to the exclusion of the dynamic interplay of language, thought and culture that characterizes genuine knowledge acquisition and understanding. Learning cannot be reduced to a routine taking-on-board of language-transported 'facts', a sender/receiver model (Shannon and Weaver, 1949) which obscures the human authorship of knowledge and culture. For Bowers (1989) microcomputers are best regarded as an extension of print technology. This then opens software to the same charges of selectivity and bias and of perpetrating cultural mythologies as the press. Bowers analyses a number of teaching programs to demonstrate how, by means of the processes of selection, reduction and amplification, they misrepresent and distort cultural values. He cites as an example particular history teaching packages that place students in the past, but with a 'presentcentric' orientation, one which fails to help them understand the socio-historically and culturally different mode of thinking in existence at that time. Present consciousness passes unquestioned and is imposed upon issues and problems of the past, which are then siphoned through the cultural parameters of the present. The outcome of such programs is to render the past 'non-historical': that is, much like the present only having occurred in the past! This technocratic view of time gives the user a grossly exaggerated and illusory sense of his/her power and autonomy (cf. Turkle, 1984). Indeed, this 'present-centredness' is the central theme of Johnson (1991), who argues that much Canadian history teaching software denies pupils any valid historical perspective in that its language simply presents to students contemporary social issues as exemplars of past events and vice versa.

A comprehensive understanding of the cultural transmission process and an ability to identify and counter distortions is, therefore, an important ingredient in all teachers' technological literacy. This is very much in line with our assertion that the contemporary definition of literacy must include the ability to understand and to use technology both for personal and democratic purposes. In order to advance his thesis Bowers (1989) refers to the different thought processes involved in literacy and orality. The alleged change in consciousness that resulted with the advent of literacy has been a major theme in the literature from Goody and Watt (1968) to, more latterly, Ong (1982), Oxenham (1980) and Street (1983). Generally it has been assumed that literacy is a 'good thing' and perhaps has principal aim of education. Yet some literacy theorists (for example, Watt, 1968) point out that it reifies words as objects, and values analytical thought over and above conversation and storytelling. Whilst it opens up new avenues of awareness and a legion of new possibilities, it nevertheless excludes the different learning opportunities associated with the oral and with analogical knowledge. The writer/reader situation is a privatised one in which the writer encodes and transmits and the reader decodes and reflects. It is a very different one from the reciprocity and immediacy of talk and the learning possibilities inherent in oracy. Indeed, some (for example, Ong, 1982) question whether literacy should be privileged over oracy to the extent it is in schooling, on the grounds that what is written can take on a false authority that can blind its readers to its origin and ideological purpose. The important role of oracy in learning in both the primary and secondary school sectors has recently been restated (for example, McLure *et al.*, 1988; and WJEC, 1991). Indeed, the claims for computers to be used more extensively as part of language development and literacy teaching must be re-examined in the light of charges that they are often incompatible with what we know about writing and about how children learn to write (cf. Peacock in this volume), an issue taken up in the next section of this paper. Similarly, microcomputers amplify the sense of individualism because communication takes place not in a dynamic, but in a passive, context characterised by an asymmetrical power relationship. However, Bowers's argument is not just that computers in classrooms determine what pupils think about, but how they think: that is, the way information is stored as data shapes the pattern and nature of thought by providing the conceptual categories with which to organise ideas, cultural orientations and values. Computers foster a 'technicist mindset' that privileges the abstract and theoretical, and a rational, problem-solving form of thought. What is easily overlooked is that the linear, 'digital' thinking involved in manipulating data excludes metaphorical, analogical thinking, which is thereby weakened and devalued. For that reason alone it is wrong to equate human and machine 'intelligence'. Computers strengthen the belief that objective data is, in fact, knowledge, and cannot represent the tacit (in Polanyi's, (1958) sense) as opposed to the explicit dimensions of knowledge. Those aspects of knowledge and knowing that cannot be organised into discrete components cannot be programmed.

Perhaps more contentious is Bowers's claim that in the Cartesian world computers evince an essentially male form of consciousness. He draws upon such writers as Keller (1985) and Bordo (1987) to argue that computers encode a concern with efficiency, logic, abstraction and problem solving. Men are typically more at ease with observation, measurement and the accumulation of facts. More contentious perhaps is the assertion that they do not value analogical, metaphorical thinking as highly as women. Bowers draws upon the developing area of communicational anthropology (for example, Saville-Troike, 1982) to suggest a congruence (if male) and a disjuncture (if female) between gendered communicational styles and person-computer interaction. Men and women, the argument goes, typically utilize different communicational and cognitive styles, in that women place a higher value on the importance of relationships in communication, whereas men view it in a more utiltarian light as a vehicle for the sending and receiving of information. In this sense at least, computers are 'male'.

Bowers speculates that one of the hidden, indirect effects of computers is that they contribute to the myth of autonomous individualism asociated with Rationalism and the philosophers Locke, Hobbes and Bentham. He regards this as not conducive to democracy because it encourages an egocentric universe in which 'decontextualised information is seen as the source of intellectual empowerment and connectedness among individuals'. It reifies the role of the self; over-values rationality; and upholds the myth of the necessarily 'progressive' nature of change. One researcher who strongly echoes this is Sherry Turkle (1984), who concluded that individulism is not just a matter of a pupil being left alone with a micro: rather, it is a message system built into much educational software which gives the user the quite erroneous impression of enormous personal authority and control. This is another facet of the 'technological mindset' which Bowers regards as a watered-down contemporary version of the Cartesian view of the individual as clinical observer/scientist who can empower and be empowered by the acquisition of objective facts.

In the light of this essentially 'cultural' critique it is important to identify how teachers are positioned in relation to educational technology and what their responsibilities are towards computer usage in their classrooms. Sketching out the nature of those responsibilities is the objective of the following section.

Section Two: Computers in Classrooms: Teachers' Responsibilities

Teachers need to regain the intellectual high ground as far as computers in classrooms are concerned, and set the in-built cultural, cognitive and communicational selectivity of educational computing against the bigger and grander enterprise, namely the aims of a liberal education. As has already been emphasised, when it comes to technology in education it is the latter which must always have primacy. Teachers must seize the initiative and, guided by accessible and relevant evaluative research, not step back and allow the agenda to be set by computer firms and software designers. It is teachers who are the practical experts in issues involving language and learning, knowledge and culture, issues at first not regarded as strictly pertinent to computing and largely ignored by technologists. To evaluate the use of computers by pupils in classrooms these must now be raised. Yet it is precisely these which have been submerged in the rush to technologise classrooms, and teachers themselves have often been pushed back from their areas of expertise in teaching and learning. By way of exemplification, I illustrate how teachers' professional knowledge and judgement is under attack (and how they, consequently, are in danger of being 'deskilled') by reference to two arenas of teacher expertise, namely (i) writing; and (ii) art education.

(i) Writing

Writing, in an educational context, is most certainly not just a medium by which facts are conveyed and, thereby, the basis for teacher assessment of pupil progress. It is, along with talking and reading, the means through which learning and understanding takes place (Rosen and Rosen, 1973; Barnes, 1970; and Wilkinson, 1989). Through it, for example, pupils shape experiences and information for different audiences and tasks along a continuum that includes the expressive, the poetic and the transactional (Britton, 1976). Papert (1981) argued that word processing would free them from the (for some obstructive) mechanics of handwriting and allow them instead to concentrate on meaning-making. Many teachers have found that programs that monitor spelling and syntax have their uses: Levine (1986), for example, claims that such aides, used intelligently to support pupil writers, can render 'the plateau of competence more easily accessible.' This argument certainly lies behind the 'writing by micro' aspect of the National Writing Project (1990), with its emphasis upon writing as a social activity, in which pupil talk and the drafting of a text are integrated activities. Yet there is an emerging body of work which ignores this collaborative, 'learning process' model of writing and seeks to 'technologise' writing by granting to the computer a heightened function. Rather than being a 'facilitator' like a pen, the computer becomes nothing less than a 'writing machine'. This is presented as having immediate and direct relevance for teachers and pupils. The spirit of the work can be readily gleaned from this extract from Williams (1989):

> We have to recognise that, whatever writing once was, it is now something else. For the computer not only gives help for conventional writing tasks, it gives us new ways of writing, through networking, electronic publishing and, perhaps most significantly, through Hypertext. The machine may even begin to write itself. (Preface)

Yazdani (1989), argues Williams, demonstrates how the 'problem' of improving users' writing might be removed by allocating the writing task entirely to the machine. He presents what he terms an 'architecture for a writing system' by building on the 'morphology of story' associated with the work of Propp (1968). He and other writers in the so-called structural poetics movement argue that the artistic qualities of any text can be accounted for by means of a finite set of technical devices. These 'rules of expressivenes' are a kind of literary version of Chomsky's (1968) transformational grammar in that they they can be shown to 'generate' a literary text, in this case children's fables. These rules (or 'devices') are the same for all texts of our culture and the immense variety of texts emerges as a result of 'a finite variety of combination of the rules and of the artistically amorphous everyday life material used by the artist.' (Drezin, 1978, quoted in Williams and Holt, 1989). On this basis Yazdani attempts to devise a complete story teller system consisting of a plot maker, a world maker, a similator, narrator and text generator.

In this respect writing as an activity is being 'deconstructed' and 'technologised' in a way which interferes with its educational purpose in terms of learning and language development. Its role is being changed from something pupils undertake to develop literacy and communicational competence towards something machines do at their behest. The educational purpose served by this shift is not at all clear: it seems to me that it is for teachers to clarify the relevance (if any) of such developments to pupils' language development and learning.

(ii) Art Education

Art has always mirrored changes in technology and art teaching has been greatly influenced by, amongst other technologies, photography, photocopiers and, recently, computer graphics. It is not surprising, then, that art teachers have been thrust into discussions concerning the classroom role of computers. They have often found themselves in a dilemma in that they know that historically artistic creativity has stagnated when it opposed technology and has taken leaps forward when it has incorporated technological advances (Janson, 1981). But the adoption of desktop publishing, colour copiers and computer graphics by some contemporary artists does not mean that art teachers, who have a subject sub-culture and syllabus in which certain areas have to be covered, should do likewise. Clark (1991) makes the point that those art teachers used to teacher-centred practical teaching, Formalism and 'still life' drawing, feel threatened by the introduction of computer-based activities into their classrooms because:

> ... should a computer-based Art activity require changes so massive that teacher security is threatened ... active resistance is likely to be experienced ... Many such teachers feel uneasy admitting to students that they are not computer experts. Others find the notion of 'computers-as-an-art medium' incompatible with the traditional Fine Arts curricula. (Clark 1991, pp. 76)

Clark restates the epistemological values of art teachers and portray them not as Luddites, but an identifiable professional group with their own long-standing and valid concerns (such as Piagetian-like, 1955, stages of art skills acquisition) whose members are seeking to discover how they might usefully employ technology to serve values which must be upheld if they are to their retain professional solidarity and credibility.

In both the above cases the re-assertion of habitual practices and established subject values does not release teachers from the obligation of becoming technologically literate. There is, of course, just as much of an obligation upon technologists to become educationally literate: that is, fully conversant with what Bowers (1989) aptly terms the 'ecology of the classroom'. Meanwhile, teachers must beware being seduced by the 'fun' and 'play' aspects of software unless these can be justified as being educationally significant on a range of language and learning criteria. They certainly must have a greater voice in both devising and evaluating such software. Johnson (1991), for example, voices the fear that

217

current software, over-zealously applied, would reduce the teaching of history and historical understanding to little more than data manipulation.

To date teachers have usually been inducted into microcomputer usage in a rushed and unsatisfactory, skills-based, technical manner. There has often been little time or encouragement to evaluate software in practice. In addition to the rigidities of the hardware most of the problems with technology in education emanate from arcane, inadequate, overpromoted software that has, at best, added little to the teaching and learning enterprise and has, at worst, disrupted and attacked it. So much software produced for the 'educational market' over the past decade has, both literally and metaphorically, been a waste of time. It is important, therefore, to highlight software that has been planned by educationalists according to what is known about how pupils learn. Two good examples would be the PEG work of Les Watson and colleagues (reported in this volume) based on a child-centredness and a learning-through-play; and the work of Peter O'Kelly, the inventor of Co-Co, which is widely used in Ontario High Schools. O'Kelly (1991) is a leading proponent of multi-user software to foster co-operative learning and he espouses many of the principles concerning language, learning and the nature of knowledge that informed the hugely influential language across the curriculum and the language and learning projects based in the English Department of the London University Institute of Education in the late 1960s and 1970s.

In spite of the impoverished and, in the long term, stultifying 'back to basics' philosophy of the present government in the United Kingdom, what must now be established is a theoretical framework within which teachers can start to raise wider cultural issues concerning technology and its future relationship to the related acts of teaching and learning. This framework will clarify teachers' responsibilities with respect to using and teaching about computers and ensure that future debates adopt a widened discourse which incorporates issues relating to language, literacy, thought, knowledge and culture. In short, we want teachers to adopt a better informed and proactive stance towards educational computing and not to allow the agenda to be set by others, such as software producers. Technology will change and go on changing as new machines and programs come into play, but what must be established are the groundrules to clarify the relationship between education (and the ways of thinking and knowing) and technology (and the ways of thinking and knowing associated with computers). Only then will computers cease to be intrusive and become genuine empowerers both of teachers and of their pupils. Apart from pockets of Luddite dismissal in schools, teachers have been inveigled into a too easy and uncritical 'acceptance' of the distinctly 'educational' benefits of computers and allowed themselves to be swept along on the 'technology as progress' wave when, in fact, a more interrogative and assertive stance must now be adopted. What must now be established is new relationship between computers and the curriculum in which the responsibility with which teachers are entrusted to ensure the effectiveness of teaching and learning is upheld. Micros must not be imposed upon classrooms in a manner which disturbs the web of interdependencies implied by Bowers's 'ecology' with its delicate network of relationships and value systems. Technology must first pass a rigorous litmus test based upon strict educational criteria relating to language, thought and culture, a set of linked concerns which unites teachers as a professional group wherever, whoever and whatever they teach. This litmus test involves questions which are essentially cultural rather than technological. These include:

(a) *Technology and language*
How do computers fit into what Moffett (1968) terms the 'universe of discourse'? Is particular software compatible with what we know about reading, writing and oracy? Does it link with the work on language and learning, and language across the curriculum? What social and conceptual traits associated with literacy are amplified by computers? How might oracy be integrated into computing?

(b) *Thought*
How should pupils 'think' and how should they think about technology? How can metaphysical thinking be safeguarded given the promotion of the computer's 'rational mindset', and might technology in education learn to value and incorporate the metaphysical, metaphorical and analogical?

(c) *Culture*
Computers have capabilities and cultural values built into them, a point well made by Johnson (1991) when she asserts that data bases are far from 'empty' software tools because they only allow certain factual data to be used. These capabilities take the form of distinct linguistic, cognitive and organisational orientations which serve particular ways of linear and analytical thinking. Teachers need to render these explicit and decide which further their educational objectives and which contradict and obstruct them. How do computers store data and what view of the world, both past and present, do pupils thereby receive? How do microcomputers 'frame' aspects of past and present cultures? How do they mediate the pupil's encounter with knowledge, values, concepts and ideas? What, thereby, is the cultural impact on pupils' thought patterns, the nature of their knowledge, and the shaping of their perspectives? What view of themselves and of the world do students need to acquire, both directly, and indirectly, and how might technology in education best be developed and employed to serve this goal? Which cultural values does particular software mediate, shape, reify or exclude?

The writers in this volume challenge teachers to review their educational responsibilities towards pupils using computers. A major responsibility is undoubtedly the need to halt the encroachment of technocratic values by using only that which supports teachers' educational and ethical priorities. To do this they must work out what is worth doing with computers and, conversely, what is manifestly not worth doing (Chandler, 1992, and Ennals, 1992). They need to spot unintended outcomes (cf. Moore in this volume; and Grint, 1992) and establish the precise nature of the interaction of design, user and use (Linn, 1991). They need to discover how computers might aid them in their administration and work outside classrooms, especially if this will eventually benefit pupils (Pole, 1992). They must appropriate computers to expand their resources and facilities, but ensure they are in control of it rather than it being in control of them (Liber, 1992; and Peacey, 1992). Teachers need to start with their pupils' needs and not with computers: only then will computers be put to beneficial use (Watson, 1992). They need to monitor their implementation and counter any gender bias (Culley, 1992; Newton and Beck, 1992; and Beynon, 1992).

In order to carry out their responsibilities, however, teachers must begin to 'question technology'. How they might do this is the subject of the next section.

Section Three: Questioning Technology

No text is neutral. However, once created it can float free of its author, take on a life of its own, and obscure the origins of its production. This is as true of computers as it is of literary texts. In looking at any machine, whether 1990s computer or a steam train of a century ago, it is easy to forget that it was designed and built under certain circumstances for certain purposes under certain constraints, and that it was probably the product of a series of compromises. Its very material being in front of us hides the series of choices and decisions the authors and designers of these literary or mechanical 'texts' chose or were forced to make. An acknowledgement of non-neutrality is the point at which any cultural analysis starts. It is this which Habermas (1987) has in mind when he argues that computers have been developed in a dangerous way in that they have had purposely incorporated within them a repressive set of panopticon-like ideologies which have the potential of locking large numbers of people into cognitive and cultural tunnel vision. If this is the case then this is one urgent reason for teachers to engage in debates as to the nature of both their own and their pupil's technological literacy. For computer-in-the-classroom substitute for the sake of argument the panopticon-in-the-classroom and the potential for abuse becomes evident. The latter would be a most attractive device for those who would seek to control the content and pedagogy of education from the outside, along with curtailing teachers' autonomy in their own classrooms.

Under three headings below (namely Technology and Literacy; Reading Technology; and the Knowledge to Read Technology) a series of questions are raised. These, it is hoped, will enable teachers to interrogate technology in a way that will allow them to establish their own agenda for the deployment of computers in teaching and learning.

(i) Technology and Literacy

The most helpful and 'teacher-friendly' books on this start with print literacy and then speculate on how computers might best be 'fitted in' and used by teachers of, usually, English (for example, Robinson, 1985; Chandler and Marcus, 1985; and Adams and Jones, 1983). However, although the term literacy is still conventionally applied to print, it has widened its applicability and incorporated other 'literacies'. This is very much in line with the manner in which definitions of literacy (and numeracy) have shifted over the past century since the great Victorian and Edwardian legislation on education in the period up to the First World War. This has not just reflected an increase in levels of competence (that is, more reading and writing), but an increase in scope and kind. For example, in recent times there has consistently been reference to television or media literacy; business and commercial literacy; computer literacy; and, most recently, self and emotional literacy. These shifts reflect changes in our ideas as to what is a 'well educated person' today from, say, that which appeared in Matthew Arnold's

Culture And Anarchy in 1869. There would be many continuities, but there would also be many changes and additions: what was regarded as functionally literate or even literate for most of the population then would clearly be grossly inadequate now.

Computer literacy must be viewed as part of a bigger enterprise, namely a literacy which empowers holders to participate in the so-called 'information society'. The history of computer literacy to date displays a far greater emphasis upon the former than the latter, so much so that the relationship between the two has been largely left unexplored. Literacy in this context has been assumed to be a kind of generalised competence in skills, often of a transitory and swiftly re-dundant kind. Levine (1986), for example, points to two definitions of com-puter literacy. One is an operational knowledge of computers; and the other a more advanced knowledge of programming. Hughie Mackay and I regard technological literacy as a more comprehensive and meaningful term than computer literacy. Firstly, it locates computers in the wider context of tech-nology and allows links to be made across various technologies and their social impact and use, whether refrigerators, pens, or whatever. Secondly, we believe that it is part of basic functional literacy in the 1990s to possess a broader grasp of technology and to appreciate it as a rapidly changing cultural phenomena that has enormous potential for good or for bad usage in our everyday experience. Thirdly, the term links technology and literacy not only in the obvious way in which micros and pens are both tools with which we can write, but in the more profound sense in that both are tools with which to think. Both are print technologies and both change (perhaps in different ways) the nature of thought from a consciousness associated with the oral to one associated with the literate. They mediate the nature of reality available to us: indeed, literacy theorists have, as previously stated, argued that one of the great watersheds in human history has been the change in thinking brought about by the move from orality to literacy (Goody and Watt, 1968; Finnigan, 1970).

There is a fourth sense in which literacy and technology can be profitably linked. We can distinguish between the computer being used to develop competence in writing (although many, including, Peacock in this volume, would question its usefulness), and itself being something that (in addition to its products) can be 'read' and critically understood as part of a new and expanded definition of literacy which includes technology. In other words, we regard the 'competences' required to 'read' technology as an essential attribute of the well-educated, literate person of the 1990s (Mackay, 1991; Middlehurst and Beynon, 1991).

If literacy is, in Freire's terms (1973), irradicably political and ideological, then not to include technological literacy as a crucial component of literacy would be to offer people a debased and inadequate version of literacy, one which had a built-in capacity for repression. It would be 'literacy-as-panopticon', every bit as dehumanising and exploitative as the neo-colonial functional literacy schemes Freire (1970) attacks. The fact is that changes to what literacy is are not dependent on just being able to read better (that is, higher order reading skills to decipher more difficult texts), but also on being able to read a range of new texts (of which televisions and computers are contemporary examples) in different kinds of ways. 'Reading' hardware or software is a related but clearly different undertaking to 'reading' a television soap opera like EastEnders, a poem by Philip Larkin, or a piece of academic discourse. But, we would argue, having the capacity to do each is the hallmark of any contemporary definition of 'being well-educated'. Teachers, as ever, have to work towards a clear concept of what 'being well-educated' really means. Technology plays a key role in our world: being part of print technology it is now at the heart of literacy rather than peripheral. Not to be able to use and 'read' it would be to render the apparently 'literate' powerless and malleable. The 'literate' would then become part of, ironically, a new 'literate illiteracy'.

(ii) Reading Technology

It is useful to distinguish between 'reading about technology' and 'reading technology'. The former may appear relatively straightforward, but is not entirely so, whilst the latter demands the kind of technological literacy we advocate. Let us consider 'reading about technology' first.

Technology was thrust into classrooms in great haste and with much confusion as a result (Beynon and Mackay, 1989). Teachers have had to cope with this and many other things during a decade of turmoil in UK education. In any case they are encapsulated within a pragmatic world of 'doing' and books which afford them clear directions and a plausible credo are more likely to be popular than ones which raise questions but do not pretend to supply direct answers. As a result of the canonical status attributed to Papert's (1981) Mindworlds, other less immediately relevant voices (for example, critics like Dreyfus and Dreyfus, 1981) have not attracted as much attention. Dreyfus and Dreyfus, for example, argue that Mindworlds advances a flawed, highly authoritarian and mechanised model of learning, one that excludes intuition and, contrary to Papert's claims, has the effect of narrowing teacher and pupil autonomy in teaching and learning. Moreover, Mindworlds is contentious in its insistence that learning starts with the particular and then moves to the abstract. It is easy to be swept along by Papert's persuasive 'how and why to do it' advocacy of LOGO and to forget how technology of any kind exerts technical, conceptual, structural and symbolic power over its users (Markus and Bjorn-Anderson, 1987). In the triad of designers, promoters and teachers, it is the first two who currently set the agenda for the latter. It is for that reason that Hughie Mackay and I argue that teachers need to read more widely and critically if they are not to be duped by answers seemingly plausible for now but which, in the long term, may well prove to lack substance. Our three edited volumes have deliberately raised issues and fuelled debates, but not offered ready and glib solutions.

If 'reading about technology' is difficult, how might teachers learn to 'read technology'? In his classic study of learning to read print, Frank Smith (1978) distinguishes between learning to read and reading. We learn to read by engaging in a kind of 'psycholinguistic guessing game', one in which we, as apprentice readers, bring our tacit 'knowledge' of how language works to bear upon the text. We make predictions, hypothesise and generate meanings in line with the evidence in front of us. To apply the analogy to technology means starting with Michael Apple's (1988) assertion that it can be treated as a 'text' and, therefore, can have its meanings and values rendered visible and 'readable'. It is interesting that Johnson (1991) suggests that models of literary criticism which make explicit the tacit dimensions of culture could provide guidelines to the development of software evaluation. We would agree with that and point to the modes of 'reading' a range of contemporary texts developed within cultural studies (for example, Punter, 1986; Turner, 1991) over the last decade in the UK as a valuable resource for teachers and one which can be profitably applied to technology. Such a reading covers both soft and hardware, as well as the context of implementation and usage, and is far more far-reaching than Johnson's 'software evaluation'. The principal object of the three volumes we have edited has been to give teachers the information and the confidence to learn to 'read technology'. So, returning to Frank Smith, what kind of 'knowledge' is required to accomplish this? Or, to express it another way, what kind of 'knowledge' underpins technological literacy?

(iii) The Knowledge To Read Technology

Young (1991) has no doubt that what is required is not a specialist know-ledge of programming but, rather, a knowledge about how technological choices are 'enmeshed in organisational, economic and political choices.' In our view technological literacy for teachers demands knowing about technology in more than a skills way (although, of course, teachers need also to be technically competent and confident). We believe there are two important sources for teachers, two inter-related domains of both explicit and tacit knowledge, namely (a) the educational and (b) the cultural:

(a) The Educational
Much of this has been outlined above. It is composed of educational principles to do with language, thought, culture, knowledge, pedagogy, subject values, epis-temology and the everyday culture of schools and classrooms. It is concerned with the educational issues to do with teaching and learning addressed by, for example, Bowers (1989) and incorporated by the term the 'ecology of the class-room'. It refers to the professional and practical knowledge of educators, acquired in their initial training; doing the job; and as part of their continuing develop-ment. A second and equally important aspect (to be addressed in the final section) is the undertaking by teachers of evaluative research of computer usage in their classrooms.

(b) The Cultural
This is composed of (1) what might best be described as the 'semiotics' of tech-nology as text (that is, the 'encoding' and 'decoding' of technology as design); and (2) locating technology's wider role in the economy. I shall comment briefly on each.

(1) *Technology as text* The development of media and cultural studies over the past decade has demonstrated how a range of texts other than the literary can be 'read'. At the heart of our version of technological literacy is this cultural, essen-tially semiotic, analysis, and an acknowledgement that technology is not, and never can be, a 'neutral' medium. Indeed, 'reading technology' has much in common with 'reading' television (Beynon *et al.*, 1983). Both have values

implicitly and explicitly built into them and represent reality in ways decided by their human authors working within technical forms and limitations, along with the constraints of presentational formulae (Masterman, 1980; Buckingham, 1991). Television news, for example, is not an exact mirror of an actual event but a representation mediated by camera crew, producers and directors and fitted in according to a dominant definition of 'newsworthiness' (Fiske, 1982; 1987; Hartley, 1982). The same is true of both computer hardware and software: they, too, have built in values and meanings which 'frame' the messages they directly and indirectly convey. In Understanding Technology In Education (1991) Hughie Mackay and I included papers of some of those who have, in different ways, sought to 'decode' and get behind the 'giveness' or fact of technology. Each paper starts from the point that any technology is designed for particular purposes and shaped by social, political, economic and, of course, market factors. This 'social shaping of technology' work (Mackenzie and Wajcman, 1985) treads in the footsteps of Raymond Williams's (1974) pioneering work on the social history of televison. In a similar vein Noble (1991) looked at the design history of numerically-controlled machine tools and the design careers they have taken (or been given). Linn (1991), meanwhile, identifies the 'use values' and the 'dead labour' designed into a particular computer and the subsequent impact of this upon the 'living labour' of its users. At the same time the 'social constructivists' (Bijker *et al.*, 1987) demonstrate how and why choices are taken in design histories (see, also, Mackay, 1991).

In an educational context Dowling (1991) argues that technology is primarily a cultural issue and that computers are best regarded as products defined by social processes rather than neutral machines. Haddon (1991), too, argues that technologies can be diverted into uses other than those for which they were designed. He looks at the stages of use: a technology's origins and design; its use; and its 're-invention' in a new context of implementation. His thesis is particularly pertinent to computers in classrooms, few of which were designed with teaching and learning in mind. Cockburn (1991) argues that technology has been designed as a 'male territory', an argument which has been taken up by feminist writers who identify male ways of thinking in both the design and deployment of individual technologies (see Arnold and Faulkner, 1985). Meanwhile Chandler (1992) and Grint (1992) interrogate computers in classrooms not as neutral and benign, but as 'politically impregnated and historically encumbered'. Medway (1992), Barnett (1992) and Capel (1992) show how another, and equally significant for teachers, technology text has been constructed, namely the study and use of technology as defined by the UK's National Curriculum. They show how the technocentric model that has emerged is a product of the history of computer education in the UK, a history which has been dominated by mathematics, its teachers and its culture.

(2) *Technology's wider role in the economy* A good understanding of the 'technology text' demands a critical understanding of technology's wider role in the economy. Only then can its relationship to education be understood. Any technology is the product of its design; the context of its implementation; and the subjectivities of its users. It is also shaped by wider social and cultural forces. Some argue (for example, Murray, 1991) that technology is at the heart of a massive social and managerial revolution, namely a movement from an economy characterised by

mass production (Fordism) to a more flexible, segmented occupational and production system (Post Fordism). Technology is seen as the major catalyst and instrument of this capitalist restructuring of labour and production (Matthews, 1991). Webster and Robins (1991) apply such arguments to education and argue that the hidden agenda of computer literacy is an ideological move to vocationalise education and teach pupils to expect to have to be trained and retrained in a life spent repeatedly in and out of work. In some ways this takes further the classic labour process thesis (Braverman, 1974), which highlights technology's role in deskilling and extending managerial control. The sociology of technology questions whether technology is emancipatory and attacks a commonly accepted technological determinism that accepts unquestioningly that it shapes society, is outside it, and fuels social change which, in turn, is seen as necessarily beneficial. The weakness of some of the sociology of technology is to substitute for technological determinism an equally inflexible social determinism. Lyons (1991) and Young (1991) are examples of writers who avoid falling into that trap by pointing to the dangers inherent in technology whilst acknowledging its democratising potential.

One of the shortcomings of much of the existing literature on computers into classroom is that it is 'trapped' inside classrooms and, as a result, encourages a dangerous myopia concerning the role of technology in education (Beynon, 1991). Education, of course, is not run by teachers: the major policy decisions are taken by others and, indeed, the voice of teachers throughout the past decade has been relatively marginal, certainly in the United Kingdom. If teachers are, therefore, to be equipped not to be taken in by the promotional 'mythinformation' of educational computing, then they must be able to marshall the ideas emerging from these debates outside education, ideas that are, nevertheless, central to understanding technology in education. Only then will they appreciate the force of Apple's (1991) argument (which, at first, may appear hyperbolic) that an uncritical acceptance of computers is a danger both to liberal education and to democracy itself. More than anything else, however, these debates must be considered and addressed in the advance from a skills-based computer literacy to something bigger, namely a revitalised definition of literacy that includes technological literacy and which can inform the delivery of the National Curriculum in the United Kingdom throughout the decade and beyond.

Section Four: Researching the Place of Technology in the Classroom

Teacher research and evaluation of computers in classrooms is a major component of what Hughie Mackay and I term technological literacy and is not peripheral to it. We have purposely sub-titled this book *More Questions Than Answers*. It is now time for teachers, as professionals, to raise those questions but, also, to start answering them. For teachers to engage in classroom-based research is the best way of ensuring that appropriate issues are articulated although, of course, they need to be supported by outside researchers. Such activity is central to the process of 'questioning' technology addressed in section three above.

Two problems immediately present themselves: the problem of teachers researching in the familiar world of their own classrooms; and of researching computers, which demands time and specific (observational) skills. For Rist (1991) the urgent need in classrooms in the USA is to ascertain how computers are used; by whom; and for what. The same is true of the UK and the immediate challenge confronting teachers who are using or proposing to use computers to enhance teaching and learning in both the primary and secondary school sectors is evaluation. They need to be able to evaluate the use of computers in their classrooms and to identify what their impact is upon the cultural 'ecology' (Bowers, 1989) of teaching and learning. As Ennals (1992) makes clear, teachers need to examine the benefits as well as the shortcomings of computers as 'mindtools' in teaching and learning. The emphasis must be upon sensitivity to context and process. Only then will insights be forthcoming such as that of Moore (1992) on a pupil achieving a correct answer but being totally mystified as to how it was done; and that of Blomeyer (1992) on different institutional and cultural contexts of computer implementation.

To do this adequately there is the need for a conceptual framework to enable teachers to 'read' technology. Much of the existing research is either inaccessible or unsuitable in that it does not pose the necessary questions, or is expressed in a manner which rarely connects with teachers' classroom concerns. Neither does it provide that wider cultural view of technology in which to contextualise the classroom deployment of computers. Teachers need to scrutinise computers (and what they purport to offer), but also to look very carefully at the 'ecology' of their own classrooms, and review the Bowers's thesis that the over-emphasis upon linear, Cartesian thought and logic is in danger not only of disturbing that delicate 'ecology', but of destroying it. Teachers must also consider ways in which educational computing represents and distorts aspects of our culture, starting with educational tasks and objectives, and only then planning how computers might be profitably integrated into the 'ecology' of teaching and learning to further these.

In 1984 the National Association for the Teaching of English (NATE) published a report on the relationship between the teaching of English and the use of computers. In many ways it was a well considered response by a highly reputable body to the increasing clamour to 'technologise' subjects. They entitled it IT's English. The clever pun is symbolic of an awful truth, namely the tendency for subjects, along with their epistemological traditions, to be diverted by a too-hasty advocacy, and 'framed' by technology rather than the reverse. It is most revealing, for example, that Johnson (1991) reports that history teachers who adopted computers saw themselves thereafter as 'doing computers' rather than teaching history.

My own fieldwork involved the systematic observation of pupils using computers in a primary school that was amongst the most 'technologised' in South Wales. Groups of pupils were constantly engaged in 'doing things' on the computers, whether word processing; using language and maths programs; using programs that involved correlating historical data and facts; making decisions in geography games; and in using LOGO and the software supplements which their enthusiastic and thoughtful teacher had prepared. But it seemed to me that little went on of real and enduring educational advantage. The computer certainly gave them lots of ordered 'things to do' and, because the teacher was well organised and very much in control of his classroom and they were generally obedient, they dutifully got on. Little blame could be attributed to their teacher, who had thought deeply about what he was asking them to do and why. But he had little time or opportunity to reach beyond the surface features of 'busyness' (Sharp and Green, 1975) and pupil 'tasks-at-hand' (Pollard, 1982) other than to inspect the visible outcomes of all this pupil activity and to assume that, for example, in LOGO certain mathematical concepts had been exercised and maybe extended. He was unaware, as far as I could ascertain, of the unintended outcomes of many of the the the computer-based activities.

Many of my reservations focussed on the high profile given to word-processing in this classroom. Pupils occasionally wrote directly onto the screen but the usual activity was the laborious typing of what they had previously hand-written so that a legible print-out was eventually manufactured. Or, alternatively, pupils engaged in 'collaborative' writing, with each composing alternate lines of what then became a multi-authored and very public (in the sense it was visible on the screen) production. I developed serious misgivings because of the time it took; how it impacted upon the writing process; and the quality of the end product. Brine (1991) voices similar concerns. His experience suggested that teachers too-easily assumed the potential of word processing and that disappointment with results followed. Text processing became obstructive to writing, so much so that composing and editing on the screen frequently 'deteriorated to a pre-occupation with the keyboard rather than the task of writing'. As a result many teachers became less developers of pupils' language and more 'computer trouble-shooters'. A careful examination of word processing activities illustrates how little is known of pupils' real-time use of computers and the impact upon language, learning, thought, concept development and knowledge. To tackle this demands that teachers develop a new attitude towards research and that the professional research community develops a new set of relationships with researching teachers.

The attempt to re-position teachers in relation to research is most commonly associated in the United Kingdom with the Centre for Applied Research in Education (CARE) at the University of East Anglia and 'illuminative evaluation'. Broadly speaking the 'illuminators' sought to engage in a democratic, non-exploitative 'brokerage' with teachers, and to involve them as partners in re-search in such a way that insights that benefitted practice would be negotiated. The closer working together of teachers and researchers in equal-partner, collaborative research could also be seen in the work of, for example, Carr and Kemmis (1986) and Thiessen (1989). In both there is an attempt to erode the boundary between research which addresses the pragmatic needs of teachers and that which generates theory. Allied to this has been the 'action research' move-ment that has encouraged teachers to be 'reflective practitioners' (Schon, 1983) concerning their own and colleagues' practices and, thereby, to arrive at a series of policy-related recommendations. In the meantime 'educational ethnography', which advanced in importance in the United Kingdom throughout the 1970s and 1980s, sought to work closely with teachers but also to generate 'grounded theory' which might offer new sets of explanatory insights to practitioners 'trapped' inside the cultural confines and pragmatics of schools, classrooms and careers. The RUCCUS project (1988–1991) on aspects of computer usage in secondary schools in Western Ontario aimed for a new paradigm which respected the abilities and needs of teachers whilst striving for theoretical insights which can 'enrich education as both an academic discipline and a professional practice' (Goodson and Mangan, 1991). Researchers were thus positioned as 'fellow professionals' willing to share insights with teachers. The project makes much of Giddens's (1985) theory of 'structuration': computers in classrooms can only be understood in terms of the intricate web of implementation — from issues arising from the technology itself, to the culture of particular sites, to teachers' lives and careers. Evaluation is not enough: rather, analysis leading to theory is needed if the impact of technology in education is to be fully understood.

Conclusion

In summary, to become technologically literate teachers must:

- become more knowledgeable about the non-neutral, cultural nature of technology.
- review and 'read' computers in the light of their professional knowledge (concerning language, thought, subject values, knowledge, etc.) and practices.
- become research-confident and undertake evaluative case studies of pupil and teacher interaction and deployment through periods of intensive data recording using observation and informal interviewing. They should be aware of and confront the problems inherent in researching their own classrooms.
- engage in debates, both as a group and in their own schools, as to the nature of both teacher and pupil technological literacy and the impact of technology upon pedagogy and curriculum in the 1990s.

Courses that are purely skills-based do not serve teachers' best interests. Too many still start with technology rather than education and force educational concerns too readily into the computer format rather than identifying the educational goals and ensuring the technology is appropriate (or adapted) to serve these. Until this tendency is reversed, teachers will continue to be in danger of being trapped into time-consuming technicism and into coping with the obstacles and disruptions the introduction of computers into classrooms occasions without first having been given the opportunity to clarify precisely why they are doing it. The 'how?' associated with skills training must always be secondary to the 'why?' associated with technological literacy.

The advent of computers in classrooms brings into play far bigger issues than the acquisition of technical skills by teachers or pupils. Our three edited volumes have sought to identify these and to present them in terms of a new and expanded definition of literacy appropriate for the 1990s.

Acknowledgment

I should like to thank my colleague and fellow editor Hughie Mackay for his insightful and supportive comments on this paper.

Bibliography

ADAMS, A. and JONES, E. (1983) *Teaching Humanities in the Microelectronics Age*, Milton Keynes, Open University Press.

ALBURY, D. and SCHWARTZ, J. (1982) *Partial Progress: The Politics of Science and Technology*, Winchester, Mass., Pluto Press.

ARNOLD, E. and FAULKNER, W. (Eds) (1985) *Smothered by Invention: Technology in Women's Lives*, London, Pluto.

APPLE, M. (1986) *Teachers and Texts: A Political Economy of Class and Gender Relations in Education*, London, Routledge and Kegan Paul.

APPLE, M. (1992) 'Is the new technology part of the solution or part of the problem in education?' in BEYNON, J. and MACKAY, H. (Eds) *op.cit.*

ARNOLD, M. (1869) *Culture and Anarchy*, London, Cambridge University Press.

BARNES, D. (1970) *From Communication to Curriculum*, Harmondsworth, Penguin.

BARNETT, M. (1992) 'Technology within the National Curriculum and elsewhere' in BEYNON, J. and MACKAY, H. (Eds) *op.cit.*

BARTHES, R. (1968) *Elements of Semiology*, London, Cape.

BEYNON, J. (1991) 'Information Technology' in GOODSON, I. and MANGAN, J.M. (Eds) *op.cit.*

BEYNON, J. and MACKAY, H. (Eds) (1991) *Technological Literacy and the Curriculum*, Basingstoke, Falmer Press.

BEYNON, J. (1990) 'Just a few micros bleeping away in the corner', in BLOMEYER, R.L. and MARTIN, C.D. (Eds) *op.cit.*

BEYNON, J. and MACKAY, H. (1989) 'I.T. education: Towards a critical perspective', *Journal of Education Policy*, Vol. 4, No. 3, pp. 245–257.

BEYNON, J., GOULDEN, H and DOYLE, B. (1983) 'The politics of discrimination', *English in Education*, Vol. 17, No. 3, Autumn.

BIJKER, W.E., HUGHES, T.P. and PINCH, T.J. (Eds) (1987) *The Social Construction of Technological Systems: New Directions in the Sociology and History of Technology*, Cambridge, Mass., M.I.T. Prees.

BLOMEYER, R.L. (1992) in this volume.

BLOMEYER, R.L. and MARTIN, C.D. (Eds) (1990) *Case Studies of Computer Aided Learning*, Basingstoke, Falmer Press.

BORDO, S. (1987) *The Flight to Objectivity: Essays on Cartesianism and Culture*, Albany, State University of New York Press.

BOWERS, C. (1989) *The Cultural Dimensions of Educational Computing*, New York, Teachers College Press.

BRAVERMAN, H. (1974) *Labor and Monopoly Capital*, New York, Monthly Press Review.

BRINE, J. (1991) 'The implicit power of educational technology' in GOODSON, I. and MANGAN, J.M. (Eds) *op.cit.*

BRITTON, J. (1976) *Language and Learning*, Harmondsworth, Penguin.

BUCKINGHAM, D. (1991) *Television Literacy: Talk, Text and Context*, Basingstoke, Falmer Press.

CAPEL, R. (1992) 'Social histories of computer education: missed opportunities?' in BEYNON, J. and MACKAY, H. (Eds) *op.cit.*

CARR, W. and KEMIS, S. (1986) *Becoming Critical: Education, Knowledge and Action Research*, Philadelphia, Falmer Press.

CHANDLER, D. (1992) 'The purpose of the computer in the classroom, in BEYNON, J. and MACKAY, H. (Eds) *op.cit.*

CHANDLER, D. and MARCUS, S. (1985) *Computers and Literacy*, Milton Keynes, Open University Press.

CHOMSKY, N. (1968) *Language and Mind*, New York, Harcourt, Brace and World.

CLARK, R.A. (1991) 'Computer-based activities in art classrooms', in GOODSON, I. and MANGAN, J.M. (Eds) *op.cit.*

COCKBURN, C. (1991) 'The gendering of technology', in MACKAY, H., YOUNG, M.F.D. and BEYNON, J. (Eds) *op.cit.*

CULLEY (1992) in this volume.

DERRIDA, J. (1976) *Of Grammatology*, Baltimore, John Hopkins University Press.

DOWLING, P. (1991) 'The dialectics of determinism: deconstructing information technology', in MACKAY, H., YOUNG, M.F.D. and BEYNON, J. (Eds) *op.cit.*

DREYFUS, H. and DREYFUS, S. (1984) 'Putting computers in their proper place', *Teachers College Record*, 85, pp. 578–601.

DREZIN, F. (1978) 'Towards a computerized generation of sacred legends', *Technical Report No. 1, Focus Project*, Haifa, University of Haifa Publication.

ECO, U. (1986) *Travels in Hyper-reality*, London, Picador.

ENNALS, R. (1992) in this volume.

FINNIGAN, R. (1981) 'Literacy and literature', in LLOYD, B. and GAY, J. (Eds) *Universals of Human Thought*, London, Cambridge University Press.

FISKE, J. (1982) *Introduction to Communication Studies*, London, Methuen.

FISKE, J. (1987) *Television Culture*, London, Methuen.

FOUCAULT, M. (1972) *The Archaeology of Knowledge*, London, Tavistock Press.

FREIRE, P. (1970) *Pedagogy of the Oppressed*, Harmondsworth, Penguin.

FREIRE, P. (1973) *Education for Critical Consciousness*, New York, Continuum Press.

GIDDENS, A. (1985) *The Nation-state and Violence*, Cambridge, Polity Press.

GOODSON, I. and MANGAN, J.M. (1991) *Computers, Classrooms and Culture*, Occasional Papers Volume 2, Ruccus Project, University of Western Ontario.

GOODY, J. (Ed.) (1968) *Literacy In Traditional Societies*, London, Cambridge University Press.

GOODY, J. and WATT, I. (1968) 'The consequences of literacy, in GOODY, J. (Ed.) *op.cit.*

GRINT, K. (1992) 'Sniffers, lurkers, actor networkers: computer, mediated communications as a technical fix', in BEYNON, J. and MACKAY, H. (Eds) *op.cit.*

HABERMAS, J. (1987) *The Theory of Communicative Action*, Boston, Beacon Press.

HADDON, L. (1991) 'The Cultural production and consumption of IT', in MACKAY, H., YOUNG, M.F.D. and BEYNON, J. (Eds) *op.cit.*

HARTLEY, J. (1982) *Understanding News*, London, Methuen.

JANSON, H.W. (1981) *A Basic History of Art*, Englewood Cliffs, N.J., Prentice-Hall.

JOHNSON, M. (1991) 'Computer tools in the history curriculum', in GOODSON, I. and MANGAN, J.M. (Eds) *op.cit.*

JOHNSON, R. (1983) *Information Technology and Cultural Studies*, Birmingham, Occasional Paper, Centre for Contemporary Cultural Studies.

KELLER, E.F. (1985) *Reflections on Gender and Science*, New Haven, Yale University Press.

KRISTEVA, J. (1990) *Le Texte du Ruman*, The Hague, Mouton.

LANE, S. and MACKAY, H. (1992) Towards a sociology of systems analysis, in WOOLGAR, S. and MURRAY, F. (Eds) *Social Perspectives on Software*, Mass. M.I.T. Press.

LEVINE, K. (1986) *The Social Context of Literacy*, London, Routledge and Kegan Paul.

LIBER, O. (1991) in this volume.

LINN, P. (1991) 'Microcomputers in education: dead and living labour', in MACKAY, H., YOUNG, M.F.D. and BEYNON, J. (Eds) *op.cit.*

LYON, D. (1991) 'The information society: ideology or utopia?', in MACKAY, H., YOUNG, M.F.D. and BEYNON, J. (Eds) *op.cit.*

MACKAY, H. (1992), 'From Computer Literacy to Technology Literacy in BEYNON, J. and MACKAY, H. (Eds) *op.cit.*

MACKAY, H., YOUNG, M.F.D. and BEYNON, J. (Eds) (1991) *Understanding Technology in Education*, Basingstoke, Falmer Press.

MACKAY, H. (1991) Introduction to MACKAY, H., YOUNG, M.F.D. and BEYNON, J. (Eds) *op.cit.*

MACKENZIE, D. and WAJCMAN, J. (Eds) (1985) *The Social Shaping of Technology*, Milton Keynes, Open University Press.

MARKUS, M.L. and BJORN-ANDERSON, N. (1987) 'Powers over users: its exercise by system professionals', *Communications of the A.C.M.* 30, pp. 498–505.

MASTERMAN, L. (1980) *Teaching About Television*, London, Macmillan.

MATTHEWS, J. (1992) 'Mass production, the Fordist system and its crisis' in MACKAY, H., YOUNG, M.F.D. and BEYNON, J. (Eds) *op.cit.*

MCLURE, M., PHILIPS, T. and WILKINSON, A.M. (Eds) (1988) *Oracy Matters*, Milton Keynes, Open University Press.

MEDWAY, P. (1992) 'Constructions of technology: reflections on a new subject', in BEYNON, J. and MACKAY, H. (Eds) *op.cit.*

MIDDLEHURST, R. and BEYNON, J. (1991) 'Competence in Communication Studies', in *Competences in British Higher Education*, Leicester, Unit for the Development of Adult and Continuing Education (U.D.A.C.E.), Training Agency Studies.

MOFFETT, J. (1968) *Teaching the Universe of Discourse*, Boston, Houghton Mifflin.

MOORE, A. (1992) in this volume.

MURRAY, R. (1991) 'Life after Henry (Ford)', in MACKAY, H., YOUNG, M.F.D. and BEYNON, J. (Eds) *op.cit.*

N.A.T.E. (1988) 'I.T.'s English: accessing English with computers', Sheffield, National Association for the Teaching of English

NATIONAL WRITING PROJECT (1990) *Writing and Micros*, London, Nelson.

NEWTON, P. and BECK, E. (1992) in this volume.

NOBLE, D. (1991) 'Social choice in machine design', in MACKAY, H., YOUNG, M.F.D. and BEYNON, J. (Eds) *op.cit.*

ONG, W. (1982), *Orality and Literacy*, London, Methuen.

O'KELLY, P. (1991) 'The evolution of groupware' in GOODSON, I. and MANGAN, J.M. (Eds) *op.cit.*

OXENHAM, J. (1980) *Literacy: Writing, Reading and Social Organisation*, London, Routledge and Kegan Paul.

PAPERT, S. (1980) *Mindstorms: Children, Computers and Powerful Ideas*, New York, Basic Books.

PEACOCK, G. (1992) in this volume.

PEACEY, N. (1992) in this volume.

PIAGET, J. (1955) *The Child's Construction of Reality*, London, Routledge and Kegan Paul.

POLANYI, M. (1958) *Personal Knowledge*, Routledge and Kegan Paul.

POLE, C. (1991) in this volume.

POLLARD, A. (1982) 'A model of coping strategies', in *British Journal of Sociology of Education*, March.

PROPP, V. (1928) *Morphology of the Folktale*, Austin, University of Texas Press.

PUNTER, D. (1986) *Introduction to Contemporary Cultural Studies*, London, Longman.

RIST, R. (1990) Introduction to BLOMEYER, R.L. and MARTIN, C.D. (Eds) *op.cit.*

ROBINSON, B. (1985) *Microcomputers and the Language Arts*, Milton Keynes, Open University Press.

ROSEN, C. and ROSEN, H. (1973) *The Language of Primary School Children*, Harmondsworth, Penguin Books.

RUCCUS PROJECT (1991) GOODSON, I. and MANGAN, J.M. (Eds) Volumes 1 and 2, London, Ontario, University of Western Ontario Publication.

SAVILLE-TROIKE, M. (1982) *The Ethnography of Communication*, Oxford, Blackwell.

SCHÖN, D.A. (1983) *The Reflective Practitioner*, New York, Basic Books.

SHANNON, C. and WEAVER, W. (1949) *The Mathematical Theory of Communication*, Illinois, University of Illinois Press.

SHARP, R. and GREEN, A. (1975) *Education and Social Control*, London, Routledge and Kegan Paul.

SMITH, F. (1978) *Understanding Reading*, New York, Holt, Rinehart and Winston.

STREET, B. (1983) *Literacy in Theory and Practice*, Cambridge, Cambridge University Press.

TURNER, G. (1990) *British Cultural Studies: an Introduction*, London, Unwin Hyman.

THIESSEN, D. (1989) 'Teachers and students' in GOODSON, I., MANGAN, J.M. and RHEA, V. (Eds) Report 1, Ruccus Project, London, Ontario, University of Western Ontario Publication.

TURKLE, S. (1984) *The Second Self: Computers and the Human Spirit*, California, Granada.

WATSON, L. (1992) in this volume.

WEBSTER and ROBINS (1991) 'The selling of the new technology', in MACKAY, H., YOUNG, M.F.D. and BEYNON, J. (Eds) *op.cit.*

WHORF, B. (1956) *Language, Thought and Reality*, London, Wiley.

WILKINSON, A.W. (Ed.) (1989) *The Writing of Writing*, Milton Keynes, Open University Press.

WILLIAMS, N. and HOLT, P. (Eds) (1989) *Computers and Writing*, Oxford, Blackwell Scientific Publications.

WILLIAMS, N. (1989) Preface to WILLIAMS, N. and HOLT, P. (Eds) *op.cit.*

WILLIAMS, R. (1974) *Television Technology and Cultural Form*, London, Fontana.

WJEC (1991) *Oracy in Schools*, Cardiff, Welsh Joint Education Committee.

YAZDANI, M. (1989) 'Computational story writing' in WILLIAMS, N. and HOLT, P. (Eds) *op.cit.*

YOUNG, M.F.D. (1984) 'I.T. and the sociology of education', *British Journal of the Sociology of Education*, 5, pp. 205–210.

YOUNG, M.F.D. (1991) 'Technology as an educational issue' in MACKAY, H., YOUNG, M.F.D. and BEYNON, J. (Eds) *op.cit.*

Notes on Contributors

Eevi Beck undertook a final-year project on girls' attitudes towards computing as part of her degree in Computer Science at the University of Manchester Institute of Science and Technology. She is now undertaking a PhD in the Department of Computer Science at the University of Liverpool.

Sheila Bellamy teaches at Gladstone Infants School, Cardiff.

John Beynon is Reader in Communication Studies at the University of Glamorgan. A former journalist, he became first an English and Social Studies teacher in schools in the comprehensive London area and then a teacher trainer. He has published widely in the ethnography of schooling (most notably *Initial Encounters in the Secondary School*, Falmer Press, 1985) and is currently completing a book on masculinity and education to be published by Routledge in 1991.

Professor Robert Blomeyer has recently moved from the University of Houston to lecture in Technology and Education at Oregon State University, Corvallis. He has authored a large number of articles on naturalistic perspectives on computer-aided learning in a range of settings and has recently edited (with Dianne Martin) *Case Studies of Computer Aided Learning* (Falmer Press, 1991).

Lorraine Culley lectures in the Department of Health and Community Studies at Leicester Polytechnic and on the MA Degree in Women's Studies at Loughborough University. She has carried out a funded research project on gender and computing in secondary schools and has published widely on gender issues.

Professor Richard Ennals came from a Cambridge humanities background to use computers in his classrooms and then to conduct and manage research into Artificial Intelligence. He is at present Professor and Head of the School of Operations Management and Quantitative Methods at Kingston Polytechnic. His latest book, *Artificial Intelligence and Human Institutions*, was published by the Springer Press in 1990.

Oleg Liber is Project Director for the Information Technology Consultancy Unit (ITCU), working on communication and education projects, including the nationwide ITEC network. Before that he was Lecturer in Education at the Institute of Education, University of London, and, previously, was Head of Mathematics at a London comprehensive school.

Patricia Lovering is a Support Teacher in Barry Island Primary School, South Glamorgan.

Hughie Mackay lectures on social aspects of technology at the University of Glamorgan and is staff tutor for social sciences at The Open University in Wales. He holds postgraduate qualifications both as a technologist and as a sociologist. Between 1981 and 1985 he carried out field-based research on school management for the Open University, most notably *Headteachers at Work* (with Valerie Hall and Colin Morgan, Open University Press, 1986). His recent research has been into the sociology of technology.

Alec Moore was a secondary school teacher of English for eighteen years. He now lectures in the Department of Postgraduate Initial Teacher Education at Goldsmiths' College, London University. Previously he was Research Fellow on the Impact Project, based at King's College, London, which is assessing the effects of classroom computer use on the way children work and learn.

Peggy Newton is a psychologist with a longstanding interest in gender issues. She has written extensively on the subject of women engineers and has more recently become involved in activities designed to attract more girls and women to computing as a career. She was a Lecturer at Huddersfield Polytechnic but is now employed as a Senior Research Fellow at the University of Manchester.

Nicholas Peacey is the Coordinator of the Special Educational Needs Joint Initiative for Training, Institute of Education, University of London. Previously he worked in comprehensive schools and in a variety of special needs provision in London before becoming INSET Coordinator for Special Education for ILEA.

Graham Peacock, formerly a teacher in primary schools in ILEA and Rotherham, is now Lecturer in Primary Education at Sheffield City Polytechnic. He is currently seconded to work in Hong Kong as a teacher trainer.

Christopher Pole is a Lecturer in Sociology at the University of Warwick where he also conducts research in the Centre for Educational Development, Appraisal and Research (CEDAR). His main teaching and research interests are in areas of the sociology of education and the use of qualitative research methods. He is currently completing a study of Records of Achievement in different kinds of secondary schools for a Midlands Local Education Authority.

Mary Shooter is Deputy Head at Gladstone Primary School, Barry, South Glamorgan.

Les Watson trained as a secondary school biology teacher and taught in comprehensive schools in Hull and Gloucester. Since 1984 he has lectured in IT/Education and is now Head of IT Services at the Cheltenham and Gloucester College of Higher Education. He is a regular contributor to the Times Educational Supplement and is currently running two school-based projects, one on Laptops in Primary Schools and the other on Knowledge Bases.

Index